STUDY PLANNER

CHAPTER 01 인칭대명사와 동사	학습일	
UNIT 01	월	일
UNIT 02	월	일
UNIT 03	월	일
UNIT 04	월	일
Review Test	월	일

KB091635

CHAPTER 02 명사, 관사, 대명사	학습일	
UNIT 05	월	일
UNIT 06	월	일
UNIT 07	월	일
Review Test	월	일

CHAPTER 03 시제	학습일	
UNIT 08	월	일
UNIT 09	월	일
UNIT 10	월	일
Review Test	월	일

CHAPTER 04 조동사	학습일	
UNIT 11	월	일
UNIT 12	월	일
UNIT 13	월	일
Review Test	월	일

CHAPTER 05 문장의 변환	학습일	
UNIT 14	월	일
UNIT 15	월	일
UNIT 16	월	일
UNIT 17	월	일
Review Test	월	일

CHAPTER 06 형용사와 부사	학습일	
UNIT 18	월	일
UNIT 19	월	일
	월	일

교 구문	학습일	
UNIT 20	월	일
UNIT 21	월	일
UNIT 22	월	일
Review Test	월	일

CHAPTER 08 to부정사	학습일	
UNIT 23	월	일
UNIT 24	월	일
Review Test	월	일

CHAPTER 09 동명사	학습일	
UNIT 25	월	일
UNIT 26	월	일
Review Test	월	일

CHAPTER 10 문장의 형식	학습일	
UNIT 27	월	일
UNIT 28	월	일
Review Test	월	일

CHAPTER 11 전치사와 접속사	학습일	
UNIT 29	월	일
UNIT 30	월	일
Review Test	월	일

SCORECARD

PASS 기준: Level 2 → 25점 이상, Level 3 → 41점 이상, Review Test → 60점 이상

CHAPTER 01 인칭대명사와 동사	Level 2	Level 3
UNIT 01	/ 30점	/ 50점
UNIT 02	/ 30점	/ 50점
UNIT 03	/ 30점	/ 50점
UNIT 04	/ 30점	/ 50점
Review Test		/ 70점

CHAPTER 02 명사, 관사, 대명사	Level 2	Level 3
UNIT 05	/ 30점	50점
UNIT 06	/ 30점	50점
UNIT 07	/ 30점	50점
Review Test		/ 70점

CHAPTER 03 시제	Level 2	Level 3
UNIT 08	/ 30점	/ 50점
UNIT 09	/ 30점	/ 50점
UNIT 10	/ 30점	/ 50점
Review Test		/ 70점

CHAPTER 04 조동사	Level 2	Level 3
UNIT 11	/ 30점	/ 50점
UNIT 12	/ 30점	/ 50점
UNIT 13	/ 30점	/ 50점
Review Test		/ 70점

CHAPTER 05 문장의 변환	Level 2	Level 3
UNIT 14	/ 30점	/ 50점
UNIT 15	/ 30점	/ 50점
UNIT 16	/ 30점	/ 50점
UNIT 17	/ 30점	/ 50점
Review Test		/ 70점

CHAPTER 06 형용사와 부사	Level 2	Level 3
UNIT 18	/ 30점	/ 50점
UNIT 19	/ 30점	/ 50점
Review Test		/ 70점

CHAPTER 07 비교 구문	Level 2	Level 3
UNIT 20	/ 30점	/ 50점
UNIT 21	/ 30점	/ 50점
UNIT 22	/ 30점	/ 50점
Review Test		/ 70점

CHAPTER 08 to부정사	Level 2	Level 3
UNIT 23	/ 30점	/ 50점
UNIT 24	/ 30점	/ 50점
Review Test		/ 70점

CHAPTER 09 동명사	Level 2	Level 3
UNIT 25	/ 30점	/ 50점
UNIT 26	/ 30점	/ 50점
Review Test		/ 70점

CHAPTER 10 문장의 형식	Level 2	Level 3
UNIT 27	/ 30점	/ 50점
UNIT 28	/ 30점	/ 50점
Review Test		/ 70점

CHAPTER 11 전치사와 접속사	Level 2	Level 3
UNIT 29	/ 30점	/ 50점
UNIT 30	/ 30점	/ 50점
Review Test		/ 70점

내신공략

중학영문법

문제풀이책

1

내신공략 중학영문법의 구성 및 특징

시리즈 구성

내신공략 중학영문법 시리즈는 중학교 영어 교과과정의 문법 사항을 3레벨로 나누어 수록하고 있으며, 각각의 레벨은 **개념이해책**과 **문제풀이책**으로 구성됩니다. 두 책을 병행하여 학습하는 것이 가장 이상적인 학습법이지만, 교사와 학생의 필요에 따라 둘 중 하나만을 독립적으로도 사용할 수 있도록 구성했습니다.

개념이해책은 문법 개념에 대한 핵심적인 설명과 필수 연습문제로 이루어져 있습니다.

문제풀이책은 각 문법 개념에 대해 총 3단계의 테스트를 통해 체계적으로 문제를 풀어볼 수 있도록 구성되어 있습니다.

특징

❶ 최신 내신 출제 경향 100% 반영

– 신유형과 고난도 서술형 문제 비중 강화

점점 어려워지는 내신 문제의 최신 경향을 철저히 분석·반영하여 고난도 서술형과 신유형 문제의 비중을 더욱 높였습니다. 이 책으로 학습한 학생들은 어떤 유형의 문제에도 대처할 수 있습니다.

– 영어 지시문 문제 제시

영어로 문제가 출제되는 최신 경향을 반영하여, 일부 문제를 영어 지시문으로 제시했습니다. 문제풀이책의 Level 3 Test는 모두 영어 지시문으로만 제시됩니다.

– 독해 지문 어법 문제 수록(문제풀이책)

독해 지문에서 어법 문제가 출제되는 내신 문제 스타일에 익숙해지도록, 독해 지문과 함께 다양한 어법 문제를 풀어볼 수 있습니다.

❷ 개념이해책과 문제풀이책의 연계 학습

문법 개념 설명과 필수 문제로 구성된 개념이해책으로 문법 개념을 학습한 후, 다양한 문제를 3단계로 풀어보는 문제풀이책으로 복습하며 확실한 학습 효과를 거둘 수 있습니다.

❸ 성취도 평가와 수준별 맞춤형 학습 제안

문제를 풀어보고 나서 점수 기준에 따라 학생의 성취도를 평가할 수 있습니다. 개념이해책에서 Let's Check It Out과 Ready for Exams 점수를 합산한 결과에 따라 문제풀이책의 어느 레벨부터 학습하면 되는지 가이드가 제시됩니다. Review Test에서는 일정 점수 이상을 받아야 다음 챕터로 넘어갈 수 있습니다.

❹ 추가 학습을 위한 다양한 학습자료 제공

다양하게 수업에 활용할 수 있는 교사용 자료가 제공됩니다. 다락원 홈페이지(www.darakwon.co.kr)에서 무료로 다운받으실 수 있습니다.

개념이해책과 문제풀이책 연계 학습법

개념이해책으로 문법 개념 학습

문제풀이책으로 문법 개념을 복습

QR코드를 찍으면 개념이해책 문법 설명이 보여요!

개념이해책 Let's Check It Out과 Ready for Exams 풀고 점수 합산

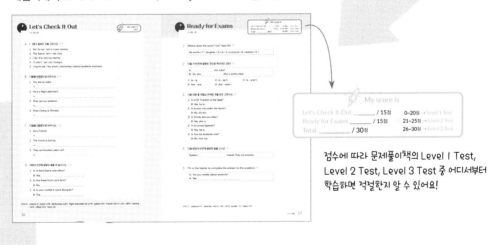

점수에 따라 문제풀이책의 Level 1 Test, Level 2 Test, Level 3 Test 중 어디서부터 학습하면 적절한지 알 수 있어요!

챕터 내용을 모두 학습한 후 Review Test 풀기

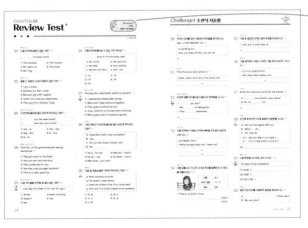

패스하면 문제풀이책의 Review Test도 풀어보고, 그것도 패스하면 다음 챕터로 넘어가요!

문제풀이책의 구성

개념이해책에서 학습한 문법 개념이 표로 더욱 간결하게 요약 제시됩니다. 핵심 용어가 빈칸으로 처리되어 있어서 학생들이 직접 내용을 채워 넣으며 개념을 복습할 수 있습니다.

● 개념이해책 연계 학습용 QR코드

QR코드를 찍으면 개념이해책 문법 개념 설명 페이지로 연결되어 내용을 즉시 확인할 수 있습니다.

Level 1 Test

학습한 문법 사항을 간단히 확인할 수 있는 드릴형 연습 문제입니다.

● VOCA

문제에 쓰인 주요 단어가 정리되어 편리하며, 문법과 단어 공부를 같이 할 수 있습니다.

Level 2 Test

중간 난이도의 문제를 풀면서 앞에서 배운 문법 사항을 실제 문제 풀이에 적용하는 연습을 합니다. 객관식과 주관식 서술형이 50% 정도로 섞인 내신 유형 문제로 구성되어 있습니다. 지시문은 한글로 제시됩니다.

● My score is

30점 만점으로 25점 이상일 때 PASS할 수 있어 학생들의 성취 욕구를 자극할 수 있으며, PASS 기준에 미달했을 때는 다시 앞부분을 복습하도록 합니다.

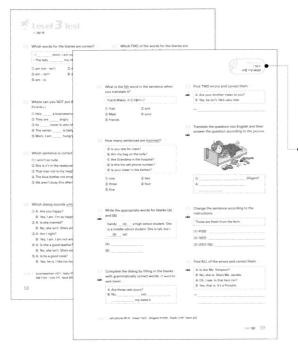

높은 난이도의 다양한 내신 유형 문제로 구성되어 있으며, 문제가 모두 영어 지시문으로 제시됩니다. 최신 유형도 포함되어 있어 내신 시험에 철저히 대비할 수 있습니다. 주관식 서술형 문제의 비중이 30퍼센트 정도로 구성되어 있습니다.

My score is

50점 만점으로 41점 이상일 때 PASS할 수 있습니다.

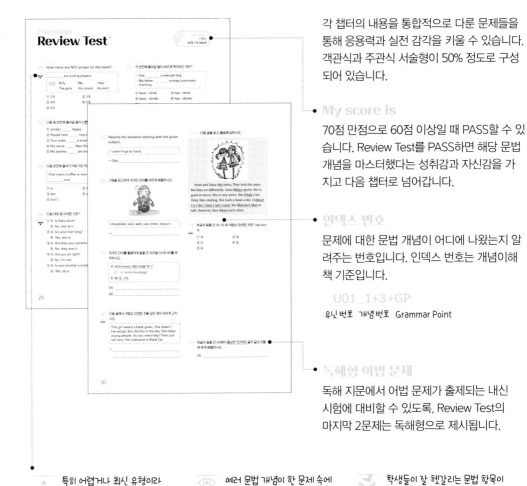

각 챕터의 내용을 통합적으로 다룬 문제들을 통해 응용력과 실전 감각을 키울 수 있습니다. 객관식과 주관식 서술형이 50% 정도로 구성되어 있습니다.

My score is

70점 만점으로 60점 이상일 때 PASS할 수 있습니다. Review Test를 PASS하면 해당 문법 개념을 마스터했다는 성취감과 자신감을 가지고 다음 챕터로 넘어갑니다.

인덱스 번호

문제에 대한 문법 개념이 어디에 나왔는지 알려주는 번호입니다. 인덱스 번호는 개념이해 책 기준입니다.

U01_1+3+GP

유닛 번호 개념번호 Grammar Point

독해형 어법 문제

독해 지문에서 어법 문제가 출제되는 내신 시험에 대비할 수 있도록, Review Test의 마지막 2문제는 독해형으로 제시됩니다.

★ 고난도 — 특히 어렵거나 최신 유형이라 익숙하지 않은 문제

👁 한눈에 쏙 — 여러 문법 개념이 한 문제 속에 들어가 있는 문제

✓ 함정 — 학생들이 잘 헷갈리는 문법 항목이거나 부주의하면 틀릴 수 있는 문제

차례

내공 중학영문법을 써본
독자들의 추천!

틀에 박힌 예문이 아니라, 학생의 생각을 살리는 예문. 틀에 박힌 문제가 아니라, 한 번 더 생각하게 하는 참신한 문제. 다양하고 새로운 유형의 문제와 예문들은 내공 중학영문법 출시 이후 줄곧 수업 교재로 채택하고 있는 이유입니다. 최근 학교 내신 시험에서도 내공과 비슷한 유형의 문제가 출제되는 걸 보면, 교재의 이름처럼 정말 대단한 내공을 가진 문법서입니다.

창원 쥬기스영어교실 원장 **이연홍**

다년간 예비중을 위한 문법 특강을 하면서 이번에 바꾸게 된 다락원 내신공략 중학영문법은 짧은 시간에 기초를 다질 수 있도록 중요 설명과 다양한 문제를 풀 수 있어 단시간에 실력 향상을 할 수 있어 학생들 모두 만족한 수업을 했습니다.

오창 로제타스톤영어학원 원장 **강보민**

평소 문법 수업에서 '아이들이 잘 이해하고 있는가'를 확인하는 것에 중점을 두는데 내공 중학영문법의 교재 구성이 이 부분에 많은 도움이 되었습니다. 개념 부분의 빈칸 문제와 두 권에 걸쳐 연습해 볼 수 있는 활용 문제들이 개념 정립과 문제 응용까지 확실하게 잡아줘서 좋았어요. 수업과 과제, 단어, 테스트까지 교재만으로도 충분히 전반적인 문법 커리큘럼을 구성할 수 있었습니다.

전주 퍼플영어학원 원장 **이서원**

다양한 유형과 풍부한 문제 풀이로 중학 기본 문법에 완벽히 대비할 수 있었다. 또한 학생들의 눈높이에 맞춘 예문들에 쉽고 정확하게 이해할 수 있는 책으로 적극 추천한다.

전남무안 이써밋영수학원 원장 **김지현**

정확하고 자세한 설명과 실제 사용할 수 있는 생생한 예문들이 많아서 좋았다. 다양한 연습 문제와 체계적인 구성들로 문법 실력에 향상을 보였다.

전남목포 홍일고 **양재동**

중학 내신에 꼭 필요한 핵심적인 문법들을 학생들이 이해하기 쉽게 설명해주고 있다. 자기 주도 학습에도 충분히 활용하게끔 문법 설명과 문제가 적절히 구성되어 있다. 탄탄한 영어 실력을 위한 영문법 책이다.

충북 청주 해피써니영어 원장 이선미

개념이해책과 문제풀이책에 있는 Fail 컷으로 공부했더니 모든 문제를 푸는 데에 있어 꼼꼼히 푸는 습관이 생겼고, 대부분 한눈에 보기 쉬운 표로 구성되어 있어 이해하기 쉬웠다. 어렵기만 하던 문법이 지금은 나의 무기가 되었다.

충북 청주 일신여고 2학년 신채은

기본부터 고난도 문제들까지 꼼꼼하게 다뤄주어서 좋다. 뻔하지 않는 다양한 문제유형과 학생들의 실책 포인트를 잘 챙겨줘서 여러 책 보지 않아도 실속 있게 챙겨주는 너무 든든한 책이다.

김포 MDS영어 원장 정지윤

외고 목표로 공부 중이다. 중1 때 만나게 된 책인데, 다양한 문제들로 실력이 향상되는 것을 느낀다. 빈칸 채우기를 하면서 개념 복습도 가능하고 나의 부족한 점을 직접 확인할 수 있어서 좋다.

학생 장예원, 한지우

미국 가서 7학년 때 처음으로 미국에서 문법을 배웠는데 내공 책으로 공부한 덕분에 문법이 쉬웠다. 8학년 때는 미국 native 현지인 학생들이 오히려 문법 부분에서 많이 어려워했는데 한국 유학생인 내가 오히려 내공 책 덕분에 좋은 점수를 받을 수 있었다.

Chaminade College Preparatory School 8학년 황인태

CHAPTER 01
인칭대명사와 동사

인칭대명사와 be동사

개념이해책
12쪽 함께 보기

■ 아래 표의 빈칸에 알맞은 내용을 써 넣으세요. **›› 정답 2쪽**

1 인칭대명사

	주격	소유격	목적격	소유대명사	주격	소유격	목적격	소유대명사
1인칭	I	1)	2)	3)	we	15)	16)	17)
2인칭	you	4)	5)	6)	you	18)	19)	20)
3인칭	he	7)	8)	9)				
	she	10)	11)	12)	they	21)	22)	23)
	it	13)	14)					

2 be동사의 현재형

주어	be동사	줄임말	주어	be동사	줄임말
I	24)	25)	he	32)	33)
we	26)	27)	she	34)	35)
you	28)	29)	it	36)	37)
they	30)	31)	this	38)	
			that	39)	40)

Level 1 Test

›› 정답 2쪽

A [ ]에서 알맞은 것을 고르시오.

1 He [is / am] in the kitchen.

2 We [is / are] so diligent.

3 You and she [is / are] soccer players.

4 She and I [is / are] kind to each other.

5 Ben [is / are] a very wise boy.

B 빈칸에 알맞은 be동사의 현재형을 쓰시오.

1 The cat's eyes _____ strange.

2 This _____ Bobby Ko.

3 Their music _____ fantastic.

4 My puppies _____ too big.

5 Jimin and I _____ in the same class.

C 문장에서 줄일 수 있는 말을 줄여서 문장을 다시 쓰시오.

1 She is a good singer.

→ _____

2 They are on the subway.

→ _____

3 He is a great gamer.

→ _____

4 It is a good idea.

→ _____

5 I am a very simple person.

→ _____

VOCA diligent 부지런한 | each other 서로 | wise 현명한 | strange 이상한 | fantastic 환상적인 | puppy 강아지

>> 정답 2쪽

01 다음 빈칸에 알맞은 것은? (답 2개) 2점

_____ are from Hong Kong.

① Jay
② Jay's friends
③ The girl
④ Their uncle
⑤ Ling Ling and Ming Ming

02 빈칸에 알맞은 말이 바르게 짝지어진 것은? 2점

• They _____ on the school bus.
• The nurse _____ very busy.

① are – are   ② are – am
③ are – is   ④ is – are
⑤ is – is

03 다음 중 빈칸에 들어갈 말이 나머지와 다른 하나는? 2점

① He _____ tall and handsome.
② My bag _____ old but nice.
③ The men _____ very strong.
④ Ms. Lim _____ a science teacher.
⑤ Their last name _____ Lee.

04 다음 중 줄임말을 바르게 쓰지 못한 학생은? 2점

① 슬기: We're good sisters.
② 지은: He's Kimmy Kim's brother.
③ 진희: That's my dog Yaya.
④ 보은: They're on the lake.
⑤ 정향: Its just the beginning.

05 다음 중 어법상 어색한 문장을 모두 고르시오. 2점

① It is very surprising.
② This is so cool!
③ His name are Jack.
④ Don and I am good friends.
⑤ They are my pets.

06 주어진 단어 중에서 필요한 것만 골라 배열하여 우리말을 영작하시오. 4점
서술형

그들은 나의 적들이다.
are, is, they, their, my, me, enemies

→ _____

07 다음 중 어법상 어색한 문장을 찾아 바르게 고쳐 쓰시오. 4점
서술형

ⓐ Theirs dog are very smart.
ⓑ The bike is mine.

(   ) → _____

08 주어진 단어들을 빈칸에 바르게 배열하시오. 4점
서술형

coke, is, drink, favorite

→ My _____ .

09 각 빈칸에 알맞은 be동사의 현재형을 쓰시오. 4점
서술형

Anna _____ warm, but her sister _____ cold.

10 그림을 묘사하는 문장을 조건에 맞게 완성하시오. 4점
서술형

• 조건 1 동사는 현재형으로 쓸 것
• 조건 2 두 단어의 첫 글자를 똑같이 쓸 것

→ They _____ on an _____ .

VOCA   nurse 간호사 | last name 성 | beginning 시작 | surprising 놀라운 | enemy 적 | favorite 제일 좋아하는 | drink 음료 | coke 콜라 | cold 냉정한

01 Which of the underlined words has a **different** meaning? 2점

① Luke <u>is</u> on the spaceship.
② Jerome <u>is</u> a nice guy.
③ They <u>are</u> in the lobby.
④ The cat <u>is</u> under the table.
⑤ Cathy <u>is</u> in the backyard.

02 Which words are correct for the blanks? 2점

- My uncle _____ Swiss.
- Sandy and Kimura _____ classmates.
- The flower _____ beautiful.

① am – are – is
② is – are – am
③ is – is – is
④ is – are – is
⑤ are – are – is

03 Which word for the blank is **different** from the others? 2점

① Your sister _____ so cute.
② Dragonflies _____ on the bench.
③ You _____ a great cook.
④ Bob and Ron _____ brothers.
⑤ Our new neighbors _____ friendly.

04 Which underlined word is **incorrect**?
(2 answers) 2점

① <u>I'm</u> a good listener.
② <u>She's</u> my mother.
③ <u>This's</u> so funny.
④ <u>Its</u> a great movie.
⑤ <u>They're</u> my new friends.

05 Which is NOT proper for the blank?
(2 answers) 2점

_____ are awesome.

① We
② You
③ Yuna Kim
④ Her student
⑤ Ryan and Laura

06 Whose correction is right? 2점

나의 할머니 할아버지는 나에게 매우 너그러우시다.
= My grandparents is very generous to me.

① 혜림: My → Me
② 규민: grandparents → grandparent
③ 가현: grandparents → grandparentes
④ 신라: is → are
⑤ 유림: me → I

07 Find ALL of the suitable words for the blank.
2점

_____ are middle school students.

① Lucy
② Chris
③ They
④ The kids
⑤ Ron and I

08 Who analyzes the sentence correctly? 2점

My Canadian friend Myles are actually from America.

① 수진: My가 아니라 Me로 써야 돼.
② 은주: Canadian을 Canada로 써야 돼.
③ 희영: Myles가 복수니까 are가 맞아.
④ 아미: 주어가 단수니까 are를 is로 바꿔야 해.
⑤ 시은: 사람이니까 America가 아니고 American이야.

VOCA spaceship 우주선 | lobby 로비 | backyard 뒷마당 | Swiss 스위스의, 스위스인(의) | classmate 같은 반 친구 | dragonfly 잠자리 | cook 요리사 | neighbor 이웃 | awesome 멋진, 끝내주는 | generous 너그러운 | actually 사실은

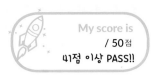
09 Which is grammatically correct? 2점

① Mr. Tong am my yoga teacher.

② He and his brother is short.

③ Sejin and Liz is fourteen years old.

④ They are yours new teachers.

⑤ *Ali Baba and the Forty Thieves* is my favorite book.

10 How many sentences are incorrect? 3점

> ⓐ Her name are Jennifer.
> ⓑ The red one are my car.
> ⓒ Your new school bag are very cool.
> ⓓ Its legs are thick and long.
> ⓔ My sister's computer am expensive.
> ⓕ Pedro are my best friend.

① one   ② two

③ three   ④ four

⑤ five

11 Which of following can make a correct sentence? (2 answers) 4점

① big / hands / . / Liam's / are

② the / . / tonight / party / are

③ bathroom / the / in / Jack / are / .

④ friends / . / are / crazy / my / best

⑤ table / are / . / on / the / the / food

12 Translate the Korean into English in 4 words. 4점

서술형

> 그들은 나의 먼 사촌이다. (distant)

→ _____

13 Fill in the blank with "am," "is," or "are." 각 1점

서술형

(1) Her kids _____ too noisy.

(2) Your new friend _____ so funny.

(3) Its cover _____ yellow.

14 Find the sentence that has an error and correct it. 4점

서술형

> ⓐ She's a lazy girl.
> ⓑ Its my cell phone number.
> ⓒ He's thirteen years old.

(   ) _____ → _____

15 Find the different word for the blanks from the others and write the word. 4점

서술형

> Amy ___(A)___ a singer. She ___(B)___ very kind. Taemin ___(C)___ a nurse. He ___(D)___ from Ilsan. Amy and Taemin ___(E)___ my father's friends.

(   ) _____

16 Look at the picture and complete the sentence according to the conditions. 5점

서술형

· Condition 1	주어는 대명사로 쓸 것
· Condition 2	직업을 쓸 것
· Condition 3	4단어로 쓸 것

→ This is my uncle. _____ .

17 Find ALL of the errors and correct them. 5점

서술형

> My dad am a driver, and my mom are a teacher. They is always busy in the morning. I'am always busy in the morning, too.

→ _____

_____

VOCA   **thieves** 도둑(thief)의 복수 | **thick** 두꺼운 | **distant** 먼 | **cousin** 사촌 | **noisy** 시끄러운 | **cover** 표지, 덮개 | **lazy** 게으른

02 be동사의 부정문과 의문문

개념이해책
15쪽 함께 보기

■ 아래 표의 빈칸에 알맞은 내용을 써 넣으세요. ≫ 정답 3쪽

1 be동사의 부정문

주어	단수	줄임말	복수	줄임말
1인칭	I am not	1)	we are not	6)
2인칭	You are not	2)	you are not	7)
3인칭	he is not	3)	they are not	8)
	she is not	4)		
	it is not	5)		

2 be동사의 의문문과 대답

be동사의 의문문		대답			
주어+be동사 ~. → 9)		긍정	10)	부정	11)

Level 1 Test

≫ 정답 3쪽

A [ ]에서 알맞은 것을 고르시오.

1 I [am / amn't] from Toronto, Canada.

2 Her brother [is not / not is] tall.

3 [She's not / She'sn't] my boss.

4 We [aren't / not] afraid of anything.

5 Charles [isn't / not is] a slow learner.

B 다음을 부정문으로 바꾸시오.

1 We are the champions.

→ _____

2 My girlfriend is a musician.

→ _____

3 It's back on the menu.

→ _____

4 This is a coin from the Joseon Dynasty.

→ _____

C 다음을 의문문으로 바꾸시오.

1 This online broadcast is fun.

→ _____

2 That is his new nickname.

→ _____

3 Sunny and Russell are in the same class.

→ _____

D 빈칸에 알맞은 말을 써 넣으시오.

1 Are you mad at me?

→ Yes, _____ _____.

2 Is our team on the field now?

→ No, _____ _____.

3 Is her brother in Taipei?

→ Yes, _____ _____.

4 Are the coupons on the table?

→ No, _____ _____.

VOCA Toronto 토론토(캐나다 동남부의 도시) | boss 사장, 상사 | afraid of ~을 두려워하는 | musician 음악가, 연주자 | coin 동전 | dynasty 왕조 | broadcast 방송; 방송하다 | nickname 별명 | mad 화난 | Taipei 타이베이(타이완의 수도) | coupon 쿠폰

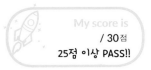

>> 정답 3쪽

01 다음 빈칸에 알맞은 것은? 2점

| Hana and Duri _____ siblings. |

① is not　　　　② not is

③ are not　　　④ not are

⑤ not

02 다음 중 밑줄 친 부분이 잘못된 것은? 2점

① It <u>isn't</u> cold.

② <u>She's not</u> a clerk.

③ <u>Its</u> back <u>isn't</u> green.

④ <u>We're not</u> twins.

⑤ <u>They arn't</u> a couple.

03 다음 대화의 빈칸에 들어갈 말로 알맞은 것은? 2점

| A: Are you from Mars?
| B: _____ . I am from Venus. |

① Yes, I am.　　　② Yes, you are.

③ No, I amn't.　　④ No, I am not.

⑤ No, you're not.

04 다음 대화를 영작할 때 필요하지 않은 말은? 2점

| A: 그녀의 남편은 경찰관입니까?
| B: 네, 그래요. |

① Is　　　　② she

③ police　　 ④ Yes

⑤ he

05 다음 중 어법상 어색한 문장은? (답 2개) 2점

① Is your math teacher strict?

② Is my keys in the car?

③ Are your password secret?

④ She's not very happy now.

⑤ My computer isn't very old.

06 다음 문장을 조건에 맞게 다시 쓰시오. 4점

서술형

| These buttons are broken.
| · 조건 1　주어를 대명사로 쓸 것
| · 조건 2　부정문으로 쓰되 줄임말을 사용할 것 |

→ _____

07 주어진 단어들과 be동사를 활용하여 현재형의 의문문을 완성하시오. 4점

서술형

| the girls, in the restroom |

→ _____

08 다음 대화의 빈칸에 알맞은 말을 쓰시오. 3점

서술형

| A: Are you in the same club?
| B: _____ , _____
| _____ . She is in the hip-hop club.
| I am in the *pansori* club. |

09 그림을 보고 답변을 완성하시오. 3점

서술형

| Q: Is she a dentist?
| A: _____ |

10 다음 문장을 부정문과 의문문으로 바꾸어 쓰고 긍정의 대답을 쓰시오. 각 2점

서술형

| It is his new laptop computer. |

(1) 부정문: _____

(2) 의문문: _____

(3) 긍정의 대답: _____

VOCA　sibling 형제자매 | clerk 점원 | back 등, 뒷부분 | twins 쌍둥이 | Mars 화성 | Venus 금성 | strict 엄격한 | broken 고장 난 | dentist 치과 의사
| laptop computer 노트북 컴퓨터

01 Which words for the blanks are correct? 2점

> • I _____ short. I am not tall.
> • The lady _____ my mom. She's my aunt.

① am not – isn't   ② am not – is

③ am – isn't   ④ amn't – isn't

⑤ am – is

02 Where can you NOT put the word "not"?
(Find ALL.) 2점

① He's _____ a businessman.

② They are _____ angry.

③ Its _____ cover is very old.

④ The ramen _____ is tasty.

⑤ Mom, I am _____ hungry.

03 Which sentence is correct? 2점

① I amn't so rude.

② She is n't in the restaurant.

③ That man not is my neighbor.

④ The blue bottles not empty.

⑤ We aren't busy this afternoon.

04 Which dialog sounds underlined{unnatural}? 2점

① A: Are you happy?
　B: Yes, I am. I'm so happy now.

② A: Is she married?
　B: No, she isn't. She's single.

③ A: Am I right?
　B: Yes, I am. I am not wrong.

④ A: Is she a good teacher?
　B: No, she isn't. She's not nice.

⑤ A: Is he a good cook?
　B: Yes, he is. I like his food.

05 Which TWO of the words for the blanks are
underlined{different} from the others? 2점

① _____ you sorry now?

② _____ the people in the town brave?

③ _____ Sabrina and you classmates?

④ _____ your child naughty?

⑤ _____ the movie *Romeo and Juliet* fun?

06 This is Kaori's translation. Which correction
is right? 2점

> 그의 규칙들은 엄격하지 않아.
> → His rules not are strict.

① His → He's   ② rules → rule

③ are → is   ④ not are → are not

⑤ are strict → strict

07 Who analyzes the sentence correctly? 2점

> This not is your fault but mine.

① 다예: This not은 Thisn't로 쓸 수도 있어.

② 기태: not은 be동사 뒤에 써야 해.

③ 솔아: your는 you의 목적격이야.

④ 치현: but은 and로도 바꿔 쓸 수 있어.

⑤ 지다: mine은 my로 바꿔 써야 해.

08 Of the two sentences, who finds an error and
writes it correctly? 2점

> ⓐ David isn't in the car.
> ⓑ My parents not at home.

① 신호탄: ⓐ David aren't in the car.

② 엄어나: ⓐ David not is in the car.

③ 최고다: ⓑ Me parents are not at home.

④ 도우너: ⓑ My parents aren't at home.

⑤ 오지게: ⓑ My parent's aren't at home.

VOCA   businessman 사업가 | tasty 맛있는 | rude 무례한 | bottle 병 | empty 텅 빈 | married 결혼한 | single 독신의 | brave 용감한 | naughty
말을 안 듣는 | rule 규칙 | fault 잘못

09 What is the 5th word in the sentence when you translate it? 2점

> Yuki와 Maki는 네 친구들이니?

① Yuki ② and
③ Maki ④ your
⑤ friends

10 How many sentences are incorrect? 3점

> ⓐ Is you late for class?
> ⓑ Am my bag on the sofa?
> ⓒ Are Grandma in the hospital?
> ⓓ Is this his cell phone number?
> ⓔ Is your sister in the kitchen?

① one ② two
③ three ④ four
⑤ five

11 서술형 Write the appropriate words for blanks (A) and (B). 각 2점

> Sandy ___(A)___ a high school student. She is a middle school student. She is tall, but I ___(B)___ tall.

(A) _____

(B) _____

12 서술형 Complete the dialog by filling in the blanks with grammatically correct words. (1 word for each blank) 4점

> A: Are those cats yours?
> B: No, _____ not. _____
> _____ my sister's.

13 서술형 Find TWO errors and correct them. 4점

> A: Are your brother mean to you?
> B: Yes, he isn't. He's very nice.

→ _____

14 서술형 Translate the question into English and then answer the question according to the picture. 5점

Q: _____ _____ diligent?
A: _____, _____
_____ .

15 서술형 Change the sentence according to the instructions. 각 2점

> Those are fresh from the farm.

(1) 부정문: _____

(2) 의문문: _____

(3) 긍정의 대답: _____

16 서술형 Find ALL of the errors and correct them. 6점

> A: Is she Ms. Simpson?
> B: No, she is. She's Ms. Jacobs.
> A: Oh, I see. Is that hers car?
> B: Yes, that is. It's a Porsche.

→ _____

VOCA cell phone 핸드폰 | mean 짓궂은 | diligent 부지런한 | fresh 신선한 | farm 농장

03 일반동사

■ 아래 표의 빈칸에 알맞은 내용을 써 넣으세요. ›› 정답 4쪽

개념이해책
18쪽 함께 보기

1 일반동사의 의미와 종류

동작	1) ___(가다),	2) ___(오다),	3) ___(앉다),	4) ___(걷다),	5) ___(뛰다),	6) ___(먹다)
상태	7) ___(가지고 있다),	8) ___(좋아하다),	9) ___(사랑하다),	10) ___(생각하다)		

2 일반동사의 3인칭 단수 현재형

대부분의 동사	+-s	11) ___(오다)	12) ___(놀다),	13) ___(걷다),	14) ___(먹다)
-s, x, -sh, -ch,-o로 끝나는 동사	+-es	15) ___(통과하다)	16) ___(씻다),	17) ___(가르치다),	18) ___(하다)
'자음+y'로 끝나는 동사	-y → -ies	study → 19) ___,	fly → 20) ___,	cry → 21) ___	
have		22) ___			

Level 1 Test

›› 정답 4쪽

A 빈칸에 알맞은 것을 [보기]에서 골라 쓰시오.

보기	play	teach	take
	wear	stay	draw

1 I _____ science.

2 On Saturdays, we _____ a walk in the park.

3 We _____ at home in the evening.

4 The students _____ the game again and again.

5 We _____ school uniforms.

6 My sisters _____ sunflowers very well.

B [ ]에서 알맞은 것을 고르시오.

1 Jasmine [dance / dances] very well.

2 Taemin [eats / eates] a hamburger for lunch.

3 My brother [haves / has] a cool bike.

4 Our English teacher [wear / wears] a tie.

5 Jiyun [misss / misses] her family.

C 동사의 뜻과 3인칭 단수 현재형을 쓰시오.

	동사	뜻	3인칭 단수 현재형
1	play		
2	walk		
3	pass		
4	do		
5	have		
6	teach		
7	study		

D 괄호 안의 동사를 빈칸에 알맞은 형태로 쓰시오.

1 My grandmother _____ cereal for breakfast. (eat)

2 My friend _____ to the shopping mall alone. (go)

3 He _____ the game. (enjoy)

4 She _____ very well. (cook)

5 Her son _____ many cards. (have)

VOCA take a walk 산책하다 | stay 머무르다 | draw 그리다 | sunflower 해바라기 | miss 그리워하다 | cereal 시리얼, 곡류 | breakfast 아침식사 | shopping mall 쇼핑몰 | alone 혼자

01 다음 빈칸에 공통으로 들어갈 알맞은 단어는? 2점

> · They _____ baseball.
> · We _____ outside.
> · Mira and Suji _____ the violin very well.

① go   ② do
③ get   ④ play
⑤ take

02 다음 중 밑줄 친 동사의 형태가 올바른 것은? 2점

① She <u>cryes</u> every night.
② Tina <u>haves</u> lunch.
③ Her sister <u>buys</u> many books.
④ Juna <u>staies</u> at the hotel.
⑤ The student <u>plaies</u> computer games.

03 다음 중 어법상 올바른 문장은? 2점

① The queen have a mirror.
② My aunt makes apple jam.
③ They writes letters to their friends.
④ Remy studys English very hard.
⑤ My sister gos to school with her friend.

04 다음 중 어법에 맞는 것은? 2점

① Daniel and Danny are have busy.
② The singers play the guitar well.
③ I has a sister and a brother.
④ He has is the only child in his family.
⑤ Her students does their homework.

05 다음 밑줄 친 단어 중 잘못 쓰인 것의 개수는? 2점

> My dad ⓐ <u>is</u> in London. He ⓑ <u>has</u> busy. He ⓒ <u>gets</u> up early. He ⓓ <u>walks</u> to the bus station. He ⓔ <u>carry</u> his umbrella every day.

① 0개   ② 1개
③ 2개   ④ 3개
⑤ 4개

06 괄호 안의 단어를 각 빈칸에 알맞은 형태로 쓰시오. 4점

서술형

> I _____ a big mouth, but my sister _____ a small mouth. (have)

07 괄호 안의 단어들을 이용하여 우리말을 영작하시오. 4점

서술형

> 그들은 매일 도서관에 간다. (go, the library, every)

→ _____

08 왼쪽의 문장을 오른쪽에 주어진 주어로 다시 쓰시오. 4점

서술형

| Birds fly in the sky. | An airplane _____ . |

09 다음 중 어법상 어색한 문장을 찾아 바르게 고쳐 쓰시오. 4점

서술형

> ⓐ I brushes my teeth after meals.
> ⓑ He has bad teeth.

(   ) → _____

10 다음은 어떤 가게의 영업 시간이다. 이를 참고해서 빈칸에 알맞은 말을 쓰시오. 4점

서술형

→ The shop _____ at 11:00 a.m. and _____ at 9:00 p.m.

VOCA   outside 밖에서 | violin 바이올린 | mirror 거울 | guitar 기타 | only child 외동 | station 정거장, 역 | teeth 치아(tooth)의 복수 | brush one's teeth 양치질하다 | meal 식사

01 Which word is correct for the blank? 2점

> The sun _____ in the east.

① rise   ② rises

③ arise   ④ rose

⑤ raises

02 Choose the best pair of words for the blanks. 2점

> A: Honey, Little Alex _____ a toy for Christmas.
> B: I don't like Christmas. People _____ too much money.

① wants – spends   ② take – get

③ takes – get   ④ wants – spend

⑤ want – gets

03 Which sentence needs a different word for the blank? ("play" or "have") 2점

① They _____ on the field.

② My students _____ baseball.

③ We _____ computer games every day.

④ Gina and Max _____ the piano together.

⑤ Our new neighbors _____ a luxury car.

04 Choose the common word for the blanks. 2점

> • The principal _____ lunch with the students.
> • A monkey _____ a long tail.
> • My patient _____ a headache.

① do   ② have

③ has   ④ eats

⑤ makes

05 How many words are NOT proper for the blank? 3점

> | 보기 | We | You |
> | --- | --- | --- |
> | | Her student | Ryan and John |
> | | Jieun | Mr. Lee |
>
> _____ stays quiet.

① 0개   ② 1개

③ 2개   ④ 3개

⑤ 4개

06 Who corrects the error in the following sentence? 2점

> My grandma water the plant every day.
> (나의 할머니는 매일 그 식물에게 물을 주신다.)

① 승현: water → waters

② 단비: the plant → to the plant

③ 정민: water → give water to

④ 승호: every day → on every day

⑤ 혜원: grandma → grandmother

07 Which of the following is grammatically incorrect? 2점

① Each person have the same book.

② The people know one another.

③ Your homework has many mistakes.

④ The human body needs food and water.

⑤ His mom mixes all the vegetables.

08 Which sentence is incorrect ? (2 answers) 2점

① We go to work by subway.

② My brothers takes a shower after dinner.

③ They feed the goats in the morning and evening.

④ Billy and Sophia comes from Italy.

⑤ My hometown has many famous sites.

09 Which is NOT proper for the blank? (Up to 3 answers) 2점

> Sujin _____ an apple every day.

① buys   ② eats
③ pickes   ④ haves
⑤ washs

10 Which of the following is grammatically correct? (2 answers) 2점

① Her name have a beautiful meaning.
② My brother likes mint chocolate chip ice cream.
③ Katie and Jack respects their English teacher.
④ Polar bears have thick fur.
⑤ He trust me, and I trust him.

11 How many sentences are grammatically <u>wrong</u>? 3점

① He weares a long coat.
② She plays soccer for her school.
③ My dog catchs the ball very well.
④ They watch a movie every night.
⑤ Her sister stays with her grandparents.

12 Write the common word for the blanks.
(simple present) 4점
서술형

> • The photographer _____ a picture of us.
> • It _____ 20 minutes to get to the park.
> • My cousin _____ care of her little brother.

→ _____

13 Translate the sentence into English by using the given words. 4점
서술형

> Cathy는 그녀의 숙제를 학교에서 한다. (do, at)

→ _____

14 Rewrite the sentence with the subject word in parentheses. 4점
서술형

> <u>My parents</u> understand me. (everybody)

→ _____

15 Write the proper word for each blank. Use the given verb. 각 3점
서술형

(1) Winter _____ the last season of the year. (be)

(2) Winter _____ before spring. (come)

16 Look at the picture and complete the sentence. 4점
서술형

→ My mom _____ every day.

17 Find ALL of the grammatically <u>incorrect</u> words and correct them. 5점
서술형

> I wakes up at 6 a.m. My brother takes the bus to school. But I go on foot. At school, my friends exercises on the playground. But my best friend Leo study in the classroom.

→ _____

→ _____

VOCA   meaning 의미 | respect 존경하다 | polar bear 북극곰 | thick 두꺼운, 숱이 많은 | fur 털 | trust 믿다 | photographer 사진사 | take care of ~을 돌보다 | understand 이해하다 | season 계절 | on foot 걸어서 | exercise 운동하다

일반동사의 부정문과 의문문

개념이해책
21쪽 함께 보기

■ 아래 표의 빈칸에 알맞은 내용을 써 넣으세요. ›› 정답 5쪽

1 일반동사의 부정문

3인칭 단수	주어 + 1)	+ 동사원형	그 외	주어 + 2)	+ 동사원형

2 일반동사의 의문문과 대답

의문문(단수)	대답	의문문(복수)	대답
Do I ~?	Yes, 3) _____ . / No, 4) _____ .	Do we ~?	Yes, 9) _____ . / No, 10) _____ .
Do you ~?	Yes, 5) _____ . / No, 6) _____ .	Do you ~?	Yes, 11) _____ . / No, 12) _____ .
Does he/she/it ~?	Yes, 7) _____ . / No, 8) _____ .	Do they ~?	Yes, 13) _____ . / No, 14) _____ .

Level 1 Test

›› 정답 5쪽

A [ ]에서 알맞은 것을 고르시오.

1 I [don't / doesn't] have a sister.

2 Kate [don't / doesn't] sing in the morning.

3 [Do / Are] you busy?

4 [Do / Does] Korea have four seasons?

5 [Does / Do] your son [draw / draws] well?

6 He [isn't / doesn't] from Mexico.

7 She [likes not / doesn't like] novels.

8 Does he [watches / watch] movies?

B 다음 문장을 부정문으로 바꾸시오.

1 My father reads the newspaper.

→ _____

2 We swim in the pool.

→ _____

3 Danny likes webtoons.

→ _____

C 다음 문장을 의문문으로 바꾸시오.

1 You have a cool smartphone.

→ _____

2 Your favorite subject is music.

→ _____

3 He comes from Argentina.

→ _____

4 Your sister has a tablet computer.

→ _____

D 대화의 빈칸에 알맞은 말을 써 넣으시오.

1 A: _____ you like cold weather?

B: Yes, _____ _____ .

2 A: _____ Jane feel good?

B: No, _____ _____ .

3 A: _____ the students have snowball fights?

B: Yes, _____ _____ .

VOCA draw 그림 그리다 | novel 소설 | webtoon 웹툰 | subject 과목 | Argentina 아르헨티나 | tablet computer 태블릿 컴퓨터 | snowball fight 눈싸움

Level 2 Test

>> 정답 5쪽

01 다음 빈칸에 들어갈 알맞은 표현은? 2점

My boyfriend _____ shopping.

① don't like   ② don't likes
③ is not like   ④ does not like
⑤ are not like

02 다음 대화의 빈칸에 알맞은 것은? 2점

A: Do they know about the contest?
B: _____.

① No, they do   ② No, they don't
③ Yes, they does   ④ Yes, they don't
⑤ No, they doesn't

03 다음 중 빈칸에 들어갈 말이 나머지와 다른 것은? 2점

① _____ the flowers smell good?
② _____ you cook well?
③ _____ your robot speak Korean?
④ _____ they live with their parents?
⑤ _____ Sam and Tom study hard?

04 다음 빈칸에 들어갈 말로 알맞지 않은 것은? 2점

Mia _____ a lot of pictures.

① takes   ② is
③ draws   ④ has
⑤ doesn't have

05 괄호 안의 지시대로 문장을 잘못 바꾼 학생은? 2점

① She runs fast. (부정문)
→ 세빈: She doesn't run fast.
② Josh does his homework. (부정문)
→ 혜림: Josh doesn't do his homework.
③ She has two turtles. (의문문)
→ 규진: Does she has two turtles?
④ My brother takes the bus. (부정문)
→ 규민: My brother does not take the bus.
⑤ They do the housework. (의문문)
→ 혜련: Do they do the housework?

06 질문에 대한 부정의 대답을 쓰시오. 4점

서술형

Q: Does your brother eat fish?
A: _____

07 다음 문장을 부정문으로 바꾸시오. 4점

서술형

The children use the Internet.

→ _____

08 괄호 안에 주어진 우리말에 맞도록 대화의 빈칸에 알맞은 말을 쓰시오. 4점

서술형

A: _____ _____
_____ music and art?
(너는 음악과 미술을 좋아하니?)
B: No, _____ _____ _____.
(아니, 좋아하지 않아.)

09 다음 문장에서 어법상 어색한 부분을 모두 바르게 고쳐 문장을 다시 쓰시오. 4점

서술형

Do he has a funny nickname?

→ _____

10 그림을 보고 빈칸에 필요한 단어를 [보기]에서 골라 넣어 문장을 완성하시오. 4점

서술형

보기	good	poor	cooks
	doesn't	sing	sings

Sally is _____ at cooking.	Mike is _____ at singing.
= Sally _____ well.	= Mike _____ _____ well.

VOCA   a lot of 많은 | turtle 거북이 | do the housework 집안일을 하다 | children 어린이(child)의 복수 | nickname 별명 | be good at ~을 잘하다
| be poor at ~을 못하다

01 Which one changes the sentence <u>incorrectly</u>? 2점

① They are singers.
→ Are they singers?
② You have a secret.
→ Do you have a secret?
③ That sounds good.
→ Does that sounds good?
④ Sumi takes off her shoes.
→ Does Sumi take off her shoes?
⑤ Ken is hungry and angry.
→ Is Ken hungry and angry?

02 Which is suitable for the blank? 2점

A: Do you take the bus to school?
B: _____. I ride my bike to school.

① Yes, I do
② No, I don't
③ Yes, you do
④ No, you don't
⑤ It's nothing

03 Which sentence is <u>incorrect</u>? 2점

① Do you respect your dad?
② I don't go to football games.
③ Does he want a cold drink?
④ Ms. Kim don't drink coffee.
⑤ Is she free today?

04 Which dialog sounds natural? 2점

① A: Does Peter work well?
B: Yes, he does.
② A: Does he raise his hands?
B: Yes, he doesn't.
③ A: Do you take a quiz?
B: No, you don't.
④ A: Does he sharpen his pencil?
B: No, he don't.
⑤ A: Does his brother do taekwondo?
B: Yes, he do.

05 Where can you put the word "Does"? 2점

① _____ she afraid of animals?
② _____ he play the guitar?
③ _____ they go to bed early at night?
④ _____ your friends play this game?
⑤ _____ you often go to the library?

06 Who understands the answer for the blank correctly? 2점

A: _____ history at school?
B: Yes, I have two history classes a week.

① 선영: 의문문은 Are로 시작하니까 Are you study로 써야 해.
② 선화: 일반동사의 의문문이니까 Do you study로 써야 해.
③ 성아: 역사 수업이 3인칭 단수니까 Does you study로 써야 해.
④ 치환: 대답을 I로 했으니까 Do I study로 써야 해.
⑤ 연수: Does he study를 넣어서 물어도 같은 대답이 나올 수 있어.

07 Which sentence is <u>incorrect</u>? (2 answers) 2점

① Does your restaurant has any specials?
② He doesn't have patience.
③ Alan don't have any money.
④ Does your school have online classes?
⑤ Do you and I understand everything?

08 How many sentences are <u>incorrect</u>? 2점

ⓐ We aren't go to school by subway.
ⓑ Jiseong does not throws his ball.
ⓒ Do you have many friends?
ⓓ My cell phone doesn't have any games.
ⓔ Does he have a TikTok account?

① 0개
② 1개
③ 2개
④ 3개
⑤ 4개

VOCA secret 비밀 | take off 벗다 | free 자유로운, 한가한 | raise 올리다, 들다 | sharpen (연필 등을) 깎다 | special특별한; (음식점의) 특별 메뉴 | patience 인내심 | throw 던지다 | account 계정

09 Which is grammatically correct? (Find ALL.) 2점

① I doesn't like your new suit.
② Mina don't eat kimchi.
③ Eric studies economics at his university.
④ Sadie don't tell any jokes.
⑤ Leo and I go skiing every winter.

10 Find ALL of the grammatical errors. 2점

ⓐ We don't likes books.
ⓑ You aren't have a sister.
ⓒ She doesn't use the Internet.

① ⓐ likes   ② ⓑ aren't
③ ⓐ likes, ⓑ aren't   ④ ⓑ have
⑤ ⓐ likes, ⓒ doesn't

11 Which of following CANNOT make a correct sentence? (2 answers) 3점

① needs / he / help / . / doesn't
② gym / does / she / the / to / ? / go
③ grow / flowers / without / don't / rain / .
④ Christmas / celebrate / ? / do / they
⑤ for / Jenna / time / has / . / me / doesn't

12 서술형 When rewriting the sentence as a question, which word appears 3rd? 4점

He tells great stories about his childhood.

➡ _____

13 서술형 Translate the underlined Korean into English. 4점

A: <u>그녀는 일찍 일어나나요?</u>
B: No, she doesn't.

➡ _____

14 서술형 Write ALL of the possible answers to the question. Use only the <u>necessary</u> words. 4점

Does your school have a music room?

| doesn't | yes | it | I | have |
| no | do | we | does | has |

➡ _____
_____

15 서술형 Translate the sentence. Use the given words. 5점

엄마는 블로그에 사진을 올리시지 않는다.
post pictures, on her blog

➡ _____

16 서술형 Fill in each blank by using "do" or "have." 4점

A: _____ Jane's brother
_____ a cat?
B: No, he _____ . He _____
a dog.

17 서술형 Complete the dialog with the proper words for blanks (A) and (B) according to the conditions. 각 3점

A: ____(A)____ ?
B: No, she doesn't. ____(B)____ .

· Words	singer, she, a, sing, well, terrible, Hannah, is, does
· Condition 1	주어진 단어를 모두 사용할 것
· Condition 2	어형을 변화하지 말고 그대로 쓸 것

(A) _____
(B) _____

VOCA suit 정장 | economics 경제학 | university 대학 | gym 헬스클럽 | childhood 어린 시절 | post (인터넷에 글·사진을) 올리다 | blog 블로그 |
terrible 형편없는

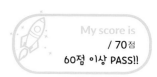

01 U01_2
한눈에 쏙
How many are NOT proper for the blank? 2점

_____ are curling players.
보기

Billy	We	They
The girls	His cousin	He and I

① 2개 　　　　② 3개
③ 4개 　　　　④ 5개
⑤ 6개

02 U01_2
다음 중 빈칸에 들어갈 말이 <u>다른</u> 하나는? 2점

① Jordan _____ happy.
② People here _____ nice to me.
③ Your sister _____ a smart girl.
④ His name _____ Nam Doil.
⑤ My teacher _____ tall and handsome.

03 U01_1+U02_1
다음 빈칸에 들어가기에 가장 적절한 것은? 2점

That man's muffler is very cool, but mine _____ cool.

① is 　　　　② is not
③ are 　　　　④ are not
⑤ don't

04 U02_2
한눈에 쏙
다음 대화 중 어색한 것은? 2점

① A: Is Sally short?
　 B: No, she isn't.
② A: Is Lucy's hair long?
　 B: Yes, she is.
③ A: Are they your parents?
　 B: No, they aren't.
④ A: Are you all right?
　 B: No, I'm not.
⑤ A: Is your brother a middle school student?
　 B: Yes, he is.

05 U03_2
각 빈칸에 들어갈 말이 바르게 짝지어진 것은? 2점

• She _____ a new pet dog.
• My father _____ orange juice every morning.

① have – drink 　　② has – drink
③ have – drinks 　　④ has – drinks
⑤ have – drinkes

06 U04_1
함정
다음 문장을 바르게 분석한 학생은? 2점

My brother isn't watches a lot of TV.

① 상원: My는 I의 목적격으로 맞게 사용됐어.
② 광수: isn't를 don't로 바꿔야 해.
③ 경미: watches를 watchs로 바꿔야 해.
④ 민재: isn't watches를 doesn't watch로 바꿔야 해.
⑤ 별이: isn't watches를 don't watch로 바꿔야 해.

07 U02_2+U04_2
Which word for the blank is <u>different</u> from the others? 2점

① _____ you hate spiders?
② _____ you play baseball?
③ _____ you have a bicycle?
④ _____ you speak British English?
⑤ _____ you really a good person?

08 U04_2
다음 대답이 나올 수 있는 질문으로 알맞은 것은? 2점

No, she doesn't.

① Is she really a K-pop star?
② Do you like horror movies?
③ Do we have any money?
④ Does Sean's sister like kimchi?
⑤ Does your father work in a beauty shop?

09 다음 중 어법상 <u>어색한</u> 것은?

U04_1

① My baby sister always cries.

② Tim doesn't studies very hard.

③ Semi and I walk to school together.

④ Siyoung doesn't do the dishes at home.

⑤ Do you want the toy? — Yes, we do.

10 다음 중 어법상 옳은 것으로 묶인 것은?

U01_1+U02_1+2

고난도

ⓐ I'm not a fighter but a lover.

ⓑ Are your new computer fast?

ⓒ Am I right? — Yes, I am.

ⓓ He still in the bathroom.

ⓔ Trân and Nguyên are not Thai.

① ⓐ, ⓔ　　　　　② ⓐ, ⓓ, ⓔ

③ ⓐ, ⓒ, ⓓ　　　　④ ⓑ, ⓒ, ⓓ

⑤ ⓐ, ⓑ, ⓓ, ⓔ

11 Which dialog is grammatically <u>incorrect</u>?

U02_2

함정

(Up to 3 answers)

① A: Are you happy?

B: Yes, we are.

② A: Are those yours?

B: Yes, those are.

③ A: Are you angry with me?

B: No, I'm not.

④ A: Is your mother a good cook?

B: Sure.

⑤ A: Are Paul Walker a singer?

B: No, he isn't.

12 두 문장이 같은 뜻이 되도록 빈칸에 알맞은 단어를 주어진 철자로 시작하여 쓰시오.

U01_1

This is his smartphone.

➡ This smartphone is h.

13 다음 대화의 빈칸에 알맞은 말을 쓰시오.

U02_2

A: Is Charlie Brown a movie director?

B: _____, _____

_____. He is a cartoon character.

14 Among the underlined words, find TWO errors and correct them.

U01_1

ⓐ Everybody loves <u>her</u>.

ⓑ <u>My</u> name is Julie.

ⓒ I don't like <u>their</u>.

ⓓ <u>It's</u> name is Heart.

ⓔ <u>Yours</u> is not good.

(　　) _____ ➡ _____

(　　) _____ ➡ _____

15 다음 빈칸에 알맞은 말을 넣어 <u>부정문</u>으로 쓰시오.

U02_1

Ray and Tesla _____ happy.

16 다음은 동채의 영작 숙제이다. <u>잘못된</u> 부분을 <u>3개</u> 찾아 바르게 고치시오.

U03_2+U04_1+2

함정

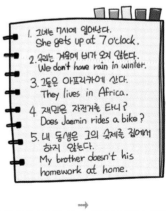

_____ ➡ _____

_____ ➡ _____

_____ ➡ _____

17 Rewrite the sentence starting with the given subject. 4점

| I catch frogs by hand. |

➜ She _____.

18 그림을 참고하여 주어진 단어를 바르게 배열하시오. 4점

| chopsticks, very, well, use, Victor, doesn't |

➜ _____

19 주어진 단어를 활용하여 밑줄 친 우리말 (A)와 (B)를 영작하시오. 각 3점

| A: (A) Emma는 매일 아침을 먹니?
　　(have, every morning)
B: (B) 응, 그래. |

(A) _____

(B) _____

20 ★ 고난도 다음 글에서 어법상 어색한 것을 <u>모두</u> 찾아 바르게 고치시오. 6점

| This girl wears a black gown. She doesn't has wings. But she flys in the sky. She helps young people. Do you need help? Then just call hers. Her nickname is Black Cat. |

➜ _____

_____

[21~22] 다음 글을 읽고 물음에 답하시오.

　　Anna and Daisy ⓐis twins. They look the same. But they act differently. Anna ⓑlikes sports. She is good at soccer. She is very active. She ⓒtalk a lot. Daisy likes reading. She reads a book a day. (A)[loud / is / she / does / not / very]. She ⓓdoesn't likes to talk. However, they ⓔlove each other.

21 ★ 고난도 윗글의 밑줄 친 ⓐ~ⓔ 중 어법상 <u>어색한</u> 것은? (정답 최대 3개) 3점

① ⓐ　　　　　　　② ⓑ

③ ⓒ　　　　　　　④ ⓓ

⑤ ⓔ

22 윗글의 밑줄 친 (A)에서 <u>필요한 5단어만</u> 골라 글의 흐름에 맞게 배열하시오. 4점

(A) _____

CHAPTER 02

명사, 관사, 대명사

UNIT 05 명사의 종류와 수량 표현

■ 아래 표의 빈칸에 알맞은 내용을 써 넣으세요. ≫≫ 정답 7쪽

개념이해책
28쪽 함께 보기

CONCEPT 1 명사의 복수형

규칙형	대부분 → -s	lake → 1) , dog → 2) , house → 3)
	-s, -sh, -ch, -x, -o → -es	bus → 4) , bench → 5) , box → 6) *예외: piano → 7) , photo → 8)
	자음+y → -ies	baby → 9) , city → 10) , party → 11)
	-f(e) → -ves	knife → 12) , leaf → 13) *예외: roof → 14)
불규칙형	불규칙	man → 15) , woman → 16) , tooth → 17) , foot → 18) , child → 19) , mouse → 20)
예외	단수와 복수가 동일	deer – 21) , fish – 22) , sheep – 23)
	항상 24)	jeans, pants, scissors, socks

CONCEPT 2 명사의 수량 표현

	25)		약간의	거의 없는
수	26)	a lot of (= 28))	30)	32)
양	27)	= 29))	31)	33)

CONCEPT 3 물질 명사의 수량 표현

a 34) p_____ of	cheese	a 35) l_____ of	bread	a 36) b_____ of	ink
a 37) c_____ of	coffee	a 38) b_____ of	chocolate	a 39) p_____ of	sugar
a 40) g_____ of	water	a 41) s_____ of	pizza	a 42) b_____ of	soup

Level 1 Test

≫≫ 정답 7쪽

A 셀 수 있는 명사는 복수형을 쓰고, 셀 수 없는 명사는 ×로 표시하시오.

1 ① car → _____ ② peace → _____

2 ① child → _____ ② apple → _____

3 ① fish → _____ ② milk → _____

4 ① air → _____ ② rice → _____

5 ① bike → _____ ② baby → _____

6 ① toy → _____ ② photo → _____

7 ① shelf → _____ ② library → _____

8 ① sheep → _____ ② bread → _____

B 빈칸에 알맞은 말을 [보기]에서 골라 쓰시오.

| 보기 | a few | little | few |

1 이 선생님은 숙제를 거의 안 내주신다.

→ Mr. Lee gives us _____ homework.

2 나는 팔 물건이 몇 개 있다.

→ I have _____ items for sale.

3 그녀는 학교에서 친구가 거의 없다.

→ She has _____ friends at school.

VOCA peace 평화 | shelf 선반 | item 물건 | for sale 판매할

32

01 명사의 복수형이 모두 옳은 것으로 구성된 것은? 2점

① mice, men, foxes

② tooth, babies, dogs

③ potatos, geese, foot

④ deer, women, oxes

⑤ ladies, roots, knifes

02 빈칸에 공통으로 들어갈 말로 적절한 것은? 2점

> • She has a lot of _____.
> • She has many _____.

① work ② money

③ homework ④ friends

⑤ bread

03 다음 중 밑줄 친 부분이 어색한 것은? 2점

① I need three boxes now.

② Those children look so cute.

③ We have five classes today.

④ There are two men and three women.

⑤ There are two truckes in the parking lot.

04 각 빈칸에 알맞은 것으로 짝지어진 것은? 2점

> • I need a _____ of paper.
> • I drink two _____ of milk a day.
> • Can I have four _____ of pizza?

① piece – glass – slices

② piece – glasses – slice

③ sheet – glass – piece

④ sheet – glasses – piece

⑤ sheet – glasses – slices

05 다음 중 어법상 어색한 문장은? 2점

① I have little friends.

② I receive a few letters.

③ She has many watches.

④ The lady speaks a few languages.

⑤ How much money do you have?

06 우리말에 맞도록 빈칸에 알맞은 말을 쓰시오. 각 2점

서술형

(1) 청바지 한 벌: _____ jeans

(2) 주스 세 잔: _____ juice

07 다음 질문에 대한 대답을 조건에 맞게 영어로 쓰시오. 4점

서술형

> Q: 문어는 다리(arm)가 몇 개인가요?
> A: _____
>
> • 조건1 4단어로 쓸 것
> • 조건2 대명사를 사용할 것

08 그림을 보고 대화를 완성하시오. 4점

서술형

> A: Would you like _____
>   _____ of pizza?
> B: No, thanks. I just need _____
>   _____ of water.

09 주어진 단어들 중 필요한 것만 골라 우리말과 일치하도록 배열하시오. 4점

서술형

> 이 동물원에는 원숭이가 거의 없어.
> there, are, is, few, a few, a little, little,
> monkeys, zoo, this, in

→ _____

10 다음 문장에서 어법상 어색한 부분 2곳을 찾아 바르게 고치시오. 4점

서술형

> The Netherlands are famous for a lot of
> things: cheeses, tulips, wooden shoes, and
> windmills.

_____ → _____

_____ → _____

VOCA parking lot 주차장 | language 언어 | the Netherlands 네덜란드 | be famous for ~로 유명하다 | windmill 풍차

01 Which noun is <u>uncountable</u>? 2점

① egg   ② ice cream
③ cook   ④ mouse
⑤ dish

02 Among the underlined words, which is <u>incorrect</u>? 2점

① I don't like <u>mice</u>.
② We have many <u>deer</u>.
③ Look at your dirty <u>feet</u>.
④ Lots of <u>geeses</u> are on the lake.
⑤ There are many <u>leaves</u> on the ground.

03 How many plural forms are correct? 2점

city – cities	wolf – wolves
knife – knives	tomato – tomatos
kid – kids	sheep – sheep
ox – oxen	child – childs
turtle – turtles	photo – photos

① 5개   ② 6개
③ 7개   ④ 8개
⑤ 9개

04 Who translates the Korean sentence into English correctly? 2점

탁자 위에 접시가 많이 있다.

① 현주: There is a lot of dishes on the table.
② 미선: There is lots of dish on the table.
③ 은지: There is many dishs on the table.
④ 혜정: There are a lot of dishes on the table.
⑤ 승준: There are plenty of dishs on the table.

05 Which blank is NOT right for the word "plenty of"? 2점

① I have _____ true friends.
② His wife has _____ sugar.
③ He knows _____ song for children.
④ He drinks _____ water every day.
⑤ They buy _____ bread in the afternoon.

06 Which underlined word is correct? 2점

① Do you have <u>many</u> homework?
② I drink <u>many</u> coke every day.
③ There is <u>a few</u> money in my wallet.
④ There were <u>little</u> people in the lobby.
⑤ <u>Few</u> people came to the party.

07 Find ALL of the answers for the blank. 2점

She has _____ notebooks in her drawer.

① few   ② a few
③ many   ④ a lot of
⑤ a little

08 Whose translation is correct? 3점

① 동호: 나는 커피 한 잔을 원해.
→ I want a loaf of coffee.
② 정균: 그는 종이 두 장이 필요해.
→ He needs two sheet of paper.
③ 경지: 난 바지가 한 벌 필요해.
→ I need a pairs of pants.
④ 선아: 그는 매일 밤 맥주 두 병을 마셔.
→ He drinks two bottles of beer every night.
⑤ 승은: 우유 세 잔을 그 속에 넣어.
→ Put three glasses of milks into it.

VOCA   dish 접시 | true 진정한, 진실한 | wallet 지갑 | lobby 로비 | notebook 공책

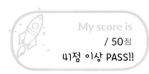
09 How many sentences are correct? 3점

> ⓐ Mr. Kim has two childrens.
> ⓑ The bird drinks little water.
> ⓒ She needs lots of chair for her customers.
> ⓓ There are few tables in the room.
> ⓔ He needs two glasses of iced coffees.

① 1개　　　　　② 2개
③ 3개　　　　　④ 4개
⑤ 5개

10 Which of following CANNOT make a correct sentence? (2 answers) 4점

① swimming / ? / like / fish / do
② coffee / a / lots / . / he / of / drinks
③ puts / salt / she / few / in / soup / . / her
④ few / . / day / me / Irene / a / times / calls / a
⑤ has / in / safes / basement / two / he / . / his

11 서술형 Find the sentence that has an error and correct it. 4점

> ⓐ We have a lot of time before the concert.
> ⓑ She puts too much sugars in her coffee.

(　) _____ ➞ _____

12 서술형 Rearrange the words and make a complete sentence. 4점

> has, of, Ryan, lot, personalities, a

➞ _____

13 서술형 Fill in the blank with a suitable word. The word must have an "F" in it. 4점

> _____ people wear Korean traditional clothes these days. But on special days, some people wear them.

14 서술형 Look at the picture and complete the sentence. 4점

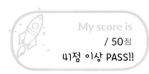

➞ She _____ her _____ after lunch.

15 서술형 Complete the translation. 4점

> 요즘에는 신사가 거의 없다.

➞ There are _____ _____ nowadays.

16 서술형 This is Peter's translation. Find TWO errors and correct them. 6점

> 프라이팬에 약간의 참기름을 넣으세요.
> ➞ Put a few sesame oils in the frying pan.

_____ ➞ _____

_____ ➞ _____

VOCA　customer 고객 | basement 지하실 | personality 인격, 성격 | traditional 전통적인 | clothes 옷, 의복 | nowadays 요즘 | sesame oil 참기름

부정관사와 정관사

개념이해책
31쪽 함께 보기

■ 아래 표의 빈칸에 알맞은 내용을 써 넣으세요. **››› 정답 8쪽**

1 부정관사 a/an

a+[자음] / an+[모음]	a cat, 1) _____ hospital, 2) _____ apple, 3) _____ uniform, 4) _____ hour

2 정관사 the

앞에 나온 5) _____ 를 다시 말할 때	I have a hamster. 6) _____ hamster is very cute.
서로 알고 있는 것을 말할 때	Please open 7) _____ window.
8) _____ 한 것을 나타낼 때	9) _____ Earth goes around 9) _____ sun.
10) _____ 이름 앞에	She often plays 11) _____ guitar.
12) _____ 의 꾸밈을 받을 때	13) _____ gift on the table is from Hara.

3 관사를 쓰지 않는 경우

식사명, 14) _____ , 학과목 앞	breakfast, lunch, dinner, baseball, math
나라 이름, 도시 이름, 사람 이름 앞	Japan, Shanghai, Jason
by+15) _____	by bus, by taxi, by subway
16) _____ 격과 함께 쓰인 명사 앞	my sister, her bag, our room
장소나 건물이 본래의 17) _____ 으로 사용될 때	go to school, go to church

Level 1 Test

››› 정답 8쪽

A 빈칸에 적절한 부정관사를 쓰고, 필요 없으면 ×표 하시오.

1 ① _____ hour   ② _____ week

2 ① _____ rice   ② _____ air

3 ① _____ children   ② _____ cheese

4 ① _____ university   ② _____ MVP

B [ ]에서 알맞은 것을 고르시오.

1 Will you close [a / the] door, please?

2 [The / A] moon is so big tonight.

3 There is [an / the] ant in your food.

4 I have a dog. [The / A] dog is very friendly.

5 [A / The] man in blue pants is my tutor.

C 빈칸에 알맞은 관사를 쓰고, 필요하지 않으면 ×표 하시오.

1 He got _____ F on the English exam.

2 Grandma has _____ breakfast at 6 in the morning.

3 We don't go to _____ school today.

4 Hilary plays _____ harp beautifully.

D 밑줄 친 부분을 바르게 고치시오.

1 Jay, pass me a salt.   → _____

2 A sky is so blue today.   → _____

3 It is a interesting book.   → _____

4 Sasaki is not from the Japan. → _____

VOCA **MVP** 최우수 선수(most valuable player) | **tutor** 과외 선생님

01 빈칸에 'a'가 들어갈 수 없는 것은? 2점

① My sister is _____ student.
② This is _____ new house.
③ There is _____ water in the bottle.
④ Carmen is _____ great dancer.
⑤ She has _____ pop-up book.

02 빈칸에 들어갈 말이 다른 하나는? 2점

① This is _____ orange from California.
② It's _____ egg, not a ball.
③ He is _____ interesting boy.
④ She still has _____ MP3 player.
⑤ He wants to wear _____ uniform.

03 각 빈칸에 들어갈 말이 바르게 짝지어진 것은? 2점

_____ moon goes around _____ Earth.

① A – a ② A – an
③ The – a ④ The – an
⑤ The – the

04 다음 문장의 빈칸에 들어갈 말에 대해 바르게 말한 학생은? 2점

Thanks for the gift! Can I open _____ box now?

① 현민: 셀 수 있는 단수 명사이므로 a가 들어가야 해.
② 수민: 앞에 a를 한 번 썼으니까 이번에도 a를 써야 해.
③ 예은: box를 서로 알고 있으므로 정관사 the를 써야 해.
④ 민준: 모음으로 시작하니까 an을 써야 해.
⑤ 보람: box는 셀 수 없으니까 아무것도 쓰면 안 돼.

05 다음 중 어법상 어색한 것은? 2점

① This is an apple.
② He is not an honest man.
③ Take an umbrella with you.
④ Can I have an yellow cap?
⑤ My uncle is an ethics teacher.

06 다음 대화의 각 빈칸에 알맞은 관사를 쓰시오. 3점

서술형

A: Is it _____ online banking app?
B: Yes, it is _____ useful app.

07 우리말을 영작한 문장의 빈칸에 들어갈 알맞은 관사를 쓰고, 필요 없으면 ×표 하시오. 3점

서술형

우리 팀의 코치님은 터키의 이스탄불 출신이셔.

→ _____ coach of our team is from _____ Istanbul, Turkey.

08 어법상 어색한 부분 2곳을 찾아 바르게 고치시오. 4점

서술형

I have an pen-mouse, but a mouse doesn't work well.

_____ → _____
_____ → _____

09 다음 우리말을 조건에 맞게 영작하시오. 6점

서술형

1년은 12개월이다.

· 조건1 관사를 사용할 것
· 조건2 아라비아 숫자를 쓰지 말 것
· 조건3 '1년'을 주어로 쓸 것
· 조건4 5단어로 쓸 것

→ _____

10 어법상 어색한 것을 모두 찾아 바르게 고치시오. 4점

서술형

I have a old dog. He has big ears, a flat nose, and a big mouth. He barks a lot. He goes to bed late. He sometimes skips the breakfast. He is my best friend.

→ _____

01 Which of the blanks does NOT need "a"? 2점

① She has _____ mountain bike.
② My cousin has _____ younger sister.
③ He brings _____ flower to me every day.
④ They need _____ rice and beans.
⑤ I want _____ new phone, Dad.

02 How many of the blanks need "a"? 2점

ⓐ She is _____ astronomer.
ⓑ The men are _____ engineers.
ⓒ It takes _____ hour and a half.
ⓓ Darling, you're my _____ angel.
ⓔ Is there _____ pet shop around here?

① one   ② two
③ three   ④ four
⑤ five

03 Which of the blank needs "the"? (2 answers) 2점

① We play _____ soccer after school.
② My mother plays _____ violin at night.
③ _____ boy in the red cap is my brother.
④ I had _____ breakfast in the morning.
⑤ He goes to school by _____ subway.

04 Which words are right for the blanks? 2점

• Can you buy _____ roses for me?
• My sister carries _____ expensive bag.
• She needs _____ umbrella.
• He plays _____ trumpet.

① x – a – an – the   ② x – an – an – the
③ a – an – a – a   ④ a – an – an – a
⑤ an – a – an – the

05 Which sentence is grammatically incorrect?
(2 answers) 2점

① Is that an olive or a grape?
② My friend, a John, is a game developer.
③ My grandfather has an old red car.
④ That animal is not a wild pig.
⑤ Those are a special toys for children.

06 Which is right for the blank? 2점

A: How long do you nap each day?
B: About half _____ hour.

① a   ② an
③ the   ④ one
⑤ 필요 없음

07 Which is NOT suitable for the blank? 2점

Look! There is an _____ on the table.

① egg   ② apple
③ orange   ④ ink bottle
⑤ melon

08 How many blanks need "a," "an," or "the"? 2점

ⓐ _____ moon is not a planet.
ⓑ I love playing _____ tennis.
ⓒ _____ milk is good for your health.
ⓓ Einstein was _____ famous scientist.
ⓔ He goes to school by _____ bus.

① one   ② two
③ three   ④ four
⑤ five

VOCA mountain bike 산악 자전거 | bean 콩 | astronomer 천문학자 | half 절반 | pet 반려동물 | carry 들고 다니다 | expensive 비싼 |
developer 개발자 | nap 낮잠 자다 | planet 행성 | scientist 과학자

09 Who corrects the error correctly? 2점

> My sister is an university student.

① 미진: My → Me
② 태선: is → are
③ 지혜: My sister → My a sister
④ 준수: an → a
⑤ 희수: student → students

10 Which sentence is correct? 3점

① Her hometown is a Daejeon.
② My father is an NBA coach.
③ Gill's uncle is my a teacher.
④ Your mother is a beautiful.
⑤ She plays a guitar every day.

11 How many sentences are grammatically <u>wrong</u>? 3점

> ⓐ I eat an apple in the morning.
> ⓑ Can you shut the door, please?
> ⓒ Is it a one-day trip?
> ⓓ He goes to school by bus.

① zero　　　　② one
③ two　　　　④ three
⑤ four

12 Find the error in the following sentences and correct it. 4점

서술형

> ⓐ She plays a piano very well.
> ⓑ The giraffe has a very long neck.
> ⓒ I am a middle school student.

(　　) _____ → _____

13 Fill in the blanks with "a," "an," or "the." 4점

서술형

> _____ neck warmer on
> _____ sofa is my sister's.

14 Look at Carol's wish list and complete the sentence. 4점

서술형

→ Carol wishes to have _____
pencil, _____ eraser, and
_____ ruler.

15 Fill in the blanks to complete the sentence. If no word is needed, put an "×." 4점

서술형

> We usually play _____ soccer for
> half _____ hour on _____
> playground.

16 Find ALL of the errors among the underlined words and correct them. 5점

서술형

> My grandfather is very short and fat. He has ⓐa gray hair and wears ⓑglasses. He loves ⓒfresh air. He has ⓓa hourglass. He watches ⓔa hourglass every evening. So ⓕhis nickname is Grand H.

→ _____

_____

17 Complete the translation. 5점

서술형

> 그는 더 이상 예술가가 아니라 UFC 챔피언이다.

→ He _____ _____
_____ any more but _____
_____ champion.

VOCA　NBA 전미 농구 협회(National Basketball Association) | one-day trip 당일 여행 | neck warmer 넥워머 | ruler 자 | playground 운동장, 놀이터 | hourglass 모래시계 | UFC 종합 격투기 대회(Ultimate Fighting Championship)

지시·재귀대명사, 비인칭 주어

개념이해책
34쪽 함께 보기

■ 아래 표의 빈칸에 알맞은 내용을 써 넣으세요. ≫› 정답 9쪽

1 지시대명사

	단수	복수
가까이 있는 것	1)	2)
멀리 있는 것	3)	4)

2 재귀대명사

	단수	재귀대명사	복수	재귀대명사
1인칭	I	5)	we	10)
2인칭	you	6)	you	11)
3인칭	he	7)	they	12)
	she	8)		
	it	9)		

3 비인칭 주어

13)	It rains a lot in summer.	17)	Brrr... It's winter now.
14)	What time is it? – It is 7:10.	18)	Look! It is bright outside.
15)	It is February 28 today.	19)	It's about 5km from Seoul.
16)	Hooray! It's Sunday.		

Level 1 Test

≫› 정답 9쪽

A [ ]에서 알맞은 것을 고르시오.

1 [This / These] are very nice.

2 Is [that / those] his new car?

3 Whose is this? – [This / It] is Sean's.

4 Are these okay? –Yes, [those / they] are.

B 다음의 재귀대명사를 쓰시오.

1 you two – _____

2 you and I – _____

3 Jim and Pat – _____

4 his sisters – _____

C 밑줄 친 'It[it]'의 쓰임이 [보기]와 같으면 =로, 아니면 ≠ 로 표시하시오.

보기	How cold is it outside?

1 It gets dark. → _____

2 It is not a frog. → _____

3 What is it in your hand? → _____

4 What date is it today? → _____

5 It's quite warm today. → _____

VOCA outside 밖에 | frog 개구리 | date 날짜 | quite 꽤

01 다음 중 밑줄 친 'That[that]'의 쓰임이 다른 하나는? 2점

① That's very nice.
② Is that girl your sister?
③ Is that her printer?
④ That is Dr. Park's office.
⑤ That's a great idea.

02 밑줄 친 단어의 쓰임이 [보기]와 다른 것은? 2점

> 보기   I'm so cute. I really love myself.

① Take care of yourself.
② Ellen herself studies at home.
③ Respect yourself first.
④ We enjoy ourselves at the pool.
⑤ Please help yourself.

03 밑줄 친 'It[it]'의 쓰임이 다른 하나는? 2점

① It rains heavily.
② It is the fourth of July today.
③ It is not your locker.
④ It is six o'clock in the morning.
⑤ Is it twenty–five meters?

04 다음 질문에 바르게 대답한 학생은? 2점

> Do you go to the Internet café alone?

① 주혜: Yes, I go there with my friends.
② 아영: Yes, I go there for myself.
③ 명순: Yes, I don't like the Internet café.
④ 다래: Yes, I go there by myself.
⑤ 다현: Yes, I go there myself.

05 어법상 어색한 문장을 모두 고르시오. 2점

① Those are my umbrella.
② We grow plants for themselves.
③ It is a beautiful autumn day.
④ My grandmother often talks to himself.
⑤ Is this bag yours? – No, this isn't.

06 다음 문장을 조건에 맞게 고쳐 쓰시오. 4점

서술형

> That is a picture of me.
>
> 조건   a picture of me를 pictures of me로 바꿀 것

→ _____

07 빈칸에 공통으로 들어갈 단어를 쓰시오. 4점

서술형

· _____ wasn't my fault.
· _____ was so rainy that night.
· _____ is November 27 today.

→ _____

08 주어진 단어 중 필요한 것만 골라 배열하여 영작을 완성하시오. 4점

서술형

> 내 남동생은 스스로 상을 차린다.
> of, the, to, himself, for, sets, table

→ My little brother _____

_____.

09 문장을 해석하고 밑줄 친 부분의 쓰임을 쓰시오. 각 2점

서술형

> How far is it to the moon?

(1) 해석: _____
(2) 쓰임: _____

10 그림을 보고 빈칸에 알맞은 말을 쓰시오. 4점

서술형

→ The mermaid looks at _____ in the
water.

VOCA   respect 존중하다 | Internet café 인터넷 카페, 피시방 | locker 사물함 | plant 식물 | often 종종 | talk to oneself 혼잣말을 하다 | fault 잘못 |
set the table 상을 차리다 | far 먼 | mermaid 인어

01 Which is NOT proper for the blank? 2점

> Is this _____ ?

① your new cell phone
② her son's computers
③ their first time in Yongsan
④ motorcycle really yours
⑤ Mr. Simpson, your neighbor

02 Which underlined word is incorrect? 2점

① These are not the same.
② That is a really nice mirror.
③ Is those your picture?
④ Whose are these sneakers?
⑤ This is your English teacher, James.

03 How many of the following are correct? 2점

> ⓐ Are those cookies yours? – Yes, those are.
> ⓑ The front door closes of himself.
> ⓒ Does she clean her room herself?
> ⓓ The boys stay at home by theirselves.

① zero ② one
③ two ④ three
⑤ four

04 Which underlined "It" is used differently than the others? 2점

① It is very far from here.
② Wake up! It's 7 o'clock.
③ Close the window. It's raining outside.
④ My favorite subject is math. It is fun.
⑤ It is winter now. I like winter very much.

05 Which underlined "It[it]" is used differently than the example? 2점

> 보기   It is early spring now.

① What time is it? – It's seven thirty.
② It is hot in summer and cold in winter.
③ Is it far from here to your school?
④ Where is your pen? – It's between the books.
⑤ It's Thursday today. Tomorrow is Friday.

06 Which is NOT necessary when translating the sentence? 2점

> 그녀는 화장실에서 자주 혼잣말을 한다.

① often ② speaks
③ her ④ to
⑤ bathroom

07 Which of the underlined words can you leave out? 2점

① Look at yourself.
② Mr. Kim introduces himself to the judges.
③ Help yourself to some pizza, Olga.
④ The girls enjoy themselves in the garden.
⑤ The man dances on the street itself.

08 Which word comes 2nd in the translation of the underlined sentence? 2점

> A: 이것이 너희 집이니?
> B: 아니야.

① it ② your
③ house ④ this
⑤ is

VOCA   neighbor 이웃 | sneakers 운동화 | front door 정문 | stay 머물다 | subject 과목 | between ~ 사이에 | introduce 소개하다 | judge 심사위원 | garden 정원

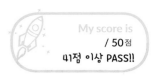
09 Which sentence is grammatically <u>incorrect</u>? 2점

① Know yourself.
② Julian loves her.
③ She says sorry to him.
④ We all enjoy us at the beach.
⑤ He learns Chinese for himself.

10 What does the underlined "it" mean? 2점

A: Is <u>it</u> very cold in here?
B: Yes, <u>it</u> is.

① time   ② day
③ month   ④ date
⑤ weather

11 Which CANNOT make a grammatically correct sentence? 4점

① dogs. / himself / He / trains
② much. / loves / She / herself / very
③ lives / neighbor / themselves. / by / My
④ children / cook / themselves. / for / The
⑤ myself / dog / walk / evening. / every / I / my

12 Look at the picture and complete the dialog. 4점 서술형

A: Is _____ your dog?
B: The one on the left? No, _____
_____ . It's Daisy's.

13 Find the error and correct it. 4점 서술형

Let me introduce herself.

_____ → _____

14 Write the common word for the blanks. 4점 서술형

• Time for bed. _____ is 9 o'clock.
• _____ is too dark outside. I'm scared.
• My sister has a computer. She uses
_____ every evening.

→ _____

15 Write one word in the blank. The two sentences must have the same meaning. 4점 서술형

We have a lot of rain in winter.

→ It _____ a lot in winter.

16 Look at the picture and fill in the blanks. 4점 서술형

A: How is the weather in Pyeongchang?
B: _____ a lot.

17 Translate the sentence according to the conditions. 6점 서술형

이 케이크들은 여러분이 직접 만드시나요?

·Condition 1   단수와 복수의 쓰임에 유의할 것
·Condition 2   주어를 강조하는 표현을 마지막에 쓸 것
·Condition 3   make를 포함하여 모두 6단어로 완성할 것

→ _____

VOCA   Chinese 중국어 | train 훈련하다 | walk 산책시키다 | scared 무서워하는

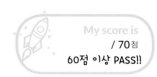

My score is
/ 70점
60점 이상 PASS!!

U05_2+GP

01 명사의 단수형과 복수형이 바르게 짝지어진 것은 모두 몇 쌍인가? 2점

city – cities	shelf – shelves
bench – benches	potato – potatos
goose – geese	deer – deer
ox – oxen	toy – toyes
rabbit – rabbits	safe – safes

① 5개   ② 6개

③ 7개   ④ 8개

⑤ 9개

U05_3

02 다음 빈칸에 알맞은 말로 짝지어진 것은? 2점

- Does she have _____ friends?
- He doesn't have _____ money.

① many – many   ② many – a lot of

③ much – many   ④ much – much

⑤ a lot of – many

U05_2

03 Which is grammatically underline incorrect? 2점

A: How ① many ② childs do you ③ have?
B: I have a ④ son and two ⑤ daughters.

U05_1+GP

04 다음 중 어법상 옳은 것을 고르시오. 3점

① We don't have times for that.

② I have plenty of homeworks.

③ I need some salts for the soup.

④ The girl brushes her tooth every day.

⑤ The man washes his feet at night.

U05_4

05 다음을 바르게 영작한 학생은? 2점

그녀는 종이 세 장과 가위 하나가 필요하다.

① 서희: She needs three papers and a scissor.

② 희연: She needs three papers and scissors.

③ 연주: She needs three pieces of papers and a pair of scissors.

④ 주아: She needs three piece of papers and a pair of scissor.

⑤ 아랑: She needs three pieces of paper and a pair of scissors.

U07_2

06 다음 중 밑줄 친 단어의 쓰임이 다른 하나는? 2점

① She often draws herself.

② He always talks to himself.

③ I don't hate myself.

④ We discovered the diamond ourselves.

⑤ The boys look after themselves.

U07_1+GP

07 In which blank can you NOT put "This[this]"? 2점

① Jerry, _____ is my sister.

② _____ graphic card is so old.

③ _____ bananas are so tasty.

④ _____ city is my hometown.

⑤ Is _____ the train from Chuncheon?

U05_1+2

08 다음 중 어법상 어색한 것은? (답 2개) 2점

① He has three little puppies.

② I like children very much.

③ I eat two apples for lunch.

④ She has four beautiful dress.

⑤ He drinks milks every morning.

09 U06_3

다음 문장에서 어법상 어색한 부분을 찾아 바르게 고친 것은? 2점

> My friend Sinji is good at the math, but she doesn't like it.

① is → are ② the → 삭제

③ doesn't → don't ④ like → likes

⑤ it → them

10 U07_3

다음 중 밑줄 친 'It[it]'의 쓰임이 같은 것끼리 묶인 것은? 2점

> ⓐ It is cold outside.
> ⓑ It is not winter here.
> ⓒ It is not cheap.
> ⓓ It is Monday today.
> ⓔ Is it very far?
> ⓕ What color is it?

① ⓑ, ⓒ, ⓓ ② ⓒ, ⓓ, ⓔ

③ ⓐ, ⓑ, ⓓ, ⓔ ④ ⓐ, ⓓ, ⓔ, ⓕ

⑤ ⓐ, ⓑ, ⓓ, ⓕ

11 U05_2+U07_1

괄호 안에 주어진 단어를 알맞게 변형하여 우리말 문장을 영작하시오. 4점

> 이것들은 너의 강아지들이니? (this, puppy)

→ _____

12 U05_2+GP

다음 중 어법상 어색한 문장을 찾아 바르게 고치시오. 4점

> ⓐ A few monkeis are in the tree.
> ⓑ I like potatoes but don't like sweet potatoes.

( )_____ → _____

13 U05_4

다음 조건에 맞게 영작을 완성하시오. 4점

> 그는 끼니 때마다 밥 두 공기를 먹는다.
>
> · 조건 1 단위 명사를 사용할 것
> · 조건 2 어휘 – bowl

→ He eats _____

every meal.

14 U05_2+U01_2

다음 그림을 보고 문장을 완성하시오. (단, be동사를 사용하고 현재 시제로 쓸 것) 4점

→ Two _____ _____ in love

with each other.

15 U05_4

Rearrange the given words and fill in the blank. 4점

> two, drinks, he, bottles, coke, of

→ _____ at a

time.

16 U03_2+U06_3

Find TWO errors and correct them. 4점

> They usually goes to school by an bus.

_____ → _____

_____ → _____

17 다음 빈칸에 공통으로 들어갈 말을 쓰시오. 3점

- This is my pet snake. _____ snake is so cute.
- _____ actress in the van is not polite.
- _____ Earth is round.

→ _____

18 그림을 보고 괄호 안에 주어진 단어를 활용하여 문장을 현재형으로 완성하시오. 4점

→ The girl _____.

(draw, she)

19 다음 각 빈칸에 적절한 관사를 쓰시오. 필요 없으면 ×표 하시오. 3점

Mr. McGuire is from _____ Ireland. He is _____ English teacher. But sometimes he teaches _____ Japanese, too.

---

20 [보기]에서 필요한 단어만 골라 영작을 완성하시오. 5점

함정

우리는 일요일마다 아침을 먹고 배드민턴을 친다.

보기	a	an	the
	breakfast	play	badminton
	Sundays	have	every

→ We _____ _____ after

_____ on _____.

[21~22] 다음 글을 읽고 물음에 답하시오.

I come home from school and open ⓐthe door. Max jumps at me and wags his tail. Kitty is on the sofa by ⓑher. She comes down and rubs her face on my feet. I open a box of cat ⓒfood and give some food to Kitty. But Max ⓓisn't want any food. He walks to the door. He barks a bit and puts his nose on ⓔit. He says, "Let's go out." (A)우리는 밖으로 나가서 공놀이를 함께 한다.

*wag: (꼬리를) 흔들다

21 윗글의 밑줄 친 ⓐ~ⓔ 중 어법상 어색한 것을 찾아 바르게 고친 것은? (정답 2개) 4점

고난도

① ⓐ the → a

② ⓑ her → herself

③ ⓒ food → foods

④ ⓓ isn't → doesn't

⑤ ⓔ it → itself

22 주어진 단어들을 이용하여 윗글의 밑줄 친 (A)를 조건에 맞게 영작하시오. 6점

---

together, out, play, ball, and, go, a, we

- 조건1 불필요한 단어를 1개 삭제할 것
- 조건2 together는 마지막에 쓸 것

→ _____

CHAPTER 03
시제

08 be동사의 과거형

개념이해책
42쪽 함께 보기

■ 아래 표의 빈칸에 알맞은 내용을 써 넣으세요. 》》 정답 10쪽

1 be동사의 과거형과 부정문

현재	과거	부정문	부정문 줄임말
am	1)	2)	3)
is	4)	5)	6)
are	7)	8)	9)

2 be동사 과거형의 의문문과 대답

의문문	대답		
10) _____ / _____ +주어 ~?	긍정	Yes, 주어+ 11) _____ / _____ .	
	부정	No, 주어+ 12) _____ / _____ .	

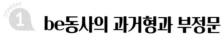

Level 1 Test

》》 정답 10쪽

A 빈칸에 알맞은 be동사의 과거형을 쓰시오.

1 Charles _____ not home.

2 She _____ interested in me.

3 You _____ out of the house last night.

4 Tony _____ late for the meeting in the morning.

B 줄임말을 사용하여 문장을 부정문으로 바꾸시오.

1 I was very sick.

→ _____

2 We were friends.

→ _____

3 Jack and Tina were in my house.

→ _____

4 The director was very happy.

→ _____

5 The rocks were from the moon.

→ _____

C 문장을 의문문으로 바꾸시오.

1 She was sad.

→ _____

2 Their dog was quiet.

→ _____

3 His father was a computer expert.

→ _____

4 You and Jimin were very close.

→ _____

D 밑줄 친 부분이 어색하면 바르게 고치시오.

1 She and I was good friends. → _____

2 Just then, there is a sound. → _____

3 The windows were not open. → _____

4 Was my coffee okay? → _____

5 Were they your brothers? → _____

VOCA be interested in ~에 관심이 있다 | director 감독 | expert 전문가 | sound 소리

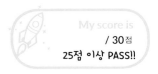
01 빈칸에 알맞은 것은? 2점

It is Monday today. It _____ Sunday yesterday.

① am ② is
③ are ④ was
⑤ were

02 문장을 부정문으로 잘못 바꾼 것은? 2점

① He was excited.
　→ He wasn't excited.
② They were disappointed.
　→ They weren't disappointed.
③ It was a great experience.
　→ It's not a great experience.
④ Jackie was at the department store.
　→ Jackie wasn't at the department store.
⑤ The visitors were nice and kind.
　→ They visitors weren't nice and kind.

03 다음 문장을 의문문으로 잘 바꾼 학생은? 2점

The school band was great last night.

① 지안: Were the school band great last night?
② 민주: Was the school band great last night?
③ 명희: The school band great last night?
④ 유리: The school band great was last night?
⑤ 지원: Was great the school band last night?

04 다음 중 어법상 어색한 문장의 개수는? 2점

ⓐ It was sunny yesterday.
ⓑ Two cats were on the chair.
ⓒ The players were in Texas now.
ⓓ Kaya wasn't at the theater last Sunday.
ⓔ Were your sister at home last weekend?
ⓕ Minji was lazy before, but now she wasn't.

① 1개 ② 2개
③ 3개 ④ 4개
⑤ 없음

05 빈칸에 공통으로 들어갈 말을 쓰시오. 3점

서술형

• _____ your dogs sick last night?
• He and I _____ at home yesterday.

→ _____

06 그림과 일치하도록 대화의 각 빈칸에 알맞은 말을 쓰시오. 4점

서술형

• before　　　　• now

A: _____ the river dirty?
B: Yes, it was. But now it _____ clean.

07 다음 중 어색한 문장을 찾아 바르게 고치시오. 4점

서술형

ⓐ Your children not was at Jason's last night.
ⓑ My axe wasn't silver, but it is silver now.

(　　) _____ → _____

08 주어진 단어를 바르게 배열해서 의문문을 만드시오. 5점

서술형

shoes, 50,000 won, were, over, those

→ _____

09 주어진 단어를 활용하여 우리말을 영작하시오. 6점

서술형

나의 증조할아버지는 독립투사셨다.
(great-grandfather, freedom fighter)

→ _____

VOCA　excited 신이 난 | disappointed 실망한 | experience 경험 | department store 백화점 | visitor 방문자, 방문객 | theater 극장 | axe 도끼
| over ~이 넘는 | great-grandfather 증조할아버지 | freedom fighter 독립투사

[01~02] Choose the correct set of words for the blanks. 각 2점

01

- Honey, I _____ so sleepy last night.
- The shops _____ very crowded yesterday.

① was – was   ② was – were

③ am – are   ④ was – are

⑤ were – were

02

- My uncle _____ at work.
- They _____ in the classroom.
- Little Joy _____ on the playground.
- Her babies _____ in the backyard.

① was – were – was – were

② was – were – were – was

③ were – was – were – was

④ was – were – was – was

⑤ were – was – was – were

[03~04] Choose the correct one for the blank in the dialog. 각 2점

03

A: _____ busy last weekend?
B: Yes, he was.

① Is your sister   ② Is Richard

③ Were the members   ④ Was your daughter

⑤ Was your father

04

A: Were Rita and Camilla in Uganda last month?
B: _____. They were in Cameroon.

① Yes, they were   ② No, they were

③ Yes, they weren't   ④ No, they weren't

⑤ No, we weren't

05 Who changes the sentence correctly? 2점

The game is popular with teens.
(과거 시제의 부정문으로)

① 채연: The game was not popular with teens.

② 동성: The game is not popular with teens.

③ 지원: The game weren't popular with teens.

④ 현진: The game not was popular with teens.

⑤ 가인: The game isn't popular with teens.

06 Which sentence is incorrect? (2 answers) 2점

① Harriet and her brother was very fast.

② His friends were kind to the old people.

③ They were in Havana three years ago.

④ *Les Misérables* were a very sad story.

⑤ John and Roy were very tired after swimming.

07 Who finds the incorrect sentence and corrects it properly? 2점

ⓐ They weren't angry yesterday.
ⓑ Was these tables heavy?

① 호연: ⓐThey wasn't angry yesterday.

② 다원: ⓐThey not were angry yesterday.

③ 탐희: ⓑThese tables was heavy?

④ 원제: ⓑWere these tables heavy?

⑤ 성준: ⓑThese tables heavy?

08 Which one is suitable for the blank? 2점

Yesterday, my friends and I played an online game together. We _____ satisfied. The game was too boring.

① were   ② was

③ are   ④ weren't

⑤ aren't

VOCA   crowded 붐비는 | backyard 뒷마당 | popular 인기 있는 | satisfied 만족한 | boring 지루한

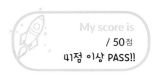

09 Which sentence is correct? (2 answers) 2점

① Were James very strong?

② Was Andrew a famous b-boy?

③ Were Mr. Taylor a taxi driver?

④ Were the neighbors close to you?

⑤ Were the pizza parlor far from their house?

10 How many sentences are correct? 3점

ⓐ Your tutor was very funny.

ⓑ His brothers was not polite.

ⓒ Kumiko and I were not friends.

ⓓ Were you on vacation now?

ⓔ Was their cat in good health?

ⓕ The weather was sunny yesterday.

① one   ② two

③ three   ④ four

⑤ five

11 Which of the following CANNOT make a correct sentence? (2 answers) 3점

① was / there / . / night / I / last

② not / right / . / Your / answer / was

③ his / players / sons / baseball / ? / Were

④ favorite / subject / . / Physics / my / were

⑤ bad / The / . / weather / is / yesterday / really

12 Look at the picture and fill in the blanks with **4 words**. Use "was" or "were." 4점

서술형

→ _____ afraid

of the dog.

13 Fill in the blanks with the *be* verb. 각 2점

서술형

Yesterday, I (A) _____ at the park with my friend Liu. She (B) _____ from China. She (C) _____ in Busan with her family now. They (D) _____ in Jeju last year.

14 Rewrite the sentence as in the example. 4점

서술형

보기   My sister is in a good mood today. (not, yesterday)

→ She was not in a good mood yesterday.

My boyfriend is with me now. (not, last night)

→ _____

15 Look at the picture and complete the dialog. 4점

서술형

A: _____ my son and your daughter at the library yesterday?

B: _____, _____ _____. They _____ at an Internet café.

16 Translate the sentence according to the conditions. 6점

서술형

당신들은 사흘 전에 그 파티에 있었나요?

· Words   be, at, ago

· Condition 1   필요하면 어형을 변화할 것

· Condition 2   모두 8단어로 쓸 것

→ _____

VOCA   close 가까운 | pizza parlor 피자 가게 | tutor 과외 선생님 | polite 예의 바른 | on vacation 휴가 중인 | afraid of ~을 무서워하는 | in a good mood 기분이 좋은 | Internet café 피시방, 인터넷 카페

일반동사의 과거형

■ 아래 표의 빈칸에 알맞은 내용을 써 넣으세요. ›› 정답 11쪽

개념이해책
45쪽 함께 보기

CONCEPT 1 일반동사의 과거형

A 규칙 동사

대부분의 동사	1)	'자음+y'로 끝나는 동사	3)
-e로 끝나는 동사	2)	'단모음＋단자음'으로 끝나는 동사	4)

B 불규칙 동사

• come – 5)	• go – 6)	• do – 7)	• have – 8)
• hit – 9)	• say – 10)	• drink – 11)	• meet – 12)
• teach – 13)	• cut – 14)	• get – 15)	• speak – 16)
• think – 17)	• find – 18)	• hurt – 19)	• buy – 20)
• bring – 21)	• take – 22)	• sit – 23)	• read – 24)

CONCEPT 2 일반동사 과거형의 부정문

25)   [26)   ]+동사원형

CONCEPT 3 일반동사 과거형의 의문문

의문문	대답		
27) +주어 ～?	긍정	Yes, 주어+28)	.
	부정	No, 주어+29)	[30)].

Level 1 Test

›› 정답 11쪽

A [ ]에서 알맞은 것을 고르시오.

1 She [studied / studied] hard last week.

2 He [enjoys / enjoyed] a movie alone yesterday.

3 The teacher [taked / took] me to the hospital.

4 They [save / saved] some money last month.

5 We [meet / met] her at the park yesterday.

6 They [played / plaid] beach volleyball.

7 She [leaved / left] the room a minute ago.

VOCA save 저축하다 | beach volleyball 비치발리볼 | bake 굽다 | collect 모으다

B 문장을 괄호 안의 지시대로 바꾸어 쓰시오.

1 My son bakes bread. (과거형)

→ _____

2 They collected cans and paper. (부정문)

→ _____

3 She lost her math textbook. (부정문)

→ _____

4 They had a pet dog. (의문문)

→ _____

5 Somebody slept in my bed. (의문문)

→ _____

01 다음 빈칸에 들어갈 말로 알맞은 것은? 2점

Sarah _____ an email to me yesterday.

① writes
② writed
③ wrotes
④ write
⑤ wrote

02 다음 빈칸에 알맞지 <u>않은</u> 것은? (답 2개) 2점

She went to the museum _____.

① last weekend
② yesterday morning
③ two days ago
④ tomorrow
⑤ next month

03 우리말을 영어로 가장 잘 옮긴 학생은? 2점

손흥민은 2020년에 푸스카스(Puskas) 상을 받았다.

① 신비: Son Heungmin win the Puskas Award in 2020.
② 가은: Son Heungmin wins the Puskas Award in 2020.
③ 이안: Son Heungmin won the Puskas Award in 2020.
④ 강림: Son Heungmin winned the Puskas Award in 2020.
⑤ 금비: Son Heungmin wined the Puskas Award 2020.

04 다음 중 어법상 옳은 문장을 <u>모두</u> 고르시오. 3점

① He didn't understood the meaning.
② She did not liked her students before.
③ Last week, she doesn't go to work.
④ We didn't go to school yesterday.
⑤ He saw Anika, but she didn't see him.

05 서술형 괄호 안의 단어를 활용하여 그림을 묘사하는 문장을 완성하시오. 5점

→ I _____ to an outlet last weekend, but I _____ _____ anything. (go, buy)

06 서술형 대화의 각 빈칸에 알맞은 말을 쓰시오. 각 2점

A: (A) _____ you swim in the sea yesterday?
B: Yes, I (B) _____.
I (C) _____ for two hours.

07 서술형 주어진 단어들을 바르게 배열하여 완전한 문장을 쓰시오. 4점

answer, the, he, not, phone, did

→ _____

08 서술형 문장을 지시대로 바꿔 쓸 때 빈칸에 알맞은 말을 쓰시오. 각 2점

Oliver puts some lotion on his skin.

(1) 과거형 → Oliver _____ some lotion on his skin.
(2) 과거형 부정문 → Oliver _____ _____ any lotion on his skin.
(3) 과거형 의문문 → _____ Oliver _____ any lotion on his skin?

VOCA   Puskas Award 푸스카스 상(FIFA가 선정하는 가장 멋진 축구 골을 넣은 선수에게 수여함) | meaning 의미 | outlet 직판점 | skin 피부

01 How many past tense forms are NOT correct? 2점

bought	ended	replyed
worried	huged	started
caught	growed	broke

① one   ② two
③ three   ④ four
⑤ five

02 Who finds the error and corrects it properly? 2점

Yesterday, I took my mom's umbrella to school and leave it there.

① 효현: took → taked
② 현주: mom's → mom
③ 주민: to school → school
④ 민서: leave → left
⑤ 서연: it → them

03 Which is NOT correct for the blank? 2점

Tim and Jin _____ last night.

① had a great time
② were at the park
③ played baseball
④ ordered chicken again
⑤ learn yoga

04 Which of the underlined phrases is incorrect? (Up to 3 answers) 3점

① He didn't drew any straight lines.
② Adrian doesn't go to the movies last night.
③ We didn't enjoy the street basketball game.
④ This subway doesn't go to Apgujeong.
⑤ Our team didn't practice soccer yesterday.

05 Which translation is correct? 2점

나는 그녀를 위해 반지를 샀지만 그녀는 오지 않았다.

① I bought a ring for her, but she doesn't come.
② I brought a ring for her, but she didn't come.
③ I bought a ring for her, but she didn't came.
④ I bought a ring for her, but she didn't come.
⑤ I buyed a ring for her, but she didn't come.

06 Among the underlined, which is incorrect? 2점

Last Sunday, Sue and I ① went shopping together. We ② saw so many cool clothes there, but we ③ didn't had much money. So I just ④ bought a cap, and she ⑤ did not buy anything.

07 Which line in the dialog is incorrect? 2점

A: ① Did you find my car key?
B: ② No, I didn't.
A: ③ I need the car right now.
B: ④ I didn't saw it anywhere.
A: ⑤ What's that in your hand?

08 How many sentences are grammatically correct? 3점

ⓐ Today, our English teacher taught math.
ⓑ My son practices the flute every Saturday.
ⓒ My father didn't reads the newspaper this morning.
ⓓ I didn't enjoy summer vacation.
ⓔ He did not be want the pink scarf.
ⓕ Did you go there? – Yes, I did.

① one   ② two
③ three   ④ four
⑤ five

VOCA   reply 응답하다 | leave 남겨놓다, 두고 오다 | order 주문하다 | straight 직선의 | clothes 옷 | scarf 스카프

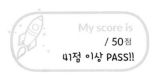

09 In which blank can you NOT put "didn't"?
(2 answers) 2점

① The wizard _____ become angry.

② I _____ get up late today.

③ He _____ sold any paintings during his life.

④ The baby _____ take any medicine.

⑤ She _____ cooks dinner every night.

10 Which set has grammatically correct sentences? 4점

(A) ⓐ He read a funny story.
　　ⓑ Did you wrote it yourself?
(B) ⓐ We plaied baseball together.
　　ⓑ I found an angel last night.
(C) ⓐ Did he really said that?
　　ⓑ We did not start the war.
(D) ⓐ Finally, they left for Quebec.
　　ⓑ She ate a lot of junk food today.
(E) ⓐ He didn't cleaned his room again.
　　ⓑ She spoke to me, but I didn't answer.

① (A)　　　　　② (B)
③ (C)　　　　　④ (D)
⑤ (E)

11 Complete the dialog. Use the word "see." 4점

서술형

A: I just _____ something. Did you _____ it?
B: No. I _____ _____ anything.

12 Find ALL of the errors and correct them. 5점

서술형

Yesterday, I pick some cherry tomatoes and was gave them to my neighbor.

→ _____

_____

13 Look at the picture and complete the sentences. Use the given words. 5점

서술형

Last night, my little sister _____ (draw) some lines on my face and _____ (make) a mustache. I _____ _____ (know) that. This morning, my dad _____ (see) it and _____ (laugh) a lot.

*mustache: 콧수염

14 Rearrange the given words and translate the Korean sentence. 4점

서술형

엄마가 나를 불렀지만 나는 일어나지 않았다.
get, but, I, me, Mom, didn't, up, called

→ _____

15 Look at the picture diary and complete the dialogs. 8점

서술형

A: _____ Janet ride a horse?
B: _____, _____ _____. She _____ a horse.

A: _____ Tony have a hamburger?
B: _____, _____ _____. He _____ spaghetti.

VOCA　wizard 마법사 | painting 그림 | medicine 약 | Quebec 퀘벡(캐나다의 도시) | pick 따다 | cherry tomato 방울토마토 | mustache 콧수염 | call 부르다 | ride 타다

진행 시제

■ 아래 표의 빈칸에 알맞은 내용을 써 넣으세요. >>> 정답 12쪽

개념이해책
48쪽 함께 보기

1 -ing 만드는 법

대부분의 동사	1)	자음+-e로 끝나는 동사	3)
-ie로 끝나는 경우	2)	단모음＋단자음으로 끝나는 동사	4)

2 현재 진행형

기본형	부정형	의문문	대답
am+-ing	5) +-ing	8) +주어+-ing ～?	Yes, 주어+11) . No, 주어+12) .
are+-ing	6) +-ing	9) +주어+-ing ～?	Yes, 주어+13) . No, 주어+14) .
is+-ing	7) +-ing	10) +주어+-ing ～?	Yes, 주어+15) . No, 주어+16) .

3 과거 진행형

기본형	부정형	의문문	대답
was+-ing	17) +-ing	19) +주어+-ing ～?	Yes, 주어+21) . No, 주어+22) .
were+-ing	18) +-ing	20) +주어+-ing ～?	Yes, 주어+23) . No, 주어+24) .

Level 1 Test

>>> 정답 12쪽

A 주어진 문장을 현재 진행형으로 바꿔 쓰시오.

1 I work on a farm.

→ _____

2 My father runs in the park.

→ _____

3 Yumi doesn't make coffee for me.

→ _____

4 She doesn't hit the nail on the wall.

→ _____

B 우리말과 일치하도록 괄호 안의 단어를 빈칸에 알맞은 형태로 쓰시오.

1 우리는 지금 패션쇼를 보는 중이야. (watch)

→ We _____ _____ a fashion show now.

2 지금은 비가 오고 있지 않아. (rain)

→ It _____ _____ right now.

3 난 그날 밤 운전을 하고 있지 않았어요. (drive)

→ I _____ _____ a car that night.

VOCA farm 농장 | nail 못

01 우리말을 영어로 바르게 옮긴 것은? 2점

> 그들은 반성문을 쓰고 있지 않다.

① They don't writing letters of apology.
② They are not writeing letters of apology.
③ They aren't writeing letters of apology.
④ They aren't writing letters of apology.
⑤ They weren't writing letters of apology.

02 다음 빈칸에 알맞은 것은? 2점

> The baby _____ some noodles.

① eat   ② is eat
③ was eat   ④ is eatting
⑤ was eating

03 문장을 괄호 안의 지시대로 잘 바꾼 학생은? 2점

> He begins the trip.

① 세나: He isn't begin the trip. (현재 시제 – 부정문)
② 나영: Did he began the trip? (과거 시제 – 의문문)
③ 영준: He is begining the trip. (현재 진행 – 평서문)
④ 준아: He wasn't beginning the trip.
   (과거 진행 – 부정문)
⑤ 아라: Is he beginning the trip? (과거 진행 – 의문문)

04 다음 중 어법상 어색한 문장의 개수는? 3점

> ⓐ Is he having lunch?
> ⓑ Are the children swiming now?
> ⓒ They aren't speak Japanese.
> ⓓ Were you washing your car?
> ⓔ She does washing her hands now.
> ⓕ Were you two crossing the street together?

① 1개   ② 2개
③ 3개   ④ 4개
⑤ 5개

05 다음 그림을 보고 질문과 대답을 완성하시오. 4점

서술형

A: What is she _____? (do)
B: _____ a dragonfly. (catch)

06 주어진 단어들을 배열하여 우리말을 영작하시오. 4점

서술형

> 누군가가 나를 어둠 속에서 지켜보고 있었어.
> was, me, in the dark, somebody, watching

→ _____

07 다음 우리말을 조건에 맞게 영작하시오. 5점

서술형

> 그녀는 오이 껍질을 벗기고 있는 중이다.
>
> - 조건 1   현재 진행형으로 쓸 것
> - 조건 2   어휘 – peel, a cucumber
> - 조건 3   5단어로 쓸 것

→ _____

08 다음 문장을 시제에 맞게 진행형으로 바꿔 쓰시오. 5점

서술형

> Foolishly, he lied to his lawyer.

→ _____

09 다음 대화의 각 빈칸에 알맞은 말을 쓰시오. 각 1점

서술형

A: (A) _____ you jogging in the park
   yesterday morning?
B: No, I (B) _____.
   I (C) _____ walking my dog.

VOCA   apology 사과 | noodle 국수 | cross 건너다 | dragonfly 잠자리 | dark 어둠 | peel 껍질을 벗기다 | cucumber 오이 | foolishly 어리석게도
       | lawyer 변호사

01 Which correction of the underlined word is NOT correct? 2점

① I am <u>drink</u> juice. → drinking
② They are <u>eat</u> dinner now. → eatting
③ I am <u>cut</u> the potatoes. → cutting
④ They are <u>come</u> to Seoul. → coming
⑤ He is <u>does</u> the dishes. → doing

02 Which is suitable for the blank? 2점

A: Is your sister in the yard?
B: Yes, she is.
A: _____ alone?
B: No, she isn't. She is playing with her rabbit.

① Does she play
② Does she plays
③ Is she playing
④ Is she play
⑤ Is she plays

03 Which sentence is <u>unnatural</u>? 2점

① He was loving the pizza.
② Zoe was coming late.
③ He was leaving home then.
④ They were having a party.
⑤ We were making a cake for you.

04 Who finds the <u>incorrect</u> underlined word or phrase and corrects it properly? 3점

Thank you, Chris. It ⓐ<u>is</u> very cold in Paju today. It ⓑ<u>is snowing</u> now. Some children ⓒ<u>are makes</u> a snowman in the park. Many people ⓓ<u>are walking</u> slowly on the road. Cars ⓔ<u>are moving</u> slowly, too. Now, back to the station.

① 효인: ⓐ → was
② 현정A: ⓑ → was snowing
③ 현정B: ⓒ → are making
④ 채연: ⓓ → is walking
⑤ 지현: ⓔ → are moveing

05 Which is NOT suitable for the blank?
(2 answers) 2점

Lucas: _____ going to the *jjimjilbang* with us?
Yoko: No. She is working today.

① Is Rosa
② Are they
③ Is your friend
④ Was Mrs. Sullivan
⑤ Is Amy's sister

06 Which words are correct for the blanks? 2점

• _____ you feed the cat?
• _____ they following us?
• _____ his brothers playing soccer?

① Were – Were – Were
② Were – Did – Did
③ Did – Was – Were
④ Did – Were – Were
⑤ Did – Were – Was

07 Which pair is correct for the blanks? 2점

• I _____ the answer.
• Brian _____ with his friend now.

① am knowing – is talking
② am knowing – was talking
③ knows – talks
④ know – is talking
⑤ know – was talking

08 Which of the following has the most grammatical errors? 2점

① The man was having a sandwich.
② Is he having a car? – I'm sorry?
③ The babys were sleeping a hour ago.
④ Honey, are you cring? – No, I don't.
⑤ Stella is a good driver. She's driving now.

VOCA yard 마당 | snowman 눈사람 | station 방송국 | feed 먹이를 주다 | follow 따라가다

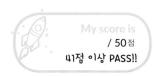
09 Which of the underlined words is different in usage than the others? 2점

① She is <u>running</u> up the hill.

② He is <u>cooking</u> in the kitchen.

③ The baby is <u>sleeping</u>.

④ I am <u>playing</u> the piano now.

⑤ The game is really <u>exciting</u>.

10 Which one does NOT answer the teacher's question correctly? (2 answers) 2점

① I was sleeping.

② I was getting dressed.

③ I did watching TV.

④ I was having breakfast.

⑤ I drank a glass of milk.

11 서술형 Translate the sentence into English. Use the given words. 4점

나 지금 필라테스 하는 중이야. (Pilates, right now)

➡ _____

12 서술형 Find the sentence that has an error and correct it. 4점

ⓐ Mina was asking a hard question.

ⓑ She is wanting a new air conditioner.

( ) _____ ➡ _____

13 서술형 Look at the picture and complete the sentence about each person. Use the proper verb. 각4점

| 보기 | play | sleep | read | water |

(1) Max _____ _____ the flowers.

(2) The grandparents _____ _____ in the chairs.

(3) The girls _____ _____ with dolls.

(4) Mr. Baker _____ _____ the newspaper.

14 서술형 Look at the picture below and complete the dialog between Lily and the officer. Use the given words. 5점

Lily: Officer, I _____ _____.

Officer: No, you _____. You just _____ a red light.
         (be, speed, run)

VOCA   get dressed 옷을 입다 | Pilates 필라테스 | air conditioner 에어컨 | speed 과속하다 | run a red light 빨간불에 멈추지 않다

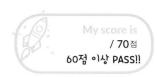

U08_1

01 다음 빈칸에 알맞은 것은? 2점

_____ it windy yesterday?

① Am   ② Is
③ Was   ④ Were
⑤ Are

U08_1

02 다음 빈칸에 들어갈 말이 바르게 짝지어진 것은? 2점

• I _____ sad at that moment.
• The baby pools _____ very crowded yesterday.

① was – was   ② was – were
③ were – were   ④ was – are
⑤ am – are

U08_1

03 다음 영작에서 어법상 어색한 곳을 바르게 고친 것은? 2점

그녀의 반려견들은 몇 년 전엔 아주 크지 않았다.
= Her pet dogs was not very big a few years ago.

① dogs → dog   ② was → were
③ was not → aren't   ④ a few → a little
⑤ years → year

U03_2+U09_1B

04 Which word for the blank is different than the others? 2점

① Artie _____ his best at the last game.
② My son _____ the laundry yesterday morning.
③ She _____ her homework early in the morning last Tuesday.
④ Last night, she _____ the dishes for her father.
⑤ My sister _____ kung fu these days.

U09_1

05 밑줄 친 부분이 어법상 어색한 것을 모두 고르시오. 3점

고난도

① Aaron falled out of a tree yesterday.
② Mark took a taxi home last night.
③ My son played tennis with her yesterday.
④ We danced at the party all night.
⑤ She washd the dishes after breakfast this morning.

U09_1+2

06 Which underlined word or phrase is incorrect? 2점

한눈에 쏙

① I did not swim in that pool.
② The musical did not start until nine.
③ Sharon didn't felt good yesterday.
④ Mike doesn't live here anymore.
⑤ My grandma does many things for me.

U09_1+3

07 대화의 각 빈칸에 들어갈 말이 바르게 짝지어진 것은? 2점

A: _____ you stay at a five-star hotel?
B: Yes, we did. The bed was very comfortable. We _____ well.

① Do – sleeped   ② Do – slept
③ Were – slept   ④ Did – sleeped
⑤ Did – slept

U09_2

08 각 빈칸에 들어갈 말을 바르게 짝지은 학생은? 2점

• He _____ invite me to his party last week.
• I'm sorry I'm late. My alarm _____ go off again.

① 태민: wasn't – didn't
② 민수: wasn't – doesn't
③ 수연: doesn't – wasn't
④ 연정: didn't – didn't
⑤ 정길: didn't – don't

09 U10_2

대화의 빈칸에 알맞은 것은? 2점

> A: What is your sister doing now?
> B: She _____ a text message.

① sent   ② send
③ sending   ④ is sending
⑤ was sending

10 U09_1+2+3+U10_1+2+3

다음 문장을 지시대로 잘 바꾼 것은? 2점

> The baby cries a lot.

① 과거 시제 긍정문: The baby cryed a lot.
② 과거 시제 부정문: The baby didn't cried a lot.
③ 과거 시제 의문문: Did the baby cried a lot?
④ 현재 진행형: The baby crying a lot.
⑤ 과거 진행형: The baby was crying a lot.

11 U08_1

빈칸에 알맞은 be동사의 형태를 쓰시오. 3점

> Yesterday, after a hard team practice, we
> _____ tired, but we _____
> very hungry. So we ended practice.

12 U01_2+U08_1+2+3

대화에서 어법상 <u>어색한</u> 문장을 찾아 바르게 고치시오. 4점

함정

Tina wasn't at school yesterday.

Oh! Was she sick?

Yes, she was. She had a high fever.

That's too bad. Was she okay now?

Yes. She is not sick now.

_____ → _____

13 U08_1+2

빈칸에 알맞은 말을 각각 한 단어로 쓰시오. 4점

함정

> I am fourteen years old. I am a middle school
> student. I _____ thirteen years old
> last year. I _____ a middle school
> student then. I was an elementary school
> student.

14 U08_3

Complete the dialog. Use the past tense form of the be verb. 4점

> Fred, at the library
>
> A: _____?
> B: No, _____.

15 U09_1B

[보기]에서 각 빈칸에 적절한 단어를 찾아 과거형으로 쓰시오. 각1점

> 보기   drive   hit   fight   make

(1) She _____ with her neighbor.
(2) He _____ his car to Seoul yesterday.
(3) The singer _____ a mistake again.
(4) The boy _____ the ball far.

16 U09_1B

다음에서 어법상 <u>어색한</u> 부분을 찾아 바르게 고치시오. 4점

> Everybody laughed and sing happily at my
> grandfather's 60th birthday party last month.

_____ → _____

17 U10_2+3

다음 문장을 시제에 맞추어 진행형으로 쓰시오. 각2점

(1) She changes her mind.

→ _____

(2) Did he cut the red ribbon?

→ _____

18 Among the underlined, find TWO errors and correct them. 4점

> Last weekend, I ⓐ<u>went</u> to London. It ⓑ<u>was</u> fantastic. I ⓒ<u>visit</u> many interesting places. In the evening, the weather ⓓ<u>was</u> fine. It didn't ⓔ<u>rained</u> a lot, and I ⓕ<u>saw</u> a beautiful rainbow.

(   ) ➡ _____

(   ) ➡ _____

19 다음 만화에서 빈칸에 알맞은 표현을 쓰시오. 각 1점

함정

(1) _____

(2) _____ _____

(3) _____

20 다음 대화를 영작할 때 필요 없는 단어를 [보기]에서 모두 골라 쓰시오. 6점
고난도

> 보기   doing   didn't   was   were
> call   study   answered
>
> A: 야! 너 내 전화 안 받았어. 너 뭐 하고 있었어?
> B: 미안. 공부하고 있었어.

➡ _____

다음 글을 읽고 물음에 답하시오.

   My mom and I went to Bukchon Hanok Village. We walked around the village. We ⓐ<u>taked</u> pictures of the old houses and alleys. It ⓑ<u>was</u> a special experience. Then, we went to Insa-dong. We ⓒ<u>saw</u> many traditional antique shops and restaurants along the street. (A)<u>나는 캐나다에 있는 나의 친구를 위해 부채를 하나 샀다.</u> We ⓓ<u>ate</u> *tteokbokki* on the street. It was good but very spicy, so I ⓔ<u>didn't finished</u> it. I want to try it again soon.

*alley: 골목 **antique: 골동품

21 윗글의 밑줄 친 ⓐ~ⓔ 중 어법상 어색한 것을 모두 고르시오. (정답 최대 3개) 3점
고난도

① ⓐ   ② ⓑ

③ ⓒ   ④ ⓓ

⑤ ⓔ

22 윗글의 밑줄 친 (A)를 조건에 맞게 영작하시오. 6점

> ·어휘   buy, a hand fan
> ·조건 1   필요하면 어형을 변화할 것
> ·조건 2   모두 10단어로 쓸 것

(A) _____

_____

CHAPTER 04
조동사

11

can, may

개념이해책
56쪽 함께 보기

■ 아래 표의 빈칸에 알맞은 내용을 써 넣으세요. ⟫⟫ 정답 14쪽

1 조동사의 쓰임

평서문	부정문
주어+조동사+동사원형	주어+ 1) _____ + 2) _____ + 3) _____
의문문	대답
조동사+주어+ 4) _____ ~?	Yes, 주어+조동사. / No, 주어+조동사+not.

2 조동사 can (과거형: 5) _____)

	평서문	부정문	의문문
형태	can+동사원형	6) _____ +동사원형	Can+주어+동사원형 ~?
능력	~할 수 있다 (= 7) _____)	~할 수 없다 (= 8) _____)	대답 Yes, 주어+can. No, 주어+can't.
가능성	~일 수도 있다	9) _____	
허락	~해도 된다 (= 10) _____)	~하면 안 된다 (= 11) _____)	

3 조동사 may (과거형: 12) _____)

	평서문	부정문	의문문
형태	may+동사원형	13) _____ +동사원형	May+주어+동사원형 ~?
약한 추측	14) _____	~이 아닐지도 모른다	대답 Yes, 주어+may. No, 주어+may not.
허락	~해도 된다 (= 15) _____)	~하면 안 된다 (= 16) _____)	

Level 1 Test

⟫⟫ 정답 14쪽

A [ ]에서 알맞은 것을 고르시오.

1 Hazel can [drive / drives] a car.

2 Your child [may / mays] not run in the lobby.

3 [Can you / Do you can] pronounce the word?

B 문장을 괄호 안의 지시대로 바꿔 쓰시오.

1 Dolphins can talk to each other. (의문문)

→ _____

2 We could make a snowman. (부정문)

→ _____

C 다음 문장을 be able to를 이용하여 바꾸어 쓰시오.

1 I can tell you the way to the amusement park.

→ _____ tell you the
way to the amusement park.

2 Can you remember the poem?

→ _____ remember the
poem?

3 They couldn't travel to Europe.

→ They _____ travel to
Europe.

VOCA   pronounce 발음하다 | snowman 눈사람 | amusement park 놀이공원 | remember 기억하다 | poem 시

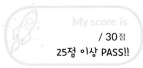
>> 정답 14쪽

01 밑줄 친 부분의 의미가 [보기]와 같은 것은? 2점

> 보기   Your brother <u>may</u> not be sick.

① <u>May</u> I help you?

② You <u>may</u> take a break now.

③ She <u>may</u> understand the question.

④ You <u>may</u> not play music loudly.

⑤ <u>May</u> we play soccer?

02 밑줄 친 부분의 의미가 [보기]와 같은 것은? 2점

> 보기   She <u>can</u> draw unique pictures.

① <u>Can</u> I join your club?

② <u>Can</u> you skate?

③ <u>Can</u> I help you?

④ You <u>can</u> go to bed now.

⑤ <u>Can</u> I close the door?

03 다음 밑줄 친 부분과 내용상 바꿔 쓸 수 있는 것은? 2점

> <u>May</u> I see your passport?

① Do   ② Will

③ Can   ④ Must

⑤ Am

04 다음 단어들로 의문문을 만들 때 3번째 올 단어는? 2점

> was, able, to, Ashley, save, him

① was   ② able

③ to   ④ Ashley

⑤ save

05 다음 중 어법상 옳은 문장은? 2점

① May I came in now?

② She can washes her car today.

③ Will you be able to lend me some money?

④ You may use not my computer.

⑤ He may not happy with the gift.

06 다음 두 문장이 같은 의미가 되도록 빈칸을 채우시오. 4점

서술형

> Cats can jump very high.

→ Cats _____ _____

_____ jump very high.

07 괄호 안의 단어를 이용하여 영작을 완성하시오. 4점

서술형

> 시끄러운 음악은 너의 귀에 해로울지도 모른다. (may, harmful)

→ Loud music _____ _____

_____ to your ears.

08 다음 우리말을 조건에 맞게 영작하시오. 각 4점

서술형

> 오늘 일을 내일로 미루어도 되나요?
>
> · 조건1 put off today's work, until을 사용할 것
> · 조건2 8단어로 쓸 것
> · 조건3 같은 의미의 표현으로 두 문장을 쓸 것

(1) _____ _____

(2) _____ _____

09 우리말과 같은 뜻이 되도록 빈칸에 알맞은 말을 쓰시오. 4점

서술형

> 다른 사람들은 같은 의견을 가지고 있지 않을지도 모른다.

→ Other people _____ _____

have the same opinion.

VOCA break 휴식 | unique 독특한 | passport 여권 | save 구하다 | lend 빌려주다 | gift 선물 | harmful 해로운 | put off 미루다 | until ~까지 |
same 같은 | opinion 의견

01 Which of the underlined words has a different meaning? 2점

① You may go shopping this afternoon.
② The test may not be difficult.
③ May I speak with your daughter?
④ You may use my pictures.
⑤ You may play with the Lego.

02 Which one has the same meaning as the underlined sentence? 2점

A: Excuse me. How can I get to City Hall?
B: Go straight two blocks and turn right. It'll be on your right. You can't miss it.

① Don't miss it.
② You can't find it easily.
③ You can find it easily.
④ You can go there.
⑤ You may miss it.

03 How many of the following are incorrect? 3점

ⓐ Sorry. I will not be able to help you.
ⓑ They may change their plans.
ⓒ She may goes to prison this weekend.
ⓓ He may can choose a yellow cap.
ⓔ She may not be my real sister.

① one   ② two
③ three   ④ four
⑤ five

04 Which is the common word for the blanks? 2점

You _____ see some of the great works by Van Gogh in the museum. You _____ also listen to an explanation with an audio player. I hope you enjoy the tour.

① can't   ② can
③ are   ④ didn't
⑤ don't

05 Which is the common word for the blanks? 2점

• Excuse me. _____ you show me the way to the palace?
• I _____ solve the problem last class, but now I can't do it.

① Couldn't[couldn't]   ② Could[could]
③ Can't[can't]   ④ May[may]
⑤ Can[can]

06 Which of the underlined words have the same meaning? 2점

ⓐ Vera can fix the rocket.
ⓑ Can she write the letters of the alphabet?
ⓒ Can you read this English book?
ⓓ Can I have some pizza now?
ⓔ Can you speak Japanese?
ⓕ Can I send a text message on your phone?

① ⓐ, ⓑ, ⓓ   ② ⓒ, ⓓ, ⓔ
③ ⓒ, ⓔ, ⓕ   ④ ⓑ, ⓒ, ⓓ, ⓕ
⑤ ⓓ, ⓕ

07 Which is suitable for the blank? 2점

He _____ be right, but I can't understand him.

① can't   ② is able to
③ may   ④ has to
⑤ doesn't

08 Which is NOT suitable as an answer? 2점

A: May I use your crayons?
B: _____

① Of course.
② Yes, you may.
③ Go ahead.
④ I'm sorry, but you can't.
⑤ No, I can't.

VOCA straight 곧장 | plan 계획 | prison 감옥 | Van Gogh 반 고흐(화가) | museum 박물관 | explanation 설명 | palace 궁전 | fix 고치다 | letter 글자, 편지 | crayon 크레용

66

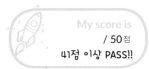
09 Which sentence is grammatically correct? 2점

① Can you be able to help me?

② What day will you can come?

③ She may not be able to buy it.

④ He can't fixes this computer now.

⑤ Thank you. I will may go there today.

10 Who corrects the error properly? 2점

> A: Can you play rugby?
> B: No, I can. Can you teach me?

① 미진: Can you play → Can't you play

② 태선: No → Yes

③ 지혜: No, I can. → No, I can't.

④ 준수: No, I can. → Yes, I can't.

⑤ 희수: Can you teach → Could you teach

11 Which sentence is grammatically wrong?
(Up to 3 answers) 3점

① Birds can fly.

② Will humans can live forever?

③ She may is late.

④ The news can't true.

⑤ Aren't you able to download the font file?

12 Find the sentence that has an error and correct it. 4점

서술형

> ⓐ A tornado can destroy buildings.
> ⓑ Many bees cannot live in one group.
> ⓒ Water cans travel all over the world.

( ) _____ → _____

13 Fill in the blanks with three words. 4점

서술형

> They couldn't work more.

→ They _____ _____

_____ work more.

14 Fill in the black with <u>1 word</u> to translate the Korean into English. 4점

서술형

> 너는 수업 시간에 휴대폰을 켜면 안 된다.

→ You _____ turn on your cell phone

in class.

15 Rewrite the sentence correctly. 4점

서술형

> He isn't may wrong. (그는 틀리지 않을지도 모른다.)

→ _____

16 Write the proper sentence in the blank. Use the given word. 4점

서술형

> A: Hello. _____ Ms. Lee?
>   (speak)
> B: This is she. Who's calling?
> A: This is your student Suho.

17 Read the following and underline the grammatically <u>wrong</u> sentence. Then, rewrite the sentence correctly. 6점

서술형

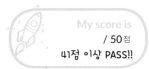

> Do you often smile? Why is a smile so important? Because of your smile, you can find a wonderful boyfriend or girlfriend. You can successful at work. You can get your dream job. You can have many friends. Smiles can make success. Don't save your smiles. Smile.

→ _____

VOCA **font** 글꼴 | **tornado** 토네이도, 회오리바람 | **destroy** 파괴하다 | **bee** 벌 | **because of** ~ 때문에 | **successful** 성공한 | **success** 성공 | **save** 아끼다, 저축하다

UNIT **11** 67

12 will, be going to

■ 아래 표의 빈칸에 알맞은 내용을 써 넣으세요. >>> 정답 15쪽

개념이해책
59쪽 함께 보기

1 조동사 will (과거형: would)

	평서문	부정문	의문문
형태	will+동사원형	1)_____+동사원형	Will+주어+동사원형 ~?
의미	~할 것이다, ~하겠다	~하지 않을 것이다, ~하지 않겠다	대답: Yes, 주어+will. No, 주어+2)_____.

2 be going to

	평서문	부정문	의문문
형태	be going to+동사원형	3)_____+동사원형	Be+주어+4)_____+동사원형 ~?
의미	~할 것이다, ~할 예정이다	~하지 않을 것이다	대답: Yes, 주어+be동사. No, 주어+be동사+not.

3 be going to의 여러 가지 뜻

5)_____	6)_____	7)_____
be going to+동사원형	be going to+장소 명사	be going to+장소 명사+미래 부사(구)

Level 1 Test

>>> 정답 15쪽

A [ ]에서 알맞은 것을 고르시오.

1 They are going [to take / take] a walk.

2 He [will / wills] have exams next week.

3 Hansu will [leave / leaves] for Las Vegas.

4 My parents are going to take care of my pet [last night / this evening].

B 우리말과 같은 뜻이 되도록 빈칸에 알맞은 말을 쓰시오.

1 내일 눈이 올까요?
→ _____ it snow tomorrow?

2 우리는 이번 주에 현장 학습을 가지 않을 것이다.
→ We're _____ _____ _____ take a field trip this week.

C 문장을 괄호 안의 지시대로 바꿔 쓰시오.

1 They will travel by boat. (부정문)
→ _____

2 You are going to cancel the meeting. (의문문)
→ _____

3 Bob will go hiking this weekend. (의문문)
→ _____

D 대화의 빈칸에 알맞은 대답을 3단어로 쓰시오.

1 A: Is your grandma going to learn yoga?
B: _____. She'll enjoy it.

2 A: Will you dive from there?
B: _____. I have a fear of heights.

VOCA take a walk 산책하다 | exam 시험 | take care of ~을 돌보다 | field trip 현장 학습 | cancel 취소하다 | fear of heights 고소 공포증

68

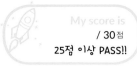
01 다음 빈칸에 알맞은 것은? 2점

> I _____ the bus to school tomorrow.

① take   ② took

③ will take   ④ don't take

⑤ taking

02 다음 각 빈칸에 순서대로 들어갈 be동사의 형태로 알맞은 것은? 2점

> • My son _____ a baby 10 years ago.
> • My son _____ a boy now.
> • My son _____ an adult in the future.

① was – is – will   ② was – is – will be

③ were – was – will is   ④ is – was – will be

⑤ is – is – will be

03 다음 빈칸에 알맞은 것은? 2점

> _____ you going to meet my parents this weekend?

① Do   ② Will

③ Are   ④ Must

⑤ Can

04 다음 중 밑줄 친 표현이 [보기]와 같은 의미인 것은? 2점

> 보기   He is going to school now.

① Are you going to accept his plan?

② I am going to Seoul tomorrow.

③ Is she going to the dentist after school?

④ They are going to get up early.

⑤ We are going to the shop now.

05 다음 중 어법상 올바른 문장은? 2점

① I won't to do it.

② She will be going to finish.

③ Will you to give up?

④ You will can pass the test.

⑤ Will it be possible?

06 친구들과 방과 후에 할 일을 이야기하는 다음 대화를 읽고, 빈칸에 공통으로 들어갈 한 단어를 쓰시오. 3점

서술형

> A: We _____ play soccer after school.
> _____ you join us?
> B: Of course, I _____.

→ _____

07 주어진 단어들을 바르게 배열하여 문장을 완성하시오. 4점

서술형

> will, divers, of, search, the bottom, the lake

→ _____

08 다음 문장과 같은 의미가 되도록 빈칸에 알맞은 말을 쓰시오. 4점

서술형

> He won't take a shower tonight.

→ He _____ _____

_____ _____ take a shower

tonight.

09 조건에 맞게 다음 우리말을 영작하시오. 3점

서술형

> 그는 내일 우리를 방문할까?
>
> 조건 5단어로 쓸 것

→ _____

10 다음 문장에서 어법상 어색한 부분을 바르게 고쳐 문장을 다시 쓰시오. 4점

서술형

> They will do not listen to me.

→ _____

VOCA   adult 성인 | in the future 미래에 | accept 받아들이다 | plan 계획 | dentist 치과 의사 | give up 포기하다 | possible 가능한 | join 함께하다
         | diver 잠수부 | search 수색하다 | bottom 바닥 | take a shower 샤워를 하다

01 Which of the following is correct for the blank? 2점

> _____ Betty going to leave Seoul soon?

① Be   ② Will
③ Is   ④ Will be
⑤ Does will

02 Which has the same meaning as the underlined words? 2점

> <u>Will you</u> study for the exam tonight?

① Do you   ② Are you going to
③ Do you will   ④ Can you
⑤ Do you have to

03 How many sentences are incorrect? 3점

> ⓐ I am going to the ballpark.
> ⓑ I will a good architect.
> ⓒ Is he going to busy tomorrow?
> ⓓ He will visited his relatives soon.
> ⓔ What you are going to do this Saturday?

① one   ② two
③ three   ④ four
⑤ five

04 Which words are correct for the blanks? 2점

> • I _____ coffee every day.
> • I _____ coffee yesterday.
> • I _____ coffee tomorrow.

① drink – drank – will drank
② drink – drank – will drink
③ drank – drank – will drank
④ am drinking – drunk – drink
⑤ drink – drink – am drinking

05 Which is the common word for the blanks? 2점

> • _____ you have some more ice cream?
> • I _____ study law in the future.

① Could[could]   ② Will[will]
③ Would[would]   ④ Are[are]
⑤ Do[do]

06 Which of the underlined words have the same meaning? 3점

> ⓐ <u>Are</u> you <u>going to</u> the gym now?
> ⓑ <u>Are</u> you <u>going to</u> call her?
> ⓒ He <u>is going to</u> Daejeon by KTX. He will arrive in an hour.
> ⓓ They <u>are going to</u> the beach this weekend.
> ⓔ <u>Is</u> she <u>going to</u> agree with me?

① ⓐ, ⓑ, ⓓ   ② ⓑ, ⓔ
③ ⓒ, ⓔ   ④ ⓑ, ⓒ, ⓓ
⑤ ⓒ, ⓓ, ⓔ

07 Which answer choice is NOT suitable for the blank? 2점

> The boss will make a decision _____.

① soon   ② in five minutes
③ before   ④ this evening
⑤ next week

08 Which is suitable for the blank? 2점

> A: Are you going to join the online book club?
> B: _____.

① I am going to the bookstore now
② Yes, I am
③ No, I don't
④ Yes, I will
⑤ I am good at reading

VOCA leave 떠나다 | ballpark 야구장 | architect 건축가 | relative 친척 | law 법, 법학 | gym 체육관, 헬스클럽 | agree with ~와 동의하다 | make a decision 결정을 내리다 | club 동아리, 동호회

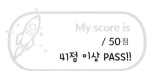

09 Who corrects the error properly? 3점

> A: Will it take a long time?
> B: No, it be won't.

① 태민: it take → take it
② 혜민: take → takes
③ 승민: it take → takes it
④ 진미: be won't → won't
⑤ 인식: won't → will

10 Which is grammatically <u>incorrect</u>? 2점

① I'll speak in English.
② Will you stay home this weekend?
③ He'll never do that again.
④ She won't be hurry.
⑤ It'll take ten years.

11 Find the sentence that has an error and correct it. 4점
서술형

> ⓐ I am very tired. I won't play soccer.
> ⓑ Be Sally going to write a letter?
> ⓒ Will it be ready by tomorrow?

(   ) _____ ➡ _____

12 Answer each question according to the dialog. 각 4점
서술형

> Sam: I'm going to do my science homework this afternoon. Can you help me?
> Danny: Okay. I'll help you after school.

(1) Is Sam going to do his math homework this afternoon? (3 words)

  ➡ _____

(2) Will Danny help Sam after school? (3 words)

  ➡ _____

13 Rewrite the sentence correctly. Change the underlined word. 5점
서술형

> Are you <u>go</u> to skip lunch?

➡ _____

[14~15] Read the following and answer each question.

> **Invitation to a Potluck Party**
>
> Let's have a potluck party with friends.
> You can bring and share your favorite food.
> We will clean up together after the party.
> • When: November 11 at 6 p.m.
> • Where: 2577 Harvard Avenue at Amy's home
> RSVP to Amy at 123-456-7890
>
> *potluck: 포트럭(각자 음식을 가져와 함께 먹는 식사)
> ** RSVP: 참석 여부 회신 바람

14 Rearrange the words and complete the sentence according to the condition. 7점
서술형

> with, a potluck party, friends, her, have, going
>
> • Condition   Add 2 more words other than the above words.

➡ Amy _____

_____ .

15 Which is NOT true according to the invitation? (Choose ALL.) 3점

① Amy's friends are going to the market.
② Amy is inviting her friends to the party.
③ Amy will have a party at her house.
④ Amy will make all of the food for the party.
⑤ Amy's friends are going to clean up after the party.

VOCA   take (시간이) 걸리다 | skip 거르다 | invitation 초대 | share 나누다

must, should

개념이해책
62쪽 함께 보기

1 조동사 must

	평서문	부정문	의문문
1)	must+동사원형: ~해야 한다 (= 2))	① 금지 3) ＿＿＿＿＿+동사원형: ~해서는 안 된다 ② 불필요 4) ＿＿＿＿＿+동사원형: ~할 필요가 없다 (= 5))	8) ＿＿＿＿＿+주어+동사원형 ~? – Yes, 주어+must. – No, 주어+must not. (금지) – No, 주어+don't/doesn't have to. (불필요)
강한 추측	must be: 6)	7) ＿＿＿＿＿ be: ~일 리가 없다	

2 조동사 should

평서문	부정문	의문문
should+동사원형: ~해야 한다 (= 9))	should not[shouldn't]+동사원형: ~해서는 안 된다 (= 10))	Should+주어+동사원형 ~? – Yes, 주어+should. – No, 주어+should not[shouldn't].

 Level **1** Test

>> 정답 16쪽

A 우리말과 뜻이 같도록 빈칸에 알맞은 말을 쓰시오.

1 너는 답을 설명할 필요가 없다.

→ You ＿＿＿＿＿ ＿＿＿＿＿ ＿＿＿＿＿ explain the answer.

2 너는 밤에 커피를 마시면 안 된다.

→ You ＿＿＿＿＿ ＿＿＿＿＿ to drink coffee at night.

3 내가 네 반려동물을 돌봐야 하니?

→ Do I ＿＿＿＿＿ ＿＿＿＿＿ look after your pet?

4 그녀는 화가 났음에 틀림없다.

→ She ＿＿＿＿＿ ＿＿＿＿＿ angry.

5 그 이야기가 사실일 리 없다.

→ The story ＿＿＿＿＿ ＿＿＿＿＿ true.

B 두 문장의 뜻이 같도록 빈칸을 채우시오.

1 You must put the remote control on the table.

→ You ＿＿＿＿＿ ＿＿＿＿＿ put the remote control on the table.

2 Must he accept the plan?

→ ＿＿＿＿＿ he ＿＿＿＿＿ accept the plan?

3 We don't need to hurry up.

→ We ＿＿＿＿＿ ＿＿＿＿＿ hurry up.

4 We should take a training course first.

→ We ＿＿＿＿＿ ＿＿＿＿＿ take a training course first.

VOCA explain 설명하다 | look after ~을 돌보다 | remote control 리모컨 | accept 받아들이다 | training course 훈련 과정

01 다음 빈칸에 알맞은 것을 고르시오. 2점

> We _____ eat too much instant food. It's not good for our health.

① must
② must not
③ have to
④ don't have to
⑤ ought to

02 다음 중 밑줄 친 부분의 의미가 다른 하나는? 2점

① She <u>must</u> be tired.
② He <u>must</u> not say that.
③ You <u>must</u> keep your promise.
④ You <u>must</u> not smoke in here.
⑤ We <u>must</u> keep quiet.

03 다음 빈칸에 들어갈 말로 알맞은 것은? 2점

> We _____ be selfish. Instead, we should be giving.

① should
② cannot
③ should not
④ don't have to
⑤ must

04 밑줄 친 부분이 비슷한 의미인 것끼리 묶인 것은? 3점

> ⓐ She <u>doesn't have to</u> go to the hospital.
> ⓑ He <u>need not</u> buy a new bike.
> ⓒ He <u>must not</u> bother her.
> ⓓ You <u>don't need to</u> be here.
> ⓔ You <u>must not</u> drink cold water.
> ⓕ She <u>should not</u> send him a letter.

① ⓐ, ⓑ, ⓒ
② ⓐ, ⓑ, ⓓ
③ ⓑ, ⓒ, ⓕ
④ ⓒ, ⓓ, ⓔ
⑤ ⓒ, ⓓ, ⓕ

05 다음 중 어법상 어색한 문장은? 2점

① He doesn't have to work today.
② She needs not wear makeup.
③ He ought not to be rude to his teachers.
④ Your brother must be very lucky.
⑤ Her sister must get some rest.

06 다음 밑줄 친 표현을 3단어로 바꿔 쓰시오. 4점

서술형

> Children <u>should not</u> play in the street.

→ Children _____ play in the street.

07 다음 우리말과 같은 의미가 되도록 빈칸을 채우시오. 4점

서술형

> 그녀는 수줍어할 리 없다.

→ She _____ _____ shy.

08 다음 우리말을 조건에 맞게 영작하시오. 6점

서술형

> 우리는 하루 종일 공부해야만 했다.
>
> · 조건 1   study, to, all day long을 포함할 것
> · 조건 2   7단어로 쓸 것

→ _____

09 다음 문장에서 어법상 어색한 부분을 바르게 고치시오. 5점

서술형

> She doesn't have to meet him yesterday.
> (그녀는 어제 그를 만날 필요가 없었다.)

_____ → _____

VOCA   instant food 즉석 음식 | promise 약속 | selfish 이기적인 | instead 그 대신에 | giving 베푸는 | bother 괴롭히다 | makeup 화장 | get some rest 휴식을 취하다 | shy 수줍어하는 | all day long 하루 종일

01 Which of the following is best for the blank?
2점

> Philip _____ clean the room. Susie cleaned it this morning.

① must
② must not
③ doesn't have to
④ has to
⑤ don't have to

02 Which has a similar meaning to the underlined words? 2점

> You <u>must not</u> use a pencil during the exam. You can only use a ballpoint pen.

① need not
② may not
③ don't have to
④ had not to
⑤ will not

03 How many of the sentences are <u>incorrect</u>? 3점

> ⓐ Must I finish this by tomorrow?
> ⓑ This kite have to have a tail.
> ⓒ You will must do several tasks.
> ⓓ You must not to make that mistake again.
> ⓔ You should be polite to Alexa.

① one
② two
③ three
④ four
⑤ five

04 Which words are correct for the blanks? 2점

> • You _____ buy tickets. I bought them for you.
> • You _____ break that bad habit.

① should – should
② don't have to – ought to
③ had to – ought to
④ should not – may not
⑤ can – ought not to

05 Which is the common word for the blanks? 2점

> • You _____ be here on time for the test.
> • He _____ be nervous about the test.

① have to
② must
③ has to
④ do
⑤ should

06 Which of the underlined words have the same meaning? 2점

> ⓐ He lost his wallet. He <u>must</u> be upset now.
> ⓑ It's a fantastic movie. You <u>must</u> see it.
> ⓒ The windows are dirty. I <u>must</u> clean them.
> ⓓ This watch <u>must</u> be old. It looks like my grandfather's.
> ⓔ That blue eraser <u>must</u> be Stella's. She likes blue.

① ⓐ, ⓓ, ⓔ
② ⓒ, ⓓ, ⓔ
③ ⓒ, ⓔ
④ ⓑ, ⓒ, ⓓ
⑤ ⓐ, ⓔ

07 Which of the following is suitable for the blank? 2점

> A: I have a terrible toothache.
> B: Really? You _____ see a dentist.

① may not
② must not
③ should
④ don't have to
⑤ are able to

08 In which blank can the word "must" NOT fit?
2점

① It _____ be expensive.
② He _____ change the plan.
③ We _____ have dreams.
④ You _____ do it last week.
⑤ They _____ carry their bags all day long.

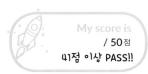
09 Which sentence is proper for the blank? 2점

> Sumi doesn't look well. _____.

① She must be sick
② She must be rich
③ She must work harder
④ She can't be ill
⑤ She must be healthy

10 Which is grammatically <u>incorrect</u>? (Up to 3 answers) 3점

① She need not arrive early.
② We need not to do that for them.
③ He must not to buy the same pants.
④ You must don't close the door.
⑤ I ought to throw this cap away.

11 Write the correct answer in the dialog. 4점

서술형

> A: Must I work on Saturday?
> B: _____. We are not open on weekends.

12 Write the proper words in the blanks. Both sentences should have the same meaning. 4점

서술형

> You should not waste water.

→ You _____ _____
_____ waste water.

13 Rewrite the sentence correctly. 4점

서술형

> Drivers ought obey the speed limit.

→ _____

14 Answer the question according to the dialog. 4점

서술형

> Teddy: Is Charles smart?
> Tommy: He must be smart.
> Shiny: He may be smart.
> Phil: He can't be smart.
> Q. Who is certain that Charles is smart?

→ _____ is certain.

15 Read the explanation below and fill in each blank. 각 2점

서술형

> To express obligation, duty, or necessity in the future or the past, "must" is not used. It is replaced by "have to."
> *obligation: 의무 **necessity: 필요

(1) We _____ book another room.
(2) We _____ book another room yesterday.
(3) We will _____ book another room later.

16 Complete the translation according to the conditions. 6점

서술형

> 나는 "그가 살아 있을 리 없잖아!"라고 혼잣말을 했다.
>
> · Words   can, say, alive
> · Condition 1   필요 시 어형 변화할 것
> · Condition 2   각 빈칸에 3단어로 쓸 것

→ I _____, "He
_____!"

VOCA   throw away 버리다 | waste 낭비하다 | obey 준수하다 | speed limit 제한 속도 | certain 확신하는 | replace 대체하다 | book 예약하다

Review Test

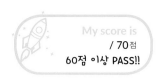
U11_3

01 다음 대화에서 대답으로 올 수 없는 것은? 2점

> A: May I try this blouse on?
> B: _____.

① Yes, you may
② No, you need not
③ No, you can't
④ No, you may not
⑤ Yes, you can

U11_2+GP

02 Which is suitable for the blank? 2점

> I am able to cook Korean food very well.
> = I _____ cook Korean food very well.

① may
② must
③ can
④ will
⑤ do

U12_1+2

03 다음 중 어법상 어색한 것은? 2점

① Are you going to meet her tomorrow?
② I am going to the music festival next month.
③ Will they going to college next year?
④ Will you do something for my family?
⑤ Are you going to Jeju-do this summer?

U11_2+GP+U13_1+2

04 주어진 문장을 부정문으로 바꾼 것이 어색한 것은? 2점

① You must save money.
　→ You don't have to save money.
② They must be from Australia.
　→ They can't be from Australia.
③ She could stand for a long time.
　→ She wasn't able to stand for a long time.
④ He ought to follow the rules.
　→ He had not to follow the rules.
⑤ You can sit there.
　→ You may not sit there.

U11_2+U12_1+U13_1

05 다음 중 밑줄 친 부분이 괄호 안의 의미에 맞지 않게 쓰인 문장의 개수는? 3점

고난도

> ⓐ She will learn the guitar next year. (미래)
> ⓑ She can't be serious. (부정의 추측)
> ⓒ Can I open the door? (허락)
> ⓓ It must be easy for a smart kid like you. (의무)

① 0개
② 1개
③ 2개
④ 3개
⑤ 4개

U12_1

06 내용상 빈칸에 이어질 말로 적절하지 않은 것은? 2점

> Will you stay here _____?

① the day before yesterday
② tonight
③ tomorrow
④ this week
⑤ next month

U12_3

07 다음 중 밑줄 친 부분의 쓰임이 다른 하나는? 2점

한눈에 쏙

① He is going to help his father.
② I am going to win first prize.
③ Are you going to meet your old friends?
④ My boss is going to go to Boston.
⑤ They are going to a mall now.

U11_GP+U13_1

08 Choose the grammatically correct sentence. 2점

함정

① Does she have to go shopping?
② You must can write a poem.
③ We don't need not turn off the phone.
④ I have change the plan.
⑤ He has to return home yesterday.

09 U11_3+U13_1+2

[보기] 중에서 빈칸에 들어갈 수 있는 단어의 개수는? 2점

보기	must	may	should	have to

You _____ not throw away the receipt.
(너는 그 영수증을 버리면 안 된다.)

① 0개　　　　　　② 1개
③ 2개　　　　　　④ 3개
⑤ 4개

10 U13_1

다음 중 밑줄 친 부분의 쓰임이 <u>다른</u> 하나는? 2점

① You <u>must</u> call your mom now.
② Your daughter <u>must</u> get there by 10.
③ <u>Must</u> he walk to school?
④ You <u>must</u> read the textbook before class.
⑤ You <u>must</u> be thirsty. I'll get a drink for you.

11 U13_2

[보기]와 같이 문장을 바꿔 쓰시오. 4점

보기	You take an umbrella with you. → You should take an umbrella with you.
He wears a school uniform.	

→ He _____ _____ a school
uniform.

12 U13_1

다음 우리말에 맞도록 빈칸에 알맞은 말을 쓰시오. 4점

우리는 방학 동안에는 일찍 일어날 필요가 없다.

→ We _____ _____
_____ get up early during vacation.

13 U11_2+GP

주어진 문장과 같은 의미가 되도록 빈칸에 알맞은 말을 쓰시오. 4점

함정

Could they find his DNA at the scene? *scene: (사고·범죄 등의) 현장

→ _____ _____
_____ _____ find his DNA
at the scene?

14 U13_1+2

Look at the pictures and write the common word for the blanks. (1 word) 4점

You _____ wear a swimming cap in the pool.	You _____ be nice to others.

15 U12_1+2

다음 밑줄 친 부분과 바꾸어 쓸 수 있는 말은? 4점

한눈에 쏙

• Justin <u>is going to</u> visit his aunt soon. • <u>Can</u> you come to my birthday party tonight?

→ _____

16 U12_2

Complete the sentence. The two sentences should have the same meaning. 4점

Will you go with me?

→ _____ _____
_____ _____ go with me?

17 U13_1

주어진 문장을 'must'를 이용하여 금지를 나타내는 말로 바꾸어 쓰시오. 4점

NO PETS ALLOWED

> You can bring your pets.

→ _____

18 U12_1

Write the appropriate answer to the question. 4점

> A: Will you drive to Jeonju?
> B: _____, _____
> _____. I will go there by KTX.

19 U13_1+GP

★ 고난도

다음 조건에 맞게 우리말 문장을 영작하시오. 6점

> 그가 집으로 가야만 했나요?
> ···
> 조건 1   go home 단어 사용할 것
> 조건 2   과거 시제로 쓸 것
> 조건 3   6단어로 쓸 것

→ _____

20 U11_3

다음 두 문장이 같은 의미가 되도록 빈칸을 채우시오. 3점

> Perhaps he is 30 years old.

→ He _____ be 30 years old.

[21~22] 다음 글을 읽고 물음에 답하시오.

You're not going to believe this! Choi Taepung, the captain of our school's soccer team, ⓐspoked to me today! He is in the third grade, and I'm in the first grade. He ⓑhas a lot of fans. Every student at my school likes him. Today, I ⓒwas walked home. I saw him next to the bus stop. And do you know what? He called me by my name and said hi to me! He ⓓknew my name. I was so surprised and happy. My face became red, and I ⓔcouldn't moved a single step. He's just awesome! (A)나는 오늘 밤 푹 잘 거야.

21 U09_1+U05_3+U10_3+U09_1+U11_2

Which of the underlined ⓐ~ⓔ is grammatically wrong? (Up to 3 answers) 3점

① ⓐ   ② ⓑ
③ ⓒ   ④ ⓓ
⑤ ⓔ

22 U12_2

주어진 표현을 이용하여 윗글의 밑줄 친 (A)를 조건에 맞게 영작하시오. 5점

> 표현   get a good night's sleep
> 조건   Write a sentence with 9 words.

→ _____

CHAPTER 05
문장의 변환

의문사 의문문

■ 아래 표의 빈칸에 알맞은 내용을 써 넣으세요. ▶▶ 정답 17쪽

개념이해책
70쪽 함께 보기

1 의문사

의문사	뜻	묻는 것	의문사	뜻	묻는 것
1)	2)	사람의 이름, 신분, 가족 관계	7)	8)	장소
3)	4)	사물 또는 사람의 직업	9)	10)	이유
5)	6)	시간, 때	11)	12)	방법, 수단, 상태

2 주의해야 할 의문사

의문사	뜻	사용	의문사	뜻	사용
13)	14)	목적격일 때(who를 써도 됨)	17)	18)	선택을 물을 때
15)	16)	소유를 물을 때	19)	20)	정도를 물을 때

3 의문사 의문문의 어순

be동사	21) + 22) + 23) ～?
일반동사	24) + 25) / / + 26) + 27) ～?

Level 1 Test

▶▶ 정답 18쪽

A [ ]에서 알맞은 것을 고르시오.

1 [When / Where] do you live?

2 [How / What] is the matter with you?

3 [How / Why] is your brother these days?

4 [When / Where] does winter vacation begin?

B 대화의 빈칸에 알맞은 의문사를 쓰시오.

1 A: _____ is he so happy?
   B: He bought a brand-new tractor.

2 A: _____ did you meet at the theater?
   B: I met my science teacher.

3 A: _____ battery charger is this?
   B: It's mine.

4 A: _____ do you go to school?
   B: My mom drives me to school.

C 질문에 알맞은 대답을 [보기]에서 고르시오.

보기	ⓐ Mr. Cho does.	ⓑ This is better.
	ⓒ It's Victor's.	ⓓ It's Friday.

1 Whose bike is this? → _____

2 What day is it today? → _____

3 Who teaches math? → _____

4 Which is better, this or that? → _____

D 주어진 단어를 바르게 배열하시오.

1 저건 누구 가방이니? (that, whose, bag, is)
   → _____

2 네 생일은 언제야? (birthday, your, when, is)
   → _____

VOCA matter 문제 | brand-new 완전히 새것의, 신상품의 | tractor 트랙터 | theater 극장 | battery charger 충전기

01 다음 대화의 빈칸에 알맞은 것은? 2점

> A: _____ sport do you like better, soccer
> or baseball?
> B: I like baseball better.

① Which　　　　② Where
③ How　　　　④ Why
⑤ When

02 다음 빈칸에 공통으로 들어갈 말은? 2점

> • _____ is on TV now?
> • _____ is your weakness?
> • _____ does she want?

① Who　　　　② What
③ How　　　　④ Where
⑤ When

03 주어진 질문에 바르게 대답한 학생은? 2점

> When do you go to the city library?

① 효민: I go there by bus.
② 우중: I study science and English.
③ 상원: It's near your home.
④ 병욱: Almost every day.
⑤ 상훈: I go there with my friends.

04 다음 중 자연스럽지 못한 대화를 고르시오. 3점

① A: Which one is your sister?
　 B: The one in the middle.
② A: Who's your favorite singer?
　 B: I love Lady Gaga. She's amazing.
③ A: What kind of music do you like?
　 B: I like hip-hop. Yeah!
④ A: How is your sister?
　 B: She is seventeen years old.
⑤ A: Who did you dance with?
　 B: I danced with Ted.

05 주어진 단어를 바르게 배열하여 <u>의문문</u>을 만드시오. 서술형

> do, live, where, you, now

➡ _____

06 조건에 맞게 대화를 완성하시오. 각 4점

서술형

> 조건1　의문사를 이용할 것
> 조건2　(A)는 두 단어, (B)는 한 단어로 쓸 것
>
> A: (A) _____ does your
> 　 grandfather usually get up?
> B: He gets up at 5:00.
> A: (B) _____ does he do at that
> 　 hour?
> B: He cooks rice for my family.

07 밑줄 친 부분을 묻는 의문문을 만들 때 빈칸에 알맞은 말을 쓰시오. 4점

서술형

> She is <u>my niece</u>.

➡ _____ is that girl on the playground?

08 다음 그림을 보고 대화문을 완성하시오.

서술형

> A: _____ _____ is your
> 　 daughter?
> B: She's five years old.

VOCA　weakness 약점 | near ~ 근처에 | almost 거의 | amazing 굉장한, 대단한 | hip-hop 힙합 | usually 주로, 보통 | niece 여자 조카 |
playground 운동장, 놀이터

01 Which words are correct for the blanks? 2점

> • _____ does she live?
>
> • _____ is your next operation?

① When – Where   ② How – Why

③ Where – What   ④ Why – How

⑤ Where – When

02 Which dialog is unnatural? 2점

① A: Where is my locker key?

    B: I don't know.

② A: How much is this scarf?

    B: It's $10.

③ A: Where is the art gallery?

    B: It's next to the green building.

④ A: Why do you go to bed so late?

    B: I usually go to bed at midnight.

⑤ A: How do I get to the subway station?

    B: I'm sorry. I'm new here.

03 Read the following and choose the best answer to the question. 2점

> Hi. I'm Jen. This is my family: Dad, Mom, my little brother Kane, and me. My father is a professor, and my mother is a doctor. I'm a middle school student. I'm 14 years old. My brother is 10 years old. He goes to elementary school. Oh, we also have a dog, Oscar. I love my family.
>
> Q: How many people are there in Jen's family?

① There are four.   ② She's fourteen.

③ She's a doctor.   ④ He's a professor.

⑤ There are five.

04 Which of the underlined words is used differently than the others? 2점

① Which city do you like better, L.A. or New York?

② Which do you like better, summer or winter?

③ Which subject do you like better, P.E. or science?

④ Which fruit do you like better, grapes or oranges?

⑤ Which color do you like better, yellow or brown?

05 Which question is NOT suitable for the given answer? (2 answers) 2점

> He's from Punggye-ri.

① Where is Lee Mincheol from?

② Where does Lee Mincheol live?

③ Where is Lee Mincheol's hometown?

④ Where is Lee Mincheol going?

⑤ Where does Lee Mincheol come from?

06 Whose answer is NOT suitable for the given question? 2점

> What's your favorite season? Why?

① 철희: I love autumn. The sky is high and clear.

② 미수: I love spring. There are so many flowers.

③ 혜수: I just hate summer. It rains a lot.

④ 애리: My favorite season is summer. I can go to the beach.

⑤ 상우: My favorite season is winter. Skiing is my favorite activity.

VOCA operation 수술 | locker 사물함 | scarf 스카프 | professor 교수 | elementary school 초등학교 | P.E. 체육(physical education) | hometown 고향 | favorite 가장 좋아하는 | activity 활동

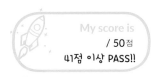
07 Which is the best answer to the question? 2점

> When do you go to your violin lesson?

① By bike.

② Every Tuesday and Thursday.

③ It's near my school.

④ I love the lesson.

⑤ I didn't go there yesterday.

08 Which question can you NOT answer according to the ad? 2점

> **Come and Enjoy the Okie–Dokie Mart!**
> • Location: 11th Street
> • Opening Hours: 10 a.m. – 11 p.m.
> • Special Event: a gift for a family with a senior citizen

① Where is the mart?

② What is the name of the mart?

③ When does the mart close?

④ Who will get a gift?

⑤ What kind of gift will they give?

09 Which is NOT necessary when translating the sentences? 2점

> • 이것은 누구의 벨소리니? (ringtone)
> • 너는 누구를 기다리고 있는 중이니? (wait for)

① who   ② whose

③ whom   ④ does

⑤ waiting

10 Fill in the blanks so that the sentences have the same meaning. 4점

서술형

> What is your favorite flavor of ice cream?

➡ _____ do you like the most?

11 Correct the underlined word. Write **2 words**.

서술형 4점

> A: <u>Where</u> do you go to bed at night?
> B: I go to bed at 1 a.m.

➡ _____

12 Rearrange the given words for blank. 4점

서술형

> A: _____ ?
>   (to, father, work, does, how, your, go)
> B: He goes to work on foot.

13 Write the common word for the blanks. 4점

서술형

> A: _____ do you like summer?
> B: I can swim in the pool. I like swimming.
> A: _____ don't you go to the pool with me this Sunday?
> B: Sounds great.

➡ _____

14 Look at the student information card and complete the dialog. 각 4점

서술형

Name	Kareem
Age	14
Nationality	Turkey
Language	Turkish

> A: (A) _____ is his name?
> B: His name is Kareem.
> A: (B) _____ _____ is he?
> B: He is fourteen years old.
> A: (C) _____ is he from?
> B: He is from Turkey.
> A: (D) _____ language does he speak?
> B: He speaks Turkish.

VOCA special 특별한 | senior citizen 노인 | ringtone 벨소리 | flavor 향, 맛 | on foot 걸어서 | nationality 국적 | language 언어 | Turkish 터키어

개념이해책
73쪽 함께 보기

■ 아래 표의 빈칸에 알맞은 내용을 써 넣으세요. ›› 정답 18쪽

1 명령문

A 긍정 명령문과 부정 명령문

	어순	해석
긍정 명령문	1) ~.	2)
부정 명령문	3) +동사원형 ~.	~하지 마라.
	4) +동사원형 ~.	절대로 ~하지 마라.

B Let's 청유문

	어순	해석
긍정 청유문	5) +동사원형 ~.	6)
부정 청유문	7) +동사원형 ~.	8)

Level 1 Test

›› 정답 18쪽

A [ ]에서 알맞은 것을 고르시오.

1 [Have / Has] a good day.

2 Do not [pick / picked] the flowers.

3 Never [talking / talk] to me again.

4 [Let's / Let] me see.

5 Let's not [hid / hide] our feelings.

B 다음을 괄호 안의 지시대로 바꿔 쓰시오.

1 You call me every thirty minutes. (긍정 명령문)

→ _____

2 Let's walk that way. (부정 청유문)

→ _____

3 You are careful. (긍정 명령문)

→ _____

4 Drive fast. (부정 명령문)

→ _____

C 빈칸에 알맞은 단어를 [보기]에서 골라 쓰시오.

보기	Be	Never	Let	Keep

1 _____ waste money!

2 _____ your promise!

3 _____ my partner.

4 _____ him have it.

D 우리말과 같은 뜻이 되도록 빈칸을 채우시오.

1 불을 켜지 마.

→ _____ turn on the lights.

2 코트를 입어.

→ _____ a coat.

3 그 문을 노란색으로 칠하자.

→ _____ _____ the door yellow.

4 그의 이야기를 믿지 말자.

→ _____ _____ _____ his story.

5 절대 여기서 길을 건너지 마.

→ _____ _____ the road here.

VOCA pick 꺾다 | hide 숨기다 | feeling 감정 | careful 조심하는 | waste 낭비하다 | promise 약속 | cross 건너다

01 다음 빈칸에 알맞은 것은? 2점

Please _____ care of my cat tonight.

① took
② take
③ taken
④ be
⑤ are

02 우리말을 영작할 때 빈칸에 알맞은 것은? (답 2개) 2점

우리 다시 만나지 말자.
= _____ meet again.

① Don't let
② Let me not
③ Let's not
④ Let's
⑤ Let not

03 다음 상황에 어울리는 명령문을 바르게 쓴 학생은? 2점

Simon eats too much chicken.

① 현우: Simon, eat too much chicken.
② 계희: Simon, eats too much chicken.
③ 명진: Simon, don't eat too much chicken.
④ 성진: Simon, let's eat too much chicken.
⑤ 매리: Simon, let's eat not too much chicken.

04 다음 대화의 빈칸에 알맞은 것은? 2점

A: Oh, my! The bus just left. Let's take a taxi.
B: _____. The next bus is coming in a minute.

① Yes, let's
② No, let's
③ Yes, we do
④ No, let's not
⑤ No, it isn't

05 다음 중 어색한 것을 고르시오. 2점

① Don't close the book yet.
② Katherine, be comb your hair.
③ Blaine, don't be angry.
④ Send this email to Mr. Lee, please.
⑤ Never speak to her like that again.

06 다음 상황 설명을 읽고, 밑줄 친 우리말에 해당하는 명령문을 쓰시오. 4점

서술형

Your friend is running too slowly in a race. You say to her, "빨리 뛰어!"

→ _____

07 주어진 단어를 이용하여 다음 안내문을 영작하시오. 4점

서술형

애완동물을 데리고 오지 마세요

bring, your pet

→ _____

08 두 문장의 의미가 같도록 빈칸에 2글자의 단어를 쓰시오. 4점

서술형

Don't make any noise, please.

→ _____ quiet, please.

09 다음을 부정 명령문으로 고치시오. 4점

서술형

Be cruel to me.

→ _____

10 다음 중 어법상 어색한 문장을 찾아 바르게 고치시오. 4점

서술형

ⓐ Never swims in this lake.
ⓑ Let's not have a party this time.

(　　) _____ → _____

VOCA take care of ~을 돌보다 | in a minute 잠시 후에, 곧 | comb 빗질하다 | slowly 느리게 | race 경주 | noise 소음 | cruel 잔인한

UNIT **15** 85

01 Which is correct for the blank? 2점

> Kevin, _____ back to me.

① comes
② come
③ was
④ came
⑤ is

02 Which change is NOT correct? 2점

① You're not kind.
➡ Be kind.
② You're not ready.
➡ Be ready.
③ You're mean.
➡ Not be mean.
④ You're so negative.
➡ Don't be so negative.
⑤ You turned off the TV.
➡ Turn on the TV, please.

03 Which is the the correct translation of the underlined Korean sentence? 2점

> Honey, did you see my message? 제발 답 문자 줘.

① Texts me back, please.
② Please texts me back.
③ Text me back, please.
④ Texting me back, please.
⑤ Please texted me back.

04 Find the suitable word for the blank. 2점

> Cathy, come on time tomorrow.
> = Cathy, _____ late tomorrow.

① is not
② not
③ be never
④ don't be
⑤ not be

05 Who translates the sentence correctly? 2점

> 그들이 그 케이크를 먹게 해줘.

① 천희: They eat the cake.
② 혜나: Let they eat the cake.
③ 효진: Let them eat the cake.
④ 도수: Let's eat the cake.
⑤ 은진: Let's them eat the cake.

06 Which of the underlined words or phrases is incorrect? 2점

① Let's put up the tent here.
② Make a shopping list first.
③ Never says goodbye.
④ Let him tell you the secret.
⑤ Please press your ID number.

07 Which dialog is unnatural? 2점

① A: Clean your room first.
B: Sure, I will.
② A: Don't touch the statue.
B: Oh, I see.
③ A: Type three H's in the box.
B: Okay.
④ A: Let's not drink this water.
B: Yes, let's not.
⑤ A: Help yourself, please.
B: Thank you.

08 How many sentences are incorrect? 3점

> ⓐ Be cool.
> ⓑ Look at the dragonflies.
> ⓒ Please never talked to me.
> ⓓ Let's walk from here.
> ⓔ Let's not spending the money.
> ⓕ Let him push the cart.

① one
② two
③ three
④ four
⑤ five

VOCA negative 부정적인 | text 문자를 보내다 | on time 제시간에, 정각에 | put up 세우다 | statue 조각상 | dragonfly 잠자리

86

09 Which one is grammatically <u>incorrect</u>? 2점

① Let's watch TV after dinner.

② Don't off the lights. It's too dark.

③ Be honest with me, please.

④ Let's go home by taxi.

⑤ Hurry up! We're late.

10 Which one is grammatically correct? 2점

① Wears a swimming cap.

② Not sit in the sun too long.

③ Uses sunblock.

④ Doesn't throw bottles.

⑤ Don't swim in deep water.

11 Which of the following can make a correct sentence? (2 answers) 4점

① speaking / Let / me / first / .

② water / some / First / . / boils / ,

③ look / . / once / at / Please / me

④ be / things / . / do / stupid / Don't

⑤ not / . / anymore / Let's / mention / it

12 Which word comes <u>3rd</u> when rearranging the given words? 4점
서술형

gifts, let's, Christmas, buy, this year, not

→ _____

13 Find the error and correct it. 4점
서술형

Hey, you! Don't be say that, please.

_____ → _____

14 Complete the translation according to the conditions. 5점
서술형

용서해라. 하지만 결코 잊지 마라.

· Condition 1   do를 사용하지 말 것
· Condition 2   f로 시작하는 두 단어를 쓸 것

→ _____ but _____

_____ .

15 Rearrange the words for the blank and translate the Korean sentence. Use the hint. 5점
서술형

제발 날 '자기'라고 부르지 마.

"*jagi*"   call   don't   me

· Hint   call A B: A를 B로 부르다

→ Please _____ .

16 Rearrange the given words and complete the sentence. One word is NOT necessary. 4점
서술형

be, let's, goodbye, say, not

→ _____

17 Fill in the blanks in the dialog according to the sign. 3점
서술형

NO PARKING HERE TO CORNER

Police officer: This is not a parking zone, sir.

_____ _____

from here to the corner.

Mr. Kim: Oh, I'm sorry. I didn't see the sign.

VOCA   swimming cap 수영 모자 | sunblock 자외선 차단제 | throw 던지다 | boil 끓이다 | mention 언급하다 | park 주차하다 | corner 구석, 모퉁이 | sign 표지판

16 부가의문문

■ 아래 표의 빈칸에 알맞은 내용을 써 넣으세요. >>> 정답 19쪽

개념이해책
76쪽 함께 보기

① 부가의문문

A 부가의문문

형태	긍정 → 1)		부정 → 2)		
동사	be동사/조동사 → 3)		일반동사 → 4)	/	/

B 명령문과 Let's 청유문의 부가의문문

명령문	~, 5)	?
Let's 청유문	~, 6)	?

Level 1 Test

>>> 정답 19쪽

A [ ]에서 알맞은 것을 고르시오.

1 Yuki is tall, [isn't / doesn't] she?

2 He can dunk, [doesn't / can't] he?

3 Close all the doors, [do / will] you?

4 Let's go camping this weekend, [shall / won't] we?

B [보기]에서 알맞은 표현을 골라 쓰시오.

> 보기   ⓐ will she   ⓑ aren't we
>   ⓒ shall we   ⓓ will you

1 She won't stop dancing, _____ ?

2 You and I are good friends, _____ ?

3 Let me hold your bag, _____ ?

4 Let's not see that movie, _____ ?

C 밑줄 친 부분을 바르게 고치시오.

1 Minsik is a bad guy, <u>isn't Minsik</u>?

→ _____

2 Dahee knows you, <u>don't you</u>?

→ _____

D 빈칸에 알맞은 말을 쓰시오.

1 Otis isn't your friend, _____ _____ ?

2 You practice yoga these days, _____ _____ ?

3 She just wants to have fun, _____ _____ ?

4 Let me go there by myself, _____ _____ ?

E 문장에서 부가의문문이 어색하면 바르게 고치시오.

1 He isn't from Seoul, is he?

→ _____

2 She doesn't cook at home, does she?

→ _____

3 You're not angry with me, aren't you?

→ _____

4 Let's share the earphones, will you?

→ _____

VOCA   dunk 덩크슛을 하다 | hold 잡다, 들다 | by oneself 혼자서 | share 같이 쓰다

01 다음 문장의 빈칸에 알맞은 것은? 2점

Hippos have pink sweat, _____?

① aren't they
② do they
③ don't they
④ have they
⑤ haven't they

02 다음 대화의 빈칸에 알맞은 것은? 2점

A: You're Tony, _____?
B: No, I'm not. I'm his twin brother.

① don't you
② are you
③ aren't you
④ are not you
⑤ isn't he

03 다음 문장에서 어법상 어색한 것을 바르게 고친 것은? 3점

There are lots of cars on the street, aren't they?

① are → is
② lots of → lot of
③ cars → car
④ aren't → are
⑤ they → there

04 밑줄 친 부분의 쓰임이 어법상 어색한 것은? 2점

① The cat isn't yours, is it?
② You don't like ballet, do you?
③ She went bowling alone, did she?
④ Sibaski plays the piano, doesn't he?
⑤ He will arrive soon, won't he?

05 다음 중 어법상 어색한 것은? 3점

① Don't push the red button, do you?
② Students like the new teacher, don't they?
③ He is a good swimmer, isn't he?
④ Usain Bolt runs very fast, doesn't he?
⑤ She has an electric guitar, doesn't she?

06 다음 문장에 알맞은 부가의문문을 쓰시오. 4점

서술형

She skipped breakfast again,
_____?

07 다음 문장에서 어법상 어색한 부분을 찾아 바르게 고치시오. 4점

서술형

Koreans eat rice every day, aren't we?

_____ → _____

08 다음 우리말을 5단어로 영작하시오. 6점

서술형

Sam은 태권도(taekwondo)를 배웠어, 그렇지 않니?

→ _____

09 그림을 보고 대화의 빈칸에 알맞은 말을 쓰시오. 4점

서술형

A: Your kid likes peanut butter, _____
_____?
B: Yes. He loves it.

VOCA hippo 하마 | sweat 땀 | twin 쌍둥이 | electric 전기의, 전기식의

01 Which words are correct for the blanks? 2점

> • Emma likes her new house, _____?
> • They won't sell the house, _____?

① does she – do they
② doesn't she – don't they
③ does she – will they
④ doesn't she – won't they
⑤ doesn't she – will they

02 Which is suitable for the blank? 2점

> A: You aren't hungry, are you?
> B _____. Let's have some pizza.

① No, I'm not   ② Yes, I am
③ No, you're not   ④ Yes, you are
⑤ No, I am

03 Who corrects the error correctly? 2점

> 다은이는 프랑스어를 못해, 그렇지?
> → Da-eun can't speak French, can da-eun?

① 경민: 앞이 부정이니까 뒤에도 can't로 써야 해.
② 동윤: 앞의 can't을 can으로 써야 해.
③ 미진: can da-eun을 can she로 써야 해.
④ 경모: 일반동사가 있으니까 doesn't she로 써야 해.
⑤ 대규: 마지막 da-eun에서 첫 글자를 대문자로 써야 해.

04 Which of the underlined words is incorrect? (2 answers) 2점

> A: Liu Fang, you are my best friend, ① don't ② you?
> B: Yes, I ③ am. And Jehun is also a good friend, ④ isn't ⑤ Jehun?

05 Which words are correct for the blanks in the dialog? 2점

> A: The robot can play the violin, _____?
> B: _____.

① can it – No, it can't
② cannot it – Yes, it can
③ can't it – Yes, it can
④ can't it – No, it can't
⑤ can't the robot – Yes, it can

06 Which is suitable for the blank? (2 answers) 2점

> _____ buy a 3D printer, shall we?

① Do   ② Don't
③ Never   ④ Let's
⑤ Let's not

07 Which translation is correct? 2점

> 너희 가족은 다섯 명이지, 그렇지 않니?

① There are five people in your family, aren't you?
② There are five people in your family, aren't there?
③ There aren't five people in your family, aren't you?
④ There are five people in your family, aren't they?
⑤ Aren't there five people in your family, are there?

08 Among the underlined phrases, which is grammatically incorrect? (2 answers) 2점

① Sara isn't sick, is she?
② He walks too slowly, isn't he?
③ We did our best, didn't we?
④ Let's just skip breakfast, will you?
⑤ She and I are rivals, aren't we?

VOCA French 프랑스어 | slowly 느리게 | do one's best 최선을 다하다 | rival 경쟁자, 라이벌

09 Which sentence is grammatically correct?
(Up to 3 answers) 3점

① He isn't your boyfriend, isn't he?
② The girls will join us, don't they?
③ Let me help you, will you?
④ She caught the ball, didn't she?
⑤ Let's not meet at 10 a.m., do we?

10 How many sentences are grammatically incorrect? 3점

ⓐ You heard me, didn't you?
ⓑ I look okay, don't I?
ⓒ Let's have a party, shall we?
ⓓ You won't be late again, will you?
ⓔ She has a pet iguana, hasn't she?
ⓕ Don't be silly, do you?

① one　　　　② two
③ three　　　④ four
⑤ five

11 Find the error and correct it. 4점

서술형

Don't bring me down again, do you?

_____ ➡ _____

12 Find TWO errors in the sentences and correct them. 4점

서술형

ⓐ This is yours, isn't this?
ⓑ Sena, comes over here, will you?

(　　) _____ ➡ _____

(　　) _____ ➡ _____

13 Fill in the blank with a question tag(부가의문문). 4점

서술형

James Kirk won't visit the White House, _____ _____?

14 Translate the Korean into English. (6 words) 5점

서술형

너 나한테 전화 안 했지, 그렇지?

➡ _____, _____?

15 Find ALL of the errors in the dialog and correct them. 5점

서술형

A: My smartphone is not working.
B: You bought it two weeks ago, did you?
A: Right. Please fix it, don't you?
B: Well, let me see it first, shall we?

➡ _____

_____

16 Look at the picture and fill in blanks (A) and (B) with the appropriate words. 각 3점

서술형

A: The boy isn't afraid of snakes, ___(A)___?
B: ___(B)___.

(A) _____

(B) _____

VOCA　iguana 이구아나 | silly 어리석은 | bring ~ down ~을 실망시키다 | White House 백악관 | fix 고치다 | afraid of ~을 무서워하는

개념이해책
79쪽 함께 보기

■ 아래 표의 빈칸에 알맞은 내용을 써 넣으세요. **>> 정답 20쪽**

1 감탄문

A What 감탄문

감탄의 대상	어순
명사	1)_____ (a/an)+ 2)_____ +명사 (주어+동사)!

B How 감탄문

감탄의 대상	어순
3)_____ 또는 4)_____	5)_____ + 6)_____ / _____ (주어+동사)!

Level 1 Test

>> 정답 20쪽

A [ ]에서 알맞은 것을 고르시오.

1 [What / How] a fun story it is!

2 [What / How] easy the exam was!

3 [What / How] a nice day you had!

4 [What / How] smart girls they are!

5 [What / How] fast time passes!

B 우리말과 일치하도록 빈칸에 알맞은 말을 쓰시오.

1 참 멋지구나!

→ _____ cool!

2 그 학생들은 참 슬펐구나!

→ _____ sad the students were!

3 참 지루한 영화군!

→ _____ a boring movie!

4 James는 참 좋은 사람이구나!

→ _____ a nice person James is!

5 넌 정말 예쁜 눈을 가졌구나!

→ _____ _____ _____

you have!

C 밑줄 친 부분이 어색하면 바르게 고치시오.

1 What nice a present!

→ _____

2 How kind are you!

→ _____

3 What strange boys you are!

→ _____

4 How the baby loudly cries!

→ _____

D 주어진 단어로 시작하는 감탄문으로 바꿔 쓰시오.

1 It is a very big cat. (What)

→ _____

2 The snail moves so slowly. (How)

→ _____

3 The tree is very tall. (How)

→ _____

4 It is a very exciting game. (What)

→ _____

VOCA **pass** 지나가다, 흘러가다 | **person** 사람 | **strange** 이상한 | **loudly** 크게, 큰 소리로 | **snail** 달팽이

01 다음 빈칸에 들어갈 말로 적절한 것은? 2점

_____ nice car he has!

① How
② What
③ How a
④ What an
⑤ What a

02 다음 중 밑줄 친 부분의 쓰임이 다른 하나는? 2점

① <u>How</u> fantastic!
② <u>How</u> cheap the bag is!
③ <u>How</u> strong Ellen is!
④ <u>How</u> does he like it?
⑤ <u>How</u> friendly the stranger was!

03 다음 단어들을 배열해서 감탄문을 만들 때 앞에서 2번째 오는 단어는? 2점

what, are, girls, tall, they

① what
② are
③ girls
④ tall
⑤ they

04 다음 문장을 바르게 고쳐 쓴 학생은? 2점

How surprised was the audience!

① 현정: What surprised was the audience!
② 선구: How surprised the audience was!
③ 준형: What a surprised was the audience!
④ 은영: How a surprised the audience was!
⑤ 진원: What surprised the audience was!

05 다음 중 어법상 어색한 것은? 2점

① How speedy!
② What a big egg it is!
③ How scary the monster is!
④ What a pretty babies they are!
⑤ What a bad singer he is!

06 그림에 나타난 상황에서 할 수 있는 말로 알맞은 영어 문장을 완성하시오. 4점

서술형

→ _____ _____! (cute)

07 다음 두 문장을 우리말로 해석하시오. 각 3점

서술형

(1) How large are your feet?

→ _____

(2) How large your feet are!

→ _____

08 주어진 단어를 배열하여 감탄문을 쓰시오. 5점

서술형

your, white, are, how, teeth

→ _____

09 다음을 감탄문으로 바꾸어 쓰고 생략할 수 있는 것에 괄호로 표시하시오. 5점

서술형

You are a very lucky person.

→ What _____!

VOCA fantastic 멋진, 환상적인 | friendly 친근한 | stranger 낯선 사람 | surprised 놀란 | audience 관중 | speedy 빠른 | scary 무서운 |
monster 괴물 | lucky 운이 좋은

01 Which word for the blank is <u>different</u> than the others? 2점

① _____ wonderful!

② _____ great engineers!

③ _____ bright they are!

④ _____ clean the monitor is!

⑤ _____ interesting the story is!

02 Which words are correct for the blanks? 2점

- _____ excellent your performance was!
- _____ old chairs you have!

① How – What an

② How – What

③ How an – What a

④ What an – What

⑤ What – How an

[03~04] Choose the appropriate one for the blank. (2 answers) 각 2점

03

What a(n) _____ !

① amazing man

② lazy girl Susan is

③ fancy restaurant is it

④ diligent your mother is

⑤ beautiful the world is

04

How clever _____ !

① they do   ② are they

③ she is   ④ you have

⑤ your dog is

05 Which one is correct for the blank? 2점

The princess's horse was so dirty.
= _____ the princess's horse was!

① What dirty

② What a dirty

③ How dirty

④ How a dirty

⑤ How very dirty

06 What is the <u>3rd</u> word when translating the sentence? 2점

넌 정말 큰 눈을 가졌구나!

① have   ② big

③ eyes   ④ what

⑤ you

07 Which has the same meaning as the given sentence? 2점

How slowly the panda eats!

① Does the panda eat slowly?

② The panda doesn't eat slowly.

③ The panda eats very slowly.

④ How slowly does the panda eat?

⑤ Why does the panda eat slowly?

08 Which translation is correct? (2 answers) 2점

이것은 참 희귀한 아이템이구나!

① How rare is this item!

② How rare this is an item!

③ How rare this item is!

④ What a rare item this is!

⑤ What a rare item is this!

VOCA engineer 엔지니어, 기술자 | performance 공연 | fancy 화려한 | diligent 부지런한 | clever 영리한 | rare 희귀한

94

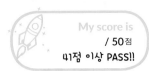
09 Which is grammatically correct? (2 answers) 2점

① What strong men they are!

② What a cute dog you have!

③ How big trees they are!

④ What pretty flower it is!

⑤ How small is your eraser!

10 How many students write <u>incorrect</u> sentences? 3점

> ⓐ 세나: How cute the character is!
>
> ⓑ 현식: What big dogs these are!
>
> ⓒ 소중: What a small world!
>
> ⓓ 규태: How slow the service is!
>
> ⓔ 인수: What poor animals they are!

① none   ② one

③ two   ④ three

⑤ four

11 Fill in each blank to make all of the sentences have the same meaning. 각 4점

서술형

> Kyle is a very honest boy.

(1) _____ honest Kyle is!

(2) _____ _____ honest boy Kyle is!

12 Change the sentence into an exclamatory sentence(감탄문). Do NOT change the subject(주어). 4점

서술형

> These shorts are very short.

→ _____

13 Read the following and complete the TWO exclamatory sentences. 각 4점

서술형

> The watch costs 3,880,000 won. It is expensive, isn't it?

(1) _____ _____ it is!

(2) What _____ _____

_____ it is!

14 Find the <u>necessary</u> words and rearrange them to make an exclamatory sentence. 4점

서술형

> mugs, have, you, pretty, what, how, a

→ _____

15 Read the following and write an exclamatory sentence about what Ari is thinking. 5점

서술형

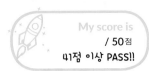

> Ari went to an Italian restaurant in the afternoon. The pasta there was very delicious. Now she is in bed. She is recalling the food. In this situation, what would she think?
>
> *recall: 떠올리다

→ _____

VOCA   eraser 지우개 | character 캐릭터 | honest 정직한 | shorts 반바지 | expensive 비싼 | mug 머그잔 | delicious 맛있는 | situation 상황

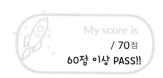

01 U14_1+2

각 빈칸에 들어갈 말이 순서대로 짝지어진 것은? 2점

A: _____ is your last name?
B: It's Lim.
A: _____ are you?
B: I'm 14.
A: _____ do you like better, English or math?
B: I like math better.

① What – How – How
② Who – How – What
③ What – How old – Which
④ How – How tall – What
⑤ What – How old – What

02 U15_1B

함정

Which sentence is incorrect? 2점

① Let's go home now.
② Let's not go anywhere tonight.
③ Let's play soccer after school.
④ Let's not eats seafood.
⑤ Let's help her children together.

03 U15_1A

다음 빈칸에 들어갈 말로 알맞은 것은? 2점

_____ kind to others.

① Do   ② Does
③ Are   ④ Be
⑤ Have

04 U16_1A+1B

한눈에 쏙

두 빈칸에 공통으로 들어가기에 알맞은 것은? 2점

• Please calm down, _____?
• You won't go to the mountain, _____?

① don't you   ② aren't you
③ will you   ④ do you
⑤ don't you

[05~06] 주어진 대답이 나올 수 있는 질문을 고르시오. 각 2점

05 U14_1

He is a principal.

① Where is your grandfather?
② How old is your grandfather?
③ What does your grandfather do?
④ What does your grandfather like?
⑤ What does your grandfather teach?

06 U14_1

I watched a movie on TV.

① Where did you watch TV?
② How did you like your new TV?
③ Which movie would you like to see?
④ What did you do in the evening?
⑤ What kinds of movies do you like?

07 U15_1A

다음은 직거래의 문자 대화이다. '개 사진 보내주세요.'를 영어로 바르게 쓴 학생은? 2점

① 수나: Sending your dog's picture, please.
② 주혜: Sent your dog's picture, please.
③ 은주: Please sending your dog's picture
④ 은영: Be send your dog's picture, please.
⑤ 가윤: Please send your dog's picture.

5️⃣

5️⃣

08 U16_1A
다음 대화의 빈칸에 알맞은 것은? 2점

> A: Your brother came home late last night, _____ ?
> B: No. He came early in the evening.

① is he   ② was he
③ did he   ④ didn't he
⑤ does he

09 U17_1A+1B
한눈에쏙
Which word for the blank is different than the others? 2점

① _____ lovely your sister is!
② _____ expensive cars they sell!
③ _____ shy his brothers are!
④ _____ deep the lake is!
⑤ _____ kind the librarian is!

10 U16_1A+1B+GP
고난도
Which set has grammatically correct sentences? 3점

> (A) ⓐ Snow is beautiful, isn't it?
>   ⓑ You don't like me, don't you?
> (B) ⓐ She never came again, did she?
>   ⓑ Take a seat, don't you?
> (C) ⓐ Something happened, wasn't it?
>   ⓑ Let's have dinner together, shall we?
> (D) ⓐ There is a park near here, isn't there?
>   ⓑ Don't work too hard, will you?
> (E) ⓐ The moon goes around the Earth, doesn't it?
>   ⓑ Please don't do that to me, will I?

① (A)   ② (B)
③ (C)   ④ (D)
⑤ (E)

11 U14_1+2+GP
다음 문장을 다른 표현으로 바꿔 쓰시오. 3점

> What is your favorite sport?

→ _____ _____ do you like the most?

12 U14_2
다음 우리말 문장을 조건에 맞게 영작하시오. 4점

> 너는 누구와 사니?
> - 조건 1 whom을 사용할 것
> - 조건 2 whom을 포함하여 5단어로 쓸 것

→ _____

13 U14_1
주어진 답변에 어울리는 질문을 완성하시오. 4점

> A: _____ eat for lunch?
> B: I ate a jumbo hotdog with a sweet Belgian waffle.

14 U15_1A
Rearrange the given words and translate the Korean sentence. 4점

> 눈을 감고 너의 미래를 상상해봐.
> future, your, your, and, imagine, eyes, close

→ _____

15 U15_1A
문장을 부정 명령문으로 전환한 것에서 어법상 어색한 곳을 찾아 바르게 고치시오. 3점

> You are very noisy. → Don't so noisy!

_____ → _____

16 U16_1B
다음 빈칸에 적절한 부가의문문을 쓰시오. 3점

> Let's not meet so early, _____ ?

17

U16_1A

그림을 보고 빈칸에 알맞은 말을 쓰시오. 4점

> A: She isn't good at singing, _____
> _____?
> B: _____, _____ _____.

18

U16_1A

Find the error and correct it. 4점

> ⓐ It's cold in Canada, isn't it?
> ⓑ You're from Greece, aren't you?
> ⓒ Palm trees grow on Jeju Island, aren't they?

( ) _____ ➡ _____

19

U17_1B

다음 문장을 같은 의미의 감탄문으로 전환하시오. 4점

> Dolphins are very smart.

➡ _____

20

U17_1A

 함정

어법상 어색한 부분을 찾아 문장을 다시 쓰시오. 4점

> What an amazing students you teach!

➡ _____

21

U17_1A

 함정

다음 우리말을 주어진 조건에 맞게 영작하시오. 4점

> 그들은 정말 멋진 음악을 연주하는구나!
>
> · 조건 1 what, great를 포함할 것
> · 조건 2 5단어로 쓸 것

➡ _____

[22~23] 다음 글을 읽고 물음에 답하시오.

A father took his child on a fishing trip. They ⓐfished for an hour. But they didn't catch anything. The son asked his father, "Dad, ⓑdo we going to catch anything here?" The father answered, "Of course, we are. ⓒBelieves me." Two hours later, they still ⓓcaught nothing. The father said, "It's too cold today. (A) 우리 집으로 돌아가자, 그럴까?" At home, the mother asked, "Son, you caught a big one, ⓔwere you?" "Yeah. Sure, Mom. A big cold, thanks to Dad," the son answered.

22

U12_2+U15_1A+U16_1A

★ 고난도

윗글의 밑줄 친 ⓐ~ⓔ 중 어법상 어색한 것으로 묶인 것은? 3점

① ⓑ, ⓒ   ② ⓓ, ⓔ
③ ⓐ, ⓓ, ⓔ   ④ ⓑ, ⓒ, ⓓ
⑤ ⓑ, ⓒ, ⓔ

23

U15_1B+U16_1B

윗글의 밑줄 친 (A)를 조건에 맞게 영작하시오. 5점

> · 어휘   go back
> · 조건 1 제안할 때 사용하는 표현을 이용할 것
> · 조건 2 부가의문문으로 마무리할 것
> · 조건 3 6단어로 쓸 것

➡ _____

CHAPTER 06
형용사와 부사

개념이해책
86쪽 함께 보기

■ 아래 표의 빈칸에 알맞은 내용을 써 넣으세요. 〉〉〉 정답 22쪽

1 형용사의 의미와 용법

1)	용법	형용사가 뒤의 명사를 직접 꾸며준다.
2)	용법	형용사가 주어로 쓰인 명사나 대명사를 간접적으로 꾸며준다.

2 수량 형용사

	많은		약간의	조금의	거의 없는
수(셀 수 있는 명사)	3)	a lot of, lots of, plenty of	5) (긍정문, 권유문)	7)	9)
양(셀 수 없는 명사)	4)		6) (부정문, 의문문)	8)	10)

3 기수와 서수

기수	one	two	three	four	five	six
서수	11)	12)	13)	14)	15)	16)
기수	seven	eight	nine	ten	eleven	twelve
서수	17)	18)	19)	20)	21)	22)
기수	thirteen	fourteen	twenty	hundred	thousand	million
서수	23)	24)	25)	26)	27)	28)

Level 1 Test

〉〉〉 정답 22쪽

A 밑줄 친 형용사의 용법이 [보기]와 같으면 =로, 아니면 ≠로 표시하시오.

> 보기   She is a <u>pretty</u> woman.

1 Be <u>careful</u>, Hannah.   → _____

2 Are you <u>ready</u> to order?   → _____

3 We had a <u>great</u> time.   → _____

4 Were they <u>curious</u> about me?   → _____

5 The old man wears <u>strange</u> clothes.   → _____

6 This summer was really <u>hot</u>.   → _____

B [ ]에서 알맞은 것을 고르시오.

1 I didn't get [many / much] sleep last night.

2 The boy asked [many / much] questions.

3 She doesn't drink [lot of / lots of] coffee.

4 [A few / A little] days ago, I lost my bag.

5 There was [few / little] water in the bucket.

6 I need [some / any] aspirin now.

7 Do you have [some / any] questions?

8 Would you like [some / any] cake?

9 The rich man had [few / little] friends.

VOCA   order 주문하다 | curious 궁금한 | strange 이상한 | bucket 양동이 | aspirin 아스피린

01 다음 빈칸에 적절하지 <u>않은</u> 것은?

> How much _____ do they have?

① power　　　　② cards
③ sugar　　　　④ time
⑤ bread

02 다음 빈칸에 알맞은 말로 짝지어진 것은?

> • Sorry, but we don't have _____ cheeseburgers. They're sold out.
> • Lisa, do you want _____ lollipops?

① any – any　　　② some – any
③ any – some　　　④ some – some
⑤ many – some

03 다음 문장에서 어법상 어색한 부분을 찾아 바르게 고친 학생은?

> A little hundred years ago, people believed in mermaids and giant sea monsters.

① 한영: A little → Little
② 영수: A little → A few
③ 수빈: years → year
④ 빈희: hundred → hundreds
⑤ 희수: people → peoples

04 다음 우리말을 영어로 바르게 옮긴 것은?

> 나의 열아홉 번째 생일은 2029년 5월 5일이야.

① My nineteenth birthday is on May fifth in two thousands twenty-nine.
② My nineteenth birthday is on May fifth in second thousand twenty-ninth.
③ My nineteens birthday is on May fiveth in two thousand twentieth-nine.
④ My nineteenth birthday is on May fifth in two thousand twenty-nine.
⑤ My nineteenth birthday is on May fifth in two thousand twentieth-nine.

05 다음 중 어법상 어색한 것을 찾아 바르게 고치시오.

서술형

> ⓐ We don't have some garlic.
> ⓑ I'll pick up some tomatoes for the salad.

(　　) _____ ➞ _____

06 주어진 단어들을 바르게 배열하여 <u>의문문</u>을 쓰시오.

서술형

> your, you, with, spend, a lot of, do, family, time

➞ _____
_____

07 Kevin이 Julia에게 할 말을 조건에 맞게 쓰시오.

서술형

Kevin♥Julia
100 Days

- 조건 1　상황: Kevin and Julia met 100 days ago.
- 조건 2　아라비아 숫자를 쓰지 말 것
- 조건 3　3단어로 쓸 것

Kevin: Julia, today is our _____
_____ of
dating.
Julia: Oh, Kevin. You're so sweet. I love you.

08 두 문장의 의미가 같도록 빈칸에 알맞은 말을 쓰시오.

서술형

> Allison had almost no visitors in the hospital.

➞ _____ people visited Allison in the hospital.

VOCA　sold out 다 팔린 | lollipop 막대사탕 | believe in ～의 존재를 믿다 | mermaid 인어 | giant 거대한 | monster 괴물 | garlic 마늘 | spend (시간을) 보내다, 쓰다 | visitor 방문객

01 Which word is NOT suitable for the blank?
(2 answers) 2점

> Ricky is a _____ guy.

① nice　　　　　② handsome
③ tough　　　　④ kindly
⑤ honest

02 Find ALL of the possible words for the blank.
2점

> She makes _____ money at the moment.

① a little　　　② little
③ plenty of　　④ lots of
⑤ many

03 Which of the underlined phrases is NOT
correct? (2 answers) 2점

① She bought a lot of pens at the store.
② How much flour do you need?
③ Many dolphins are swimming in the water.
④ Lot of dogs were running after me.
⑤ I saw many cute sheeps on the hill.

04 Who finds the error and corrects it? 2점

> A: Would you please give me hot something?
> B: Sure. How about some tea?

① 창민: give → gives
② 민서: hot → hotly
③ 서연: hot something → something hot
④ 연주: Sure → Surely.
⑤ 주선: some → any

05 Which is proper for the blank? 2점

> Frank has _____ friends in his new town.
> So he feels very lonely.

① some　　　　② a lot of
③ few　　　　 ④ little
⑤ many

06 Which of the pairs has the same meaning? 2점

① He has a lot of cars.
　= He has few cars.
② The actor received a few fan letters.
　= The actor received few fan letters.
③ This plant needs a little water.
　= This plant needs little water.
④ Sarah taught a lot of students.
　= Sarah taught many students.
⑤ The family made little money.
　= The family made very much money.

07 Which is NOT true according to the picture?
2점

① Plenty of vacationers are at the beach.
② The boy is holding a lot of candy.
③ Some people are playing volleyball.
④ A few cars are on the street.
⑤ A few people are getting suntans.

08 Which underlined word is incorrect? 2점

> My ① teachers ② give ③ little homework, so I
> have ④ lot of free ⑤ time.

VOCA　guy 남자 | at the moment 지금 | flour 밀가루 | dolphin 돌고래 | lonely 외로운 | receive 받다 | vacationer 행락객, 피서객 | suntan 햇
볕에 태움, 선탠 | free time 자유 시간

09 Which word is NOT necessary when translating the sentence? 2점

> 그는 여러 번 그녀에게 청혼했지만, 그녀의 대답은 항상 거절이었다.

① proposed   ② much
③ times   ④ answer
⑤ always

10 How many sentences are incorrect? 3점

> ⓐ He doesn't have some pets.
> ⓑ Will you have some more bread?
> ⓒ Do you have some problems?
> ⓓ The students didn't do something.
> ⓔ Is anything wrong with you?

① one   ② two
③ three   ④ four
⑤ five

11 Which sentence is grammatically incorrect? (Up to 3 answers) 3점

① Do you want new something?
② Is there any cheese in the fridge?
③ We had plenty of chicken wings.
④ Can you come back in a little hours?
⑤ We're getting off on the twelfth floor.

12 Change the underlined words into 2 words. 4점

서술형

> African countries like Angola have plenty of diamonds but need medicines.

→ _____

13 Rearrange the given words and make a complete sentence. 4점

서술형

> passed, a few, test, students, hard, the

→ _____

14 Translate the sentence according to the conditions. 6점

서술형

> 아미(Ami)는 시간이 거의 없지만 일은 많다.
> · Words   but, lots, has, work
> · Condition 1   주어진 어휘를 변형하지 말 것
> · Condition 2   8단어로 쓸 것

→ _____

15 Translate the Korean into English by using the given words. 5점

서술형

> 그 영화는 특별한 것이 아니었다. (be, nothing)

→ _____

16 Find the error and correct it. 4점

서술형

> ⓐ I'd like to have some more food.
> ⓑ We don't need some new ideas now.

(   ) _____ → _____

17 Look at the picture and fill in the blanks. Use person A's words. Do NOT use Arabic numerals(아라비아 숫자). 3점

서술형

> A: What grade are you in?
> B: I'm in the _____ _____.
> A: Me, too.

19 부사

개념이해책
89쪽 함께 보기

■ 아래 표의 빈칸에 알맞은 내용을 써 넣으세요. ›› 정답 23쪽

1 부사의 역할과 형태

1)	수식	She doesn't cook well.	3)	수식	Thank you very much.
2)	수식	She was a very clever girl.	4)	수식	Luckily, they had enough time.

대부분의 형용사	5)	kind → 6) , slow → 7)
'자음+y'로 끝나는 경우	8)	easy → 9) , happy → 10)

2 주의해야 할 부사

형용사와 형태가 같은 부사	11) (빠른; 빨리), 12) (이른; 일찍), 13) (힘든, 딱딱한; 열심히),
	14) (늦은; 늦게), 15) (예쁜; 꽤)
-ly를 붙여 뜻이 달라지는 부사	16) (늦은; 늦게) – 17) (최근에),
	18) (열심히) – 19) (거의 ~ 않는),
	20) (가까이) – 21) (거의),
	22) (높은; 높게) – 23) (매우)
too와 either	24) 는 긍정문에, 25) 는 부정문에 쓴다.
well	well이 부사이면 '26) '이란 뜻이고, 형용사이면 '27) '이란 뜻이다.

3 빈도부사

28)	29)	30)	31)	32)	33)
항상	대개, 보통	자주, 흔히	가끔, 때때로	좀처럼 ~ 않는	결코 ~ 아닌

Level 1 Test

›› 정답 23쪽

A [ ]에서 알맞은 것을 고르시오.

1 He [quiet / quietly] walked out.

2 My son is a [great / greatly] inventor.

3 The final exam won't be very [easy / easily].

4 Don't get up [late / lately] tomorrow.

5 I'm going to study English [hard / hardly].

6 The shark swims very [fast / fastly].

7 She didn't like him [too / either].

8 We [final / finally] won a gold medal.

B 밑줄 친 부분이 어색하면 바르게 고치시오.

1 You did well on the test.

→ _____

2 All the players ran very hardly.

→ _____

3 I'm not hungry. – Me too.

→ _____

4 Mr. Kim is a high successful businessman.

→ _____

5 It snows sometimes in spring here.

→ _____

VOCA inventor 발명가 | successful 성공한 | businessman 사업가

Level 2 Test

>> 정답 23쪽

01 다음 빈칸에 들어갈 말로 알맞지 <u>않은</u> 것은?

> She pushed the shopping cart _____.

① well ② smoothly
③ easily ④ cheerfully
⑤ lovely

02 각 빈칸에 들어갈 말이 바르게 짝지어진 것은?

> • They didn't like the new program _____.
> • I hide money under my bed, _____.

① either – either ② either – too
③ neither – too ④ too – either
⑤ too – neither

03 어법상 어색한 부분을 찾아 바르게 고친 것은?

> Be careful! That car near hit your dog.

① Be → Are ② careful → carefully
③ near → nearly ④ hit → hitted
⑤ your → yours

04 다음 중 어법상 옳은 것은?

① He makes sometimes a mistake.
② She never was on time.
③ We can help often them.
④ My dog always feels hungry.
⑤ I don't do often my homework.

05 다음 중 어법상 어색한 문장의 개수는?

> ⓐ Everybody likes someone kind.
> ⓑ Your mom cooks very good.
> ⓒ My brother often is scary.
> ⓓ These books are usefully to me.
> ⓔ Our English teacher speaks Japanese, too.

① 1개 ② 2개
③ 3개 ④ 4개
⑤ 5개

06 다음 빈칸에 공통으로 들어갈 단어를 쓰시오.

서술형

> • The game was _____ boring.
> • A: I'm nervous. Aren't you nervous?
>   B: I'm nervous, _____.

→ _____

07 다음 중 어법상 <u>어색한</u> 문장을 찾아 바르게 고치시오.

서술형

> ⓐ I am not very well today.
> ⓑ She hard ever visits her friends.

( ) _____ → _____

08 다음 그림을 보고 각 빈칸에 알맞은 단어를 쓰시오.

서술형

(1) She is _____ at horseback riding.

(2) She rides horses _____.

09 주어진 단어를 넣어 다음 문장을 다시 쓰고, 우리말로 해석하시오.

서술형

> The boss praises his employees. (seldom)

(1) 다시 쓰기 → _____

(2) 해석 → _____

10 밑줄 친 부분에 유의하여 문장을 우리말로 해석하시오.

서술형

(1) He was very <u>late</u>.

→ _____

(2) I got up <u>late</u> this morning.

→ _____

UNIT **19** 105

01 Which is NOT correct for the blank? 2점

> A: How often does your brother use your computer?
> B: He _____ uses it.

① almost   ② always
③ sometimes   ④ never
⑤ seldom

02 Which is proper for the blank in the dialog? 2점

> A: What are you doing?
> B: I'm waiting for the 8 o'clock school bus. It's 8:30 now.
> A: That's unusual. The bus isn't _____ late.

① always   ② never
③ seldom   ④ usually
⑤ sometimes

03 Where does the given word best fit? 2점

> Warren (①) tells (②) lies, (③) so (④) I trust (⑤) him. (never)

04 Which words are correct for the blanks? 2점

> • I loved the musical. My parents liked it, _____.
> • Jessica didn't come to school today, and Amy didn't come _____.
> • A: I'm not afraid of ghosts.
>   B: Me _____.

① either – either – neither
② either – too – neither
③ too – too – either
④ too – either – neither
⑤ too – neither – either

05 Which of the underlined words is used differently than the example? 2점

> 보기   He runs very fast.

① Mom wakes me up too early.
② We prepared dinner well.
③ Yunho is always friendly.
④ Dad, please drive safely.
⑤ She and I walked quietly.

06 Who listens to K-pop the second most often? 2점

① Yaoming never listens to K-pop.
② Luis always listens to K-pop.
③ Masai sometimes listens to K-pop.
④ Roberto doesn't listen to K-pop.
⑤ Nattapong often listens to K-pop.

07 Which translation is correct? 2점

> 그는 자신의 목표를 이루기 위해 거의 열심히 노력하지 않았다.

① He did not work hard for his goals.
② He hardly worked hard for his goals.
③ He hard worked hard for his goals.
④ He didn't hardly works hard for his goals.
⑤ He hardly worked hardly for his goals.

08 Which sentence is grammatically incorrect? (2 answers) 2점

① I see my cousins seldom.
② Is often she like this?
③ Amy is always late for school.
④ Sometimes she eats alone.
⑤ What kind of game do you usually play?

VOCA   almost 거의 | unusual 이상한 | trust 믿다 | musical 뮤지컬 | afraid of ~을 무서워하는 | ghost 유령 | K-pop 케이팝(가요)

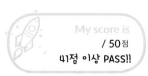
09 How many sentences are grammatically correct? 3점

> ⓐ The kids quick ran home.
> ⓑ That table is pretty heavy.
> ⓒ Do you have an early class?
> ⓓ It rains heavily in summer here.
> ⓔ Lucky, I had some coins in my pocket.
> ⓕ My grandfather is a high educated man.

① one　　　　　② two
③ three　　　　④ four
⑤ five

10 Which word comes 5th when translating the sentence? 2점

> 왜 그 가게는 늘 붐비지?

① is　　　　　② the
③ store　　　　④ always
⑤ crowded

11 Rewrite the sentence. Use the correct form of the given word. 4점
서술형

> The thirsty man drank the water. (quick)

→ _____

12 Rearrange the given words correctly and make a question. 4점
서술형

> put up, do, decorations, Halloween, when, usually, you

→ _____

13 Find the grammatically incorrect sentence and rewrite the sentence correctly. 4점
서술형

> Mr. Parker lives in my neighborhood. ⓐ He always gets up early in the morning. ⓑ He often walks his dog after breakfast. ⓒ He usually doesn't drive to work. ⓓ He never misses work. ⓔ But sometimes he is late for work.

(　　) → _____

14 Translate the Korean into English according to the conditions. 7점
서술형

> 최근에 내 딸이 집에 늦게 와요.
>
> · Condition 1　어휘 – get home
> · Condition 2　문장 전체를 수식하는 부사를 맨 앞에 쓸 것
> · Condition 3　'late'를 두 번 사용하되 적절한 형태로 쓸 것

→ _____

15 Look at Cathy's schedule and answer each question. Use an adverb of frequency(빈도부사). 각 4점
서술형

할 일	월	화	수	목	금	토	일
샤워하기	○	○	○	○	○	○	○
아침 먹기	○	○	○	○	○		
TV 보기							○

> Q: How often does Cathy take a shower?
> A: ____(A)____
> Q: How often does Cathy have breakfast?
> A: ____(B)____
> Q: How often does Cathy watch TV?
> A: ____(C)____

(A) _____

(B) _____

(C) _____

VOCA　heavily 심하게 | educated 교육받은 | crowded 붐비는 | thirsty 목이 마른 | put up decorations 장식하다 | neighborhood 동네 | walk 산책시키다 | miss 거르다, 빠지다 | take a shower 샤워하다

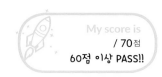

My score is
/ 70점
60점 이상 PASS!!

U18_3

01 다음 서수 중 잘못된 것의 개수는? 2점

first	fifth	forth
nineth	thirteenth	eighteenth
twentieth	thirty-threeth	hundredth

① 1개　　　　　　② 2개
③ 3개　　　　　　④ 4개
⑤ 5개

U18_1

02 밑줄 친 부분의 쓰임이 [보기]와 같은 것끼리 묶인 것은?
2점

> 보기　It was a <u>lovely</u> day.
>
> ⓐ I have a <u>perfect</u> girlfriend.
> ⓑ The question wasn't <u>easy</u>.
> ⓒ That's a <u>beautiful</u> park.
> ⓓ I felt a little <u>sad</u> today.
> ⓔ The food here is really <u>fresh</u>.

① ⓐ, ⓑ　　　　　② ⓐ, ⓒ
③ ⓐ, ⓓ, ⓔ　　　④ ⓑ, ⓓ
⑤ ⓑ, ⓓ, ⓔ

U18_1

03 Which is NOT proper for the blank? 2점

> The weather was _____ yesterday.

① rainy　　　　　　② hot
③ cool　　　　　　④ cold
⑤ cloud

U18_2

04 다음 빈칸에 알맞은 말로 짝지어진 것은? 2점

> • Actually, the man doesn't have _____ money.
> • My daughter has _____ pretty dolls.

① a few – many　　② many – a little
③ much – plenty of　④ much – much
⑤ a lot of – much

U19_2A

05 다음 중에서 형용사와 부사로 모두 사용되는 단어가 <u>아닌</u> 것은? 2점

① good　　　　　　② pretty
③ early　　　　　　④ well
⑤ hard

U19_1+2A

06 다음 빈칸에 알맞지 <u>않은</u> 것은? 2점

함정

> The president ran _____.

① fast　　　　　　② well
③ in the park　　　④ hardly
⑤ in the morning

U18_1

07 다음 문장에서 <u>어색한</u> 것을 찾아 바르게 설명한 학생은? 2점

> My grandmother knows many stories interesting.

① 미연: '나의'는 Mine으로 써야 맞아.
② 수진: 주어가 3인칭 단수라 knows를 know로 써야 해.
③ 현수: many를 a lot of나 lots of로 써야 해.
④ 철희: stories가 아니라 story가 맞아.
⑤ 규진: interesting stories가 맞아. 앞에서 꾸며야 해.

U18_1+U19_1

08 다음 빈칸에 들어갈 말이 바르게 짝지어진 것은? 2점

> • A turtle has a _____ shell on its back.
> • She always listens to his advice _____.

① hardly – careful　　② hard – carefully
③ hard – care　　　　④ hardly – carefully
⑤ hard – careful

09 U19_2B

다음 문장에서 <u>어색한</u> 부분을 찾아 바르게 고친 것은? 2점

> Strangely, the visitors arrived lately last night.

① Strangely → Strange
② visitors → visiters
③ arrived → arrive
④ lately → late
⑤ last → lastly

10 U19_3+GP

Which one is grammatically <u>incorrect</u>? 2점

① Do you always get up at six?
② Linda never misses her English class.
③ I often dream about going to the moon.
④ She usually walks to school on Mondays.
⑤ Who doesn't sometimes do homework?

11 U18_2

밑줄 친 부분과 바꾸어 쓸 수 있는 표현을 주어진 철자로 시작하여 2단어로 쓰시오. 4점

> She drinks <u>a lot of</u> water.

→ p_____ _____

12 U18_1

[보기]와 같이 주어진 문장을 바꿔 쓰시오. 4점

> 보기 That girl is tall.
>   → She is a tall girl.
> ⋯⋯⋯⋯⋯⋯⋯⋯⋯⋯⋯⋯⋯⋯
> This movie is interesting.

→ _____

13 U18_2

우리말을 영작할 때 빈칸에 알맞은 말을 쓰시오. 4점

남자 1호는 돈이 거의 없지만 저는 많습니다. 저를 뽑아주십시오.

→ The number-one guy has _____
money, but I have _____
_____ _____ money.
Please pick me.

14 U18_3

Find the error and correct it. 4점

> Thanksgiving Day is a public holiday on the four Thursday in November.

_____ → _____

15 U18_GP

다음을 영작할 때 5번째로 올 단어를 쓰시오. 4점

그 농구 팀은 키가 크고 빠른 누군가가 필요하다.

→ _____

16 U18_1+U19_1

다음에서 <u>어색한</u> 부분을 2개 찾아 고치시오. 4점

> Fortunate, he survived the suddenly attack.

_____ → _____

_____ → _____

17 두 문장이 같은 뜻이 되도록 빈칸에 알맞은 한 단어를 쓰시오. 4점

> Our part-timer is always on time.

→ Our part-timer is _____ late.

18 다음 시험 결과를 보고 빈칸에 알맞은 말을 쓰시오. 각 1점

Name	미란	소연	용섭	동준	혁종
Pass/Fail	P	P	F	F	F

(1) Miran _____ the exam.

(2) Soyeon _____ the exam,

_____ .

(3) Yongseop _____ the exam.

(4) Dongjun didn't _____ the exam.

(5) Hyeokjong didn't _____ the exam

_____ .

19 Translate the Korean into English. Choose the <u>necessary</u> words and rearrange them. 4점

> 빠른 달리기 선수들은 대개 다리가 꽤 길다.
> runners, long, pretty, have, usually, seldom, fast, legs

→ _____

_____

20 다음 중 어법상 어색한 문장을 찾아 바르게 고쳐 쓰시오.

★ 고난도

4점

> Yebin is my favorite classmate. ⓐ She and I always do things together. ⓑ Yesterday, we went to a K-pop concert and had a lot of fun there. ⓒ However, we got back home too lately. ⓓ Her parents are seldom angry with her. ⓔ But yesterday, they were very angry.

( ) → _____

[21~22] 다음 글을 읽고 물음에 답하시오.

　　ⓐEllie and Janice were in the 2st grade. They were best friends. ⓑThey did always everything together. They walked to school together every morning. ⓒThey ate lunch together. They took the same classes. (A)그들은 모든 것을 빨리 배웠다. But Ellie wasn't good at math. ⓓJanice wasn't good at it, too. They helped each other a lot. They wanted to go to the same high school. However, ⓔEllie moved to another city recently.

21 윗글의 밑줄 친 ⓐ~ⓔ 중 어법상 <u>어색한</u> 것의 개수는? 4점

★ 고난도

① 1개　　　　　　② 2개

③ 3개　　　　　　④ 4개

⑤ 5개

22 다음은 윗글의 밑줄 친 (A)를 영작한 것이다. 어법상 어색한 것을 <u>모두</u> 찾아 바르게 고쳐 문장을 다시 쓰시오. 4점

> They learnd everything fastly.

→ _____

CHAPTER 07
비교 구문

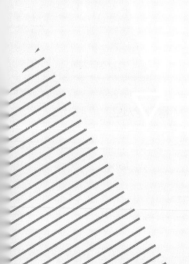

20 비교 변화, 동등 비교

■ 아래 표의 빈칸에 알맞은 내용을 써 넣으세요. ›› 정답 24쪽

개념이해책
96쪽 함께 보기

1 비교 변화

A 규칙 변화

대부분	+-er/-est	tall – 1)	– 2)
-e로 끝나는 경우	+-r/-st	large – 3)	– 4)
'자음+y'로 끝나는 경우	y → i+-er/-est	busy – 5)	– 6)
'단모음+단자음'으로 끝나는 경우	마지막 자음+-er/-est	hot – 7)	– 8)
대부분의 2음절, 3음절 이상	more/most+원급	famous – 9)	– 10)

B 불규칙 변화

good/well – 11)	– 12)	bad/ill – 13)	– 14)
many/much – 15)	– 16)	little – 17)	– 18)
late(시간이 늦은) – 19)	– 20)	late(순서가 늦은) – 21)	– 22)

2 동등 비교

기본 형태	23) +원급+ 24)
원급의 부정	not ~ 25) +원급+ 26)

Level 1 Test

›› 정답 24쪽

A [ ]에서 알맞은 것을 고르시오.

1 You're as brave [so / as] my brother.

2 I love soccer as [many / much] as baseball.

3 They are [as not / not as] diligent as you.

4 Her horse is as fast as [yours / you].

B 밑줄 친 부분이 어색하면 바르게 고치시오.

1 He is as intelligent as Sara.

→ _____

2 I am not as heavily as you.

→ _____

3 Math is as not difficult as science.

→ _____

C 다음 우리말과 같은 뜻이 되도록 빈칸을 채우시오.

1 네 손톱은 그녀의 것만큼 길어.

→ Your fingernails are _____ long

_____.

2 저 책은 이 책만큼 어렵지 않아.

→ That book is _____ _____

_____ _____ this one.

3 그는 나의 선생님만큼 쉽게 그 문제를 풀었다.

→ He solved the question _____

_____ _____ my teacher.

VOCA brave 용감한 | diligent 부지런한 | intelligent 지적인 | fingernail 손톱

112

01 다음 중 'not'이 들어가기에 적절한 곳은?

The tree (①) was (②) as (③) tall (④) as (⑤) I.

02 다음 빈칸에 알맞은 것은?

Sam didn't study as _____ as I did.

① hard
② harder
③ hardest
④ more hard
⑤ the hardest

03 다음 중 어법상 옳은 것은?

① She is as brilliant so I.
② Your puppy is as small as my.
③ That door isn't clean as this one.
④ Sam works as careless as his brother.
⑤ The donkey ran as fast as the zebra.

04 다음 우리말을 바르게 영작한 학생은?

그의 고양이는 너의 고양이만큼 많은 우유를 마신다.

① 민준: His cat drinks as milk as your cat.
② 지후: His cat drinks as many milk as yours.
③ 준서: His cat drinks as much milk as yours.
④ 건우: His cat drinks much milk as your cat.
⑤ 현준: His cat drinks as much milk so your cat.

05 다음 중 어법상 틀린 것만 골라 바르게 고친 것으로 짝지어진 것은?

ⓐ Andy isn't have as much shoes so Jack.
ⓑ You can eat as many as you wants.

① ⓐ so → as ⓑ as you → so you
② ⓐ as → so ⓑ wants → want
③ ⓐ much → many ⓑ many → much
④ ⓐ Jack → Jack's ⓑ you → yours
⑤ ⓐ isn't → doesn't ⓑ as → so

06 주어진 단어들을 바르게 배열하여 완전한 문장을 쓰시오.

서술형

I, am, you, hungry, not, as, as

→ _____

07 다음 문장에서 어법상 어색한 부분을 찾아 바르게 고치시오.

서술형

Sam is as not fast as Morris.

_____ → _____

08 다음 조건에 맞게 우리말을 영작하시오.

서술형

너의 눈은 그의 눈만큼 커.

- 어휘   eyes, big, as, he, your, yours, his
- 조건 1   주어진 어휘 중 필요한 단어만 쓰고 그 외에 필요한 단어는 보충해서 쓸 것
- 조건 2   7단어로 쓸 것

→ _____

09 다음 그림을 보고 빈칸에 알맞은 말을 쓰시오.

서술형

→ The money is _____ _____

_____ the chicken. (heavy)

VOCA   brilliant 총명한 | careless 부주의한 | donkey 당나귀 | zebra 얼룩말

01 Which CANNOT make a grammatically correct sentence? 3점

① as / is / not / . / sister / me / old / as / My

② English / as / . / boring / is / Math / as

③ as / Comics / magazines / not / are / . / as / funny

④ mine / Your / as / . / good / guess / is / as

⑤ Superman / as / flew / as / highly / . / Gomez

02 Which is correct for the blank? 2점

> He plays the guitar as _____ as you do.

① many   ② well

③ better   ④ best

⑤ good

03 Which describes the picture correctly? 2점

12000 원   18000 원

① The black shirt is as cheap as the white one.

② The black shirt is not as expensive as the white one.

③ The white shirt is not as expensive as the black one.

④ The white shirt is as cheap as the black one.

⑤ The black shirt isn't as cheap as the white one.

04 Which of the underlined words is incorrect? 2점

> My score ① is ② not ③ as ③ good ④ as ⑤ you.

05 Which is the most suitable for the blank? 2점

> A: How tall are you?
> B: I'm 181 centimeters tall. How about you?
> A: I'm also 181 centimeters tall.
> B: Then _____.

① I'm not tall

② You're tall

③ you are not as tall as I

④ I am not as tall as you

⑤ you are as tall as I

06 Who finds the error and corrects it properly? 2점

> Their dog barks as happy as yours.

① 동현: Their → Theirs

② 준형: barks → bark

③ 민수: 앞의 as → like

④ 성호: happy → happily

⑤ 재민: 뒤의 as → so

07 Which order of height is correct? 2점

> Emma is very tall. Marie is not as tall as Emma. Lisa is as tall as Emma.

① Emma < Marie < Lisa

② Lisa = Emma < Marie

③ Marie = Lisa < Emma

④ Marie < Lisa = Emma

⑤ Emma = Marie < Lisa

08 Which correction is right? 2점

> He has not as many coins as she does.

① has → have

② has not → doesn't have

③ many → a lot of

④ not as → as not

⑤ as she does → as hers

VOCA comics 만화책 | score 점수 | bark 짖다 | coin 동전

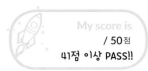
09 Which is grammatically correct? 2점

① Your car is as fast as me.

② Sally is beautiful as her sister.

③ Write your letter as simply as mine.

④ Your weapon is as not powerful as mine.

⑤ She has not as much money as I.

10 Which sentence is incorrect? 2점

① Your cell phone is as old as mine.

② Jenny is not as friendly as her sister.

③ That tower is as tall as this one.

④ This backpack is not expensive as that one.

⑤ They didn't have as much time as we did.

11 Which set has grammatically correct sentences? 3점

(A) ⓐ Paris isn't as big as Seoul.
  ⓑ My computer runs as fast as Jimmy.

(B) ⓐ She isn't as active as her brother.
  ⓑ She walks as beautiful as a model.

(C) ⓐ I can sing as well as you can.
  ⓑ Your bag is as heavily as mine.

(D) ⓐ Tennis isn't as popular as soccer.
  ⓑ You can eat as much as you want.

(E) ⓐ He is as handsome as his father.
  ⓑ Monkeys aren't as dangerously as tigers.

① (A)   ② (B)

③ (C)   ④ (D)

⑤ (E)

12 Find the sentence that has an error and correct it. 4점

서술형

ⓐ He does not work as well as I do.

ⓑ The second racer turned as graceful as the first racer.

(   ) ＿＿＿＿＿＿＿ ➡ ＿＿＿＿＿＿＿

13 Find the error and correct it. 4점

서술형

Son, be as bravely as a lion.

＿＿＿＿＿＿＿ ➡ ＿＿＿＿＿＿＿

14 Rearrange the given words and make a complete sentence. 4점

서술형

he, I, time, does, need, much, as, as

➡ ＿＿＿＿＿＿＿＿＿＿＿＿＿＿

15 Translate the sentence into English. 5점

서술형

그 풍선은 그 연만큼 높이 날았다. (8단어)

➡ ＿＿＿＿＿＿＿＿＿＿＿＿＿＿

16 Fill in the blanks with the appropriate words. 4점

서술형

Sunny has 10,000 won. Narae has 10,000 won, too.

➡ Sunny has ＿＿＿＿＿ ＿＿＿＿＿

money ＿＿＿＿＿ Narae.

17 Look at the picture and complete the sentence according to the conditions. 5점

서술형

조건1 동등 비교를 사용할 것
조건2 과거 시제로 쓸 것
조건3 어휘 – clear, crystal

➡ The salt lake in Turkey ＿＿＿＿＿

＿＿＿＿＿＿＿＿＿＿＿＿＿ .

비교급

개념이해책
99쪽 함께 보기

■ 아래 표의 빈칸에 알맞은 내용을 써 넣으세요. ▶▶ 정답 25쪽

① 비교급의 의미와 기본 형태

형태	의미
-er than… 또는 more ~ than…	1)

② 비교급의 부정과 열등 비교

	형태	의미
비교급의 부정	not ~+2) _____ +than …	…보다 ~하지 않은[않게]
열등 비교	3) _____ +원급+than …	4)

③ 비교급 강조 부사

5) m _____ [6) s _____ , 7) e _____ , 8) f _____ , a lot]+비교급+than ~

Level 1 Test

▶▶ 정답 25쪽

A [ ]에서 알맞은 것을 고르시오.

1 Andy is [quiet / quieter] than John.

2 My mom is [more old / older] than my father.

3 She is [more careful / carefuler] than Sena.

4 He works less [harder / hard] than his boss.

5 The red bike is [very / much] more expensive than the green one.

B 괄호 안의 단어들을 바르게 배열하시오.

1 Tina is (younger, you, than).

→ _____

2 The little boy is (much, me, wiser, than).

→ _____

3 Badminton is (interesting, less, than, tennis).

→ _____

4 This question is (than, easy, one, less, that).

→ _____

C 밑줄 친 부분이 어색하면 바르게 고치시오.

1 She is lazyer than her sister.

→ _____

2 Your phone case is more prettier than mine.

→ _____

3 The room is less larger than that one.

→ _____

4 The sun is much bigger than the Earth.

→ _____

D 우리말과 같은 뜻이 되도록 빈칸을 채우시오.

1 너의 여동생은 나보다 어리다.

→ Your sister is _____ _____

_____.

2 9월은 8월보다 덥지 않다.

→ September _____ _____

_____ August.

VOCA **careful** 신중한 | **phone case** 핸드폰 케이스

My score is
/ 30점
25점 이상 PASS!!

01 다음 빈칸에 가장 적절한 것은? 2점

> Hippos can be _____ than lions.

① dangerous ② dangerouser
③ dangerest ④ more dangerouser
⑤ more dangerous

02 다음 빈칸에 가장 알맞은 것은? 2점

> This cap is too small for my boyfriend. Can you show me a _____ size?

① large ② larger
③ largest ④ smaller
⑤ small

03 다음 각 빈칸에 알맞은 것으로 짝지어진 것은? 2점

> I went to a terrible restaurant last night.
> The food was _____, and the service was even _____.

① better – best ② good – better
③ bad – worse ④ worse – worst
⑤ tasty – excellent

04 그림과 일치하지 <u>않는</u> 것을 모두 고르시오. 2점

Ian Willy

① Ian is shorter than Willy.
② Ian is as fat as Willy.
③ Willy is taller than Ian.
④ Willy isn't fatter than Ian.
⑤ Willy isn't thinner than Ian.

05 주어진 단어를 활용하여 우리말을 영작하시오.

서술형

> 이 반지가 저것보다 더 작나요?
> this ring, small, that one

→ _____

06 그림을 보고 조건에 맞게 빈칸을 채우시오.

서술형

· 조건1 모두 크기를 비교할 것
· 조건2 (1)과 (2)는 괄호 안의 단어를 이용하여 비교할 것
· 조건3 'not'을 사용하지 말 것

(1) A cherry is _____ _____ an apple. (small)
(2) An apple is _____ _____ a cherry. (big)
(3) An apple is _____ _____ _____ a watermelon.

07 다음 문장에서 <u>어법상</u> 어색한 것을 찾아 고치시오.

서술형

> The telephone pole is much less higher than the tower.

_____ → _____

08 다음 성적표를 보고, 조건에 맞게 문장을 완성하시오.

서술형

REPORT CARD
NAME: Vince

Math	F
Science	F
English	F
Ethics	A
P.E.	A

· 조건1 비교 구문을 이용할 것
· 조건2 many를 활용할 것

→ Vince got _____ F's _____ A's.

VOCA hippo 하마 | terrible 형편없는, 끔찍한 | telephone pole 전봇대 | report card 성적표

01 Which is suitable for the blank? 2점

> Toronto is a lot less large than Busan.
> = Busan is _____ than Toronto.

① smaller　　　　② larger
③ much smaller　　④ less large
⑤ much larger

02 Which is suitable for the blank? (2 answers) 2점

> We had _____ snow this year than last year.

① many　　　　② much
③ more　　　　④ less
⑤ little

03 Which is true according to the table? 2점

	Omar	Mark
Go to bed	1:00 (a.m.)	11:00 (p.m.)
Get up	7:30 (a.m.)	6:30 (a.m.)

① Omar gets up earlier than Mark.
② Omar sleeps more than Mark.
③ Omar goes to bed earlier than Mark.
④ Mark sleeps longer than Omar.
⑤ Mark goes to bed later than Omar.

04 How many sentences are grammatically correct? 3점

> ⓐ Ted is busyier than Micky.
> ⓑ A bus is less convenient than a car.
> ⓒ I need a bigger box than this.
> ⓓ This is more stylish than that.
> ⓔ My phone is less expensive than you.

① 1개　　　　　② 2개
③ 3개　　　　　④ 4개
⑤ 5개

05 Which pair has a different meaning? 2점

① He drinks less water than she.
 = She drinks more water than he.
② Men are simpler than women.
 = Women are less simple than men.
③ The red chair is more comfortable than the blue chair.
 = The blue chair is less comfortable than the red chair.
④ He walks more slowly than his brother.
 = His brother walks less slowly than he.
⑤ These pears are cheaper than those.
 = Those pears are less expensive than these.

06 Which correction is right? 2점

> My class picked up trash much more hardly than my friend's class yesterday.

① picked → pick　　② trash → trashes
③ much → very　　　④ hardly → hard
⑤ more hardly → harder

07 Which has the same meaning as the given sentence? 2점

> Artie's beard is longer than Hunter's.

① Artie's beard isn't as long as Hunter's.
② Hunter's beard is longer than Artie's.
③ Hunter's beard is less long than Artie's.
④ Both Artie's beard and Hunter's aren't long.
⑤ Artie's beard isn't long, but Hunter's is long.

08 Find ALL of the grammatically incorrect sentences. 3점

① Dogs are still more faithful than cats.
② My grandma is far older than my grandpa's.
③ Dave is even heavier than before.
④ Luna is much more happy than her friends.
⑤ My uncle's truck is so bigger than your dad's.

VOCA　convenient 편리한 | stylish 멋진, 유행을 따르는 | pear 배(과일) | pick up 줍다 | trash 쓰레기 | beard 턱수염 | faithful 충실한

118

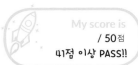
09 How many words are NOT necessary when translating the sentence? 2점

> Claire는 Judy보다 훨씬 더 많은 영화를 본다.
>
> ⓐ very　　　ⓑ still　　　ⓒ more
> ⓓ Judy's　　ⓔ watches

① zero　　　　② one
③ two　　　　④ three
⑤ four

10 서술형 Fill in the blank with one word. The two sentences should have the same meaning. 4점

> Karl isn't as active as his brother.

→ Karl is _____ active than his brother.

11 서술형 Read the following and complete the answer to the question. 4점

> Juan is four years older than David. David is a year older than Sarah. Sarah is fourteen years old.
>
> Q: How old is Juan?
> A: He is _____.

12 서술형 Find the sentence that has an error and correct it. 4점

> ⓐ The Indian elephant is smaller than the African elephant.
> ⓑ It rains a lot more heavy in summer than in spring.

(　　) _____ → _____

13 서술형 Translate the Korean into English in **9 words**. Use the given word. 5점

> 이 식당은 저 식당보다 훨씬 더 안 좋다. (bad)

→ _____

14 서술형 Look at the picture and complete the sentence according to the conditions. 4점

·Condition 1	부정문을 쓰지 말 것
·Condition 2	비교급을 이용할 것
·Condition 3	'm'으로 시작하는 강조 부사를 쓸 것
·Condition 4	어휘 – strong

→ The small car is _____

_____ _____ the big car.

15 서술형 Look at the picture and complete the sentences by using the given words. 각 3점

21kg　　12kg

(1) The white suitcase is _____
_____. (light, 5 words)
(2) The black suitcase is _____
_____. (heavy, 5 words)
(3) The white suitcase isn't _____
_____. (big, 6 words)

VOCA　active 활동적인, 적극적인 | suitcase 여행 가방

개념이해책
102쪽 함께 보기

■ 아래 표의 빈칸에 알맞은 내용을 써 넣으세요. ▶▶ 정답 26쪽

1 최상급의 의미와 기본 형태

형태	의미
the -est 또는 most ~	1)

2 최상급과 전치사

형태		의미
최상급+ 2)	+복수 명사(비교 대상)	… 중에서 가장 ~한[– 히, – 게]
최상급+ 3)	+단수 명사(장소, 집단)	…에서 가장 ~한[– 히, – 게]

3 one of the+최상급+복수 명사

형태		의미
one of the+최상급+ 4)	명사	5)

Level 1 Test

▶▶ 정답 26쪽

A [ ]에서 알맞은 것을 고르시오.

1 Today is the [colder / coldest] day of the year.

2 This cabbage is [the biggest / bigger] of all.

3 This is one of the nicest [restaurant / restaurants] in town.

4 She is the strongest [in / of] all my friends.

B 괄호 안의 단어를 빈칸에 알맞게 고쳐 쓰시오.

1 The Nile is the _____ river in the world. (long)

2 Soccer is _____ than baseball. (tough)

3 This tractor has the _____ engine of all. (powerful)

4 December is the _____ month of the year. (late)

C 밑줄 친 부분이 어색하면 바르게 고치시오.

1 Which country is the colder in Europe?

→ _____

2 The rocket flew highest than it did before.

→ _____

D 다음 우리말과 일치하도록 빈칸을 채우시오.

1 어제는 내 인생 최악의 날이었다.

→ Yesterday was the _____ _____ of my life.

2 수아는 우리 반에서 가장 노래를 잘 한다.

→ Suah is _____ _____ singer in our class.

3 너는 누구를 가장 존경하니?

→ Who do you _____ _____ ?

VOCA cabbage 양배추 | tough 힘든 | tractor 트랙터 | life 인생 | respect 존경하다

Level 2 Test

》》 정답 26쪽

01 다음 빈칸에 가장 적절한 것은? 2점

> This is _____ convenience store in this city.

① large
② larger
③ the largest
④ largest
⑤ larger than

02 다음 각 빈칸에 알맞은 것으로 짝지어진 것은? 2점

> • Ryan runs _____ faster than Lee.
> • He is the _____ brilliant boy in our village.

① much – more
② much – most
③ very – more
④ very – most
⑤ more – very

03 다음 그림의 내용과 일치하는 것은? 2점

101살 502살 248살

① The first witch is the oldest of all.
② The second witch is the youngest of all.
③ The third witch is younger than the first one.
④ The second witch isn't as old as the third one.
⑤ The first witch is much younger than the second one.

04 다음 문장을 바르게 분석한 학생은? 3점

> The Louvre is one of the most famous museum in the world.

① 미연: 여기선 비교급으로 more famous로 써야 해.
② 채니: 비교급이니까 much famouser로 써야 해.
③ 현주: famous의 최상급을 famousest로 써야 해.
④ 동주: museum을 복수 museums로 써야 해.
⑤ 현철: in the world를 of the world로 써야 해.

05 두 문장이 같은 뜻이 되도록 빈칸에 알맞은 말을 쓰시오. 4점

서술형

> All the other girls were slower than Hani.

→ Hani was _____ _____ _____ all the girls.

06 다음 그림을 보고 조건에 맞게 빈칸을 채우시오. 각 3점

서술형

> • 조건1 (1)은 높이를 비교할 것
> • 조건2 (2)와 (3)은 크기를 비교할 것
> • 조건3 모두 한 단어로만 쓸 것

(1) The black block is the _____.
(2) The gray block is the _____ of all.
(3) The white block is the _____ of all.

07 괄호 안의 단어를 어법에 맞게 배열하여 빈칸을 채우시오. 4점

서술형

> Kim Sunbin is _____ _____. (shortest, the, shortstops, of, one).
> *shortstop: 유격수

08 주어진 두 문장을 바탕으로 빈칸을 채우시오. 4점

서술형

> Eric is braver than Louis. Ethan is less brave than Louis.

→ Ethan is the _____ _____ of all. (cowardly)

VOCA convenience store 편의점 | brilliant 총명한 | witch 마녀 | museum 박물관 | cowardly 겁 많은

01 Which word is correct for the blank? 2점

> • Is this the _____ style in fashion?
> • The actress was the _____ dresser of all.

① late – bad
② later – worse
③ last – worst
④ latest – worst
⑤ latest – worse

02 Which correction is right? 2점

> The mobile phone is one of the most useful invention in history.

① is → are
② most → best
③ useful → usefulest
④ invention → inventions
⑤ in → of

03 Which TWO of the following words are NOT necessary when translating the sentence? 2점

> 극락전은 한국 역사상 가장 오래된 건물입니다.

① most
② oldest
③ buildings
④ in
⑤ Korean

04 Which pair has a different meaning? 2점

① I walk faster than Susie.
= Susie doesn't walk as fast as I.
② Love is more important than money.
= Money is less important than love.
③ Midan isn't as intelligent as Miri.
= Miri is more intelligent than Midan.
④ Sora is the politest girl in class.
= Every girl in class is politer than Sora.
⑤ My son came home earlier than my daughter.
= My daughter came home later than my son.

05 Which is true according to the table?
(2 answers) 2점

Name	Daniel	Eric	Kevin	Lucy
Height	161cm	181cm	162cm	162cm

① Kevin is a lot taller than Lucy.
② Lucy isn't as short as Daniel.
③ Kevin is the shortest of all.
④ Eric is the tallest in the group.
⑤ Daniel and Eric are taller than Kevin.

06 Which is correct for the blank? (2 answers) 2점

> It's _____ in the world.

① the best parks
② the most safest bike
③ the highest mountain
④ one of the best universities
⑤ one of the hotter place

07 Which sentence is correct? (2 answers) 2점

① Her handwriting was the worse of all.
② Jill is the most quiet student in the room.
③ The first comedian was the funniest of all.
④ Love is the most important thing in the world.
⑤ Dana has the most longest legs of them.

08 How many sentences are correct? 3점

> ⓐ Brian is the strongest of the three.
> ⓑ This duck is the largest of my animals.
> ⓒ Who is the most famous actor in your country?
> ⓓ What is the most biggest island in Korea?
> ⓔ You are the happiest person in the world.
> ⓕ This is one of the most interesting books of the library.

① one
② two
③ three
④ four
⑤ five

VOCA in fashion 유행하는 | actress 여배우 | dresser ~하게 옷을 입는 사람 | mobile phone 핸드폰 | invention 발명(품) | intelligent 지적인 | polite 예의 바른 | university 대학 | handwriting 손글씨, 필체 | comedian 코미디언 | actor 배우 | country 나라

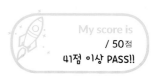
09 Which of following can make a correct sentence? (2 answers) 3점

① can / most / . / swim / fastest / Dave / the
② of / all / pitcher / is / the / most / . / Ryu
③ of / . / is / month / January / the / coldest / the / year
④ Beavers / . / are / diligent / animal / of / the / most / one
⑤ is / planet / . / our / solar system / the / biggest / Jupiter / in

10 Find the sentence that has an error and correct it. 4점

서술형

ⓐ Black is the darkest of all the colors.
ⓑ Math is the best difficult subject of all.
ⓒ What is the longest river in Europe?

(   ) _____ ➡ _____

11 Rearrange the words correctly in the blank. 4점

서술형

of, of, most, things, one, important, is, the, all

➡ Health _____

_____ .

12 Write the correct form of "cute" in each blank. 4점

서술형

There are three dogs in my house; Ki, Yo, and Mi. Ki is _____ than Yo. Mi isn't as _____ as Yo. So _____ is the _____ of the three.

13 주어진 단어를 활용하여 다음 우리말을 영작하시오. 4점

서술형

가장 마른 가수가 가장 큰 소리로 노래했다.
(thin, loudly)

➡ _____

14 Write the correct form of "hard" in each blank. 각 1점

서술형

Eric: What is the (A) _____ word to spell in Korean?
Karen: I think it's 희한하다.
Eric: Actually, there is a (B) _____ word than that.
Karen: What is it?
Eric: It's 괜찮아. Or is it 괜찮아?
Karen: 괜찮아 is correct.
Eric: I should study Korean (C) _____ than now.

15 Look at the picture and fill in the blanks according to the conditions. 각 2점

서술형

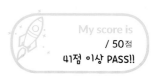

· 조건 1   (1)~(3) 모두 'big'을 이용할 것
· 조건 2   원급, 비교급, 최상급을 모두 이용할 것

(1) The fish on the right isn't _____ _____ _____ the other ones.
(2) The fish in the middle has the _____ tail.
(3) The fish on the left has _____ eyes than the others.

16 Translate the given sentence into English. 5점

서술형

무관심이 세상에서 가장 무서운 것이다.
(scary, indifference)

➡ _____

VOCA   Jupiter 목성 | planet 행성 | solar system 태양계 | subject 과목 | thin 마른 | loudly 크게, 큰 소리로 | spell 철자를 쓰다 | tail 꼬리 | scary 무서운 | indifference 무관심

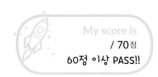

U20_1A+1B

01 다음 중 비교 변화가 나머지와 <u>다른</u> 하나는? 2점

① ill
② well
③ hot
④ much
⑤ little

U20_2B

02 다음 우리말과 뜻이 같도록 할 때, 빈칸에 알맞은 것은? 2점

> 해운대는 여느 때만큼 붐비지 않는다.
> → Haeundae is _____ it usually is.

① as not crowded as
② as crowded as not
③ as crowded not as
④ not as crowded as
⑤ not as more crowded as

U20_2+U21_1

03 Which word for the blank is <u>different</u>? 2점

① The boy ate more _____ me.
② Mr. Choi is younger _____ Mrs. Choi.
③ He feels a lot better _____ he did yesterday.
④ You waited longer _____ thirty minutes.
⑤ He wakes up as early _____ his grandfather.

U21_2

04 다음 표의 내용과 일치하지 <u>않는</u> 것은? 2점

이름	키	몸무게	시력(좌/우)
Amy	159cm	48.5kg	2.0 / 1.3
Bob	173cm	53.5kg	1.0 / 1.5

① Amy is not taller than Bob.
② Bob is heavier than Amy.
③ Amy weighs more than Bob.
④ Bob's right eye isn't worse than Amy's.
⑤ Amy's left eye is better than Bob's.

U20_1B+U21_1

05 다음 빈칸에 공통으로 들어갈 말은? 2점

> • She plays online games _____ than you.
> • He wanted to be a _____ person.

① bad
② well
③ better
④ most
⑤ best

U20_1B+U21_1

06 밑줄 친 부분 중 어법상 <u>어색한</u> 것은? 2점

① America is <u>bigger than</u> I heard.
② Bolt is <u>faster than</u> I expected.
③ Today is <u>bad than</u> yesterday.
④ This pin is <u>more useful than</u> I thought.
⑤ Bo-gum is <u>more handsome than</u> Hae-in.

U21_3+GP

07 다음 빈칸에 알맞지 <u>않은</u> 것을 <u>모두</u> 고르시오. 2점

> Light travels _____ faster than sound.

① far
② more
② even
④ still
⑤ very

U20_2+U21_1+3+U22_1

08 Which CANNOT make a grammatically correct sentence? 4점

① day / my life / was / of / the / it / . / happiest
② than / much / bigger / . / New York is / Boston
③ as / snails / . / they / as / walked / slowly
④ than / farther / even / . / ran / yesterday / Kevin
⑤ than / the roof / flew / . / the rock / more / highly

09 다음 표와 일치하지 <u>않는</u> 문장으로 짝지어진 것은? ^{2점}

U21_1+U22_1+2

한눈에 쏙

	Age	Height (cm)	Weight (kg)
Gong	18	171	48
Kyle	13	165	52
Nicky	14	156	73

ⓐ Gong is the oldest of all.
ⓑ Kyle isn't taller than Nicky.
ⓒ Kyle is the lightest among them.
ⓓ Of the three, Gong is the tallest.
ⓔ Nicky is the heaviest in the group.

① ⓐ, ⓑ
② ⓑ, ⓒ
③ ⓑ, ⓒ, ⓓ
④ ⓑ, ⓒ, ⓔ
⑤ ⓒ, ⓓ, ⓔ

10 다음 빈칸에 적절하지 <u>않은</u> 것은? ^{2점}

U20_1+U22_1

This game is the most _____ one in our store.

① exciting
② interesting
③ popular
④ hard
⑤ expensive

11 Fill in the blanks with the proper words. ^{4점}

U20_2

I love you _____ _____ _____ you love me.
(나는 네가 날 사랑하는 만큼 많이 널 사랑해.)

12 두 문장이 같은 뜻이 되도록 빈칸을 채우시오. ^{4점}

U21_1

The dragon didn't fly as fast as the princess.

→ The princess _____ _____ _____ the dragon.

13 다음을 영작한 것 중 <u>어색한</u> 부분을 2개 찾아 고치시오. ^{4점}

U20_1B+U21_1

나는 지난 주말에 두 편의 영화를 보았다. 첫 번째 영화가 두 번째 영화보다 더 재미있었다.

= I watched two movies latest weekend. The first one was more funnier than the second one.

_____ → _____
_____ → _____

14 다음 대화를 읽고, 두 번째 문장의 오타를 바르게 고쳐 문장을 다시 쓰시오. ^{4점}

U21_1+2

함정

What's the matter with your bf?
He always #!$#%# money @$^%# I do.
What? What's that?
I always pay more than him.
Break up with him! kkkk

*bf: boyfriend의 줄임말

→ He always _____ _____ money _____ I do.

15 Rearrange the given words and make a complete sentence. Do NOT use one word. ^{4점}

U21_1+GP+U06_2

plays, I, she, the, guitar, very, much, better, than

→ _____

16 괄호 안의 단어를 활용하여 우리말을 영작하시오. ^{4점}

U20_1+U22_2

Juri는 나의 사촌들 중 가장 어리다. (young)

→ _____

17 다음을 영작한 것 중 <u>어색한</u> 부분을 <u>2개</u> 찾아 고치시오. 4점

함정

> 삶에서 가장 필요한 것은 고통이다.
> = The best necessary things in life is pain.

_____ → _____

_____ → _____

18 그림과 일치하지 <u>않는</u> 문장을 찾아 밑줄을 치고 바르게 고치시오. 4점

> Ken is fatter than J.J. He isn't as tall as John. He is slimmer than Dave. Dave is wearing the same cap as John.

→ _____

19 두 문장 중 어법상 <u>어색한</u> 것을 찾아 바르게 고치시오. 4점

> ⓐ The rose is the most beautiful flowers.
> ⓑ My grandmother was one of the best dressers in her hometown.

( ) _____ → _____

20 밑줄 친 단어를 활용하여 각 빈칸에 알맞은 말을 쓰시오. 4점

> I was <u>ill</u> yesterday. I became much _____ today. I wanted to go to the hospital, but there was nobody at home. I ate nothing until the evening. Today is the _____ day of my life.

[21~22] 다음 글을 읽고 물음에 답하시오.

> I am a robot developer. I have two robots. ⓐThey are Yummy-O and G27. What ⓑare they do? Yummy-O cooks meals for me, and G27 plays music for me. They are just great. Yummy-O is a ©good cook than my mother. She is the ⓓbest cook in the world. (A)[me / anyone / than / understands / well / G27]. He is the ⓔcaringest robot in the world. Would you like to have a robot like them?

21 윗글의 밑줄 친 ⓐ~ⓔ 중 어법상 옳은 것은? (정답 2개) 4점

고난도

① ⓐ   ② ⓑ

③ ©   ④ ⓓ

⑤ ⓔ

22 윗글의 (A)에 주어진 단어를 어법에 맞게 바르게 배열하시오. (한 단어는 변형하여 쓸 것) 4점

→ _____

CHAPTER 08
to부정사

명사적 용법

■ 아래 표의 빈칸에 알맞은 내용을 써 넣으세요. ›› 정답 28쪽

개념이해책
110쪽 함께 보기

1 to부정사

형태	to부정사	전치사
뒤에 오는 것	to + 1)	to + 2)
해석	~하는 것, ~하는, ~하기 위해 등	~로, ~에게

2 to부정사의 명사적 용법

문장 성분	위치	예문
3)	문장 앞	To learn a foreign language is hard. = 4)＿＿＿ is hard 5)＿＿＿＿＿ a foreign language.
6)	be동사[seem] 뒤	My dream is 7)＿＿＿＿＿ a model.
8)	일반동사 뒤	I want 9)＿＿＿＿＿ a lawyer.

3 의문사+to부정사 = 의문사+주어+10)＿＿＿＿＿ +동사원형

형태	의미	형태	의미
what+to부정사	11)	when+to부정사	13)
how+to부정사	12)	where+to부정사	14)

Level 1 Test

›› 정답 28쪽

A 밑줄 친 to가 '부정사'의 to인지 '전치사'인지 구분하시오.

1 I walked to the bus station. → ＿＿＿＿＿

2 To play table tennis is fun. → ＿＿＿＿＿

3 She doesn't know what to do. → ＿＿＿＿＿

B [ ]에서 알맞은 것을 고르시오.

1 [Bully / To bully] someone is wrong.

2 We want to [living / live] in the country.

3 We sat down to [catch / catching] our breath.

4 His dream is [be / to be] a voice actor.

5 [To read / To reads] books is good for you.

C 밑줄 친 to부정사를 '주어', '보어', '목적어'로 구분하시오.

1 I want to have some pizza. → ＿＿＿＿＿

2 My wish is to travel abroad. → ＿＿＿＿＿

3 I don't know where to go. → ＿＿＿＿＿

4 It is hard to get up early. → ＿＿＿＿＿

D 밑줄 친 부분을 바르게 해석하시오.

1 To be a doctor is my dream.

→ ＿＿＿＿＿＿＿＿＿＿ 나의 꿈이다.

2 It is good to be kind to others.

→ 다른 사람들에게 ＿＿＿＿＿＿＿＿ 좋다.

3 He likes to talk with you.

→ 그는 너와 ＿＿＿＿＿＿＿＿ 좋아한다.

VOCA table tennis 탁구 | bully 약자를 괴롭히다 | country 시골 | catch one's breath 숨을 고르다 | voice actor 성우 | travel 여행하다 | abroad 해외로

정답 28쪽

01 다음 대화의 빈칸에 알맞은 것은?

> A: What are you going to do this weekend?
> B: I plan _____ camping with my friends.

① go   ② went
③ to going   ④ to go
⑤ going

02 각 빈칸에 알맞은 말이 순서대로 나열된 것은?

> • My job is _____ teach children.
> • _____ is fun to run on ice.
> • You need _____ sleep now.

① to – That – to   ② to – It – to
③ for – It – to   ④ to be – It – to
⑤ it – It – it

03 밑줄 친 부분의 쓰임이 [보기]와 같은 것은?

> 보기   He loves to eat ice cream.

① It is bad to watch too much TV.
② I don't want to stay here.
③ My history homework is to write an essay.
④ Is it easy to make rice cake?
⑤ To finish the work is impossible.

04 밑줄 친 부분이 어법상 올바른 것은?

① Remember every password is not easy.
② They went to be the river.
③ Do you want to come here?
④ To I, the box is very precious.
⑤ My wish is to meets IU.

05 빈칸에 들어갈 말로 알맞은 것은?

> Let me know when _____.

① start   ② to start
③ starting   ④ starts
⑤ started

06 주어진 문장과 같은 뜻이 되도록 빈칸에 알맞은 말을 쓰시오.

서술형

(1) To use this machine is easy.

→ _____ is easy _____

_____ this machine.

(2) I don't know what to say.

→ I don't know _____

_____ _____

_____.

07 다음 문장에서 어법상 어색한 부분을 찾아 바르게 고치시오.

서술형

> I am not sure whom to trusting.

_____ → _____

08 다음 우리말을 조건에 맞게 영작하시오.

서술형

> 그녀는 밤에 별을 보는 것을 좋아한다.
>
> 조건 1   like, watch, the stars, at night을 포함할 것
> 조건 2   8단어로 쓸 것

→ _____

09 그림을 보고 주어진 단어를 이용해서 영작을 완성하시오.

서술형

> 폭풍이 오기 전에 바다에서 수영하는 것은 위험하다.
> swim, in the sea, dangerous, it

→ _____

before a storm.

VOCA   **plan** 계획하다 | **go camping** 캠핑 가다 | **essay** 글쓰기 과제 | **rice cake** 떡 | **impossible** 불가능한 | **password** 비밀번호 | **precious** 소중한
| **machine** 기계 | **trust** 신뢰하다 | **storm** 폭풍

01 Which translation is correct? 2점

> 너는 무엇을 사기를 원하니?

① What you want to buy?
② What do you want to buy?
③ What do you want buy?
④ What you to buy want?
⑤ What do you want to buying?

02 Which underlined part is used in the same way as in the given sentence? 2점

> She wants to get a new backpack.

① To save money is not easy.
② She expects to buy a car next year.
③ My job is to guide tourists.
④ It is helpful to have a mentor.
⑤ He sent a package to me.

03 Which is the common word for the blanks? 2점

> • It is my dream _____ visit India.
> • He seems _____ be okay now.

① for   ② to
③ in   ④ with
⑤ at

04 Which underlined "to" is used differently than the others? 2점

① He loves to play outside.
② I often go to the mountain.
③ It's a great pleasure to meet you.
④ Mina needs to study hard.
⑤ I want to buy some clothes.

05 Look at the picture and choose the correct words for the blanks. 3점

> Child: What are you doing, Dad? Play with me!
> Father: I want _____ with you, but I'm _____ now.

① to play – working   ② play – work
③ to play – work   ④ playing – working
⑤ to play – to work

06 Which of the following is correct for the blank? 2점

> Sunny will learn _____ this winter.

① how to ski   ② how to skiing
③ what ski to   ④ when should ski
⑤ where ski

07 Whose translation is correct? 2점

> 네 잎 클로버를 보는 것은 행운이다.

① 형택: Find a four-leaf clover is good luck.
② 소원: To find a four-leaf clover is good luck.
③ 형규: To finding a four-leaf clover is good luck.
④ 대종: A four-leaf clover finding is good luck.
⑤ 영탁: A four-leaf clover to find is good luck.

08 Which word is correct for the blank? 2점

> _____ is fun to make cupcakes.

① It   ② That
③ What   ④ How
⑤ This

VOCA   expect 기대하다 | guide 안내하다 | tourist 관광객 | mentor 멘토 | package 소포, 택배 | seem to ~처럼 보이다 | pleasure 기쁨 | four-leaf clover 네 잎 클로버 | luck 운, 행운 | cupcake 컵케이크

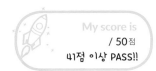
09 Which is NOT necessary when translating the given sentence? 3점

> 물 없이 사는 것은 불가능하다.
> = _____ _____ impossible _____
> _____ _____ _____.

① to ② it
③ this ④ live
⑤ without

10 How many sentences are grammatically <u>incorrect</u>? 3점

> ⓐ She wants go home.
> ⓑ Her dream is be a makeup artist.
> ⓒ We planned to start a flower shop.
> ⓓ It is wonderful to be married.
> ⓔ I hope to live in a large house.
> ⓕ What to do is the problem.

① one ② two
③ three ④ four
⑤ five

11 Look at the picture and complete the sentence. Use the given words. 6점 서술형

> dangerous, touch, the jellyfish, it, to

→ _____

12 Rearrange the given words in the blank. 4점 서술형

> Please tell me _____ you back. (I, call, should, when)

13 Read the dialog and complete the answer to the question. 5점 서술형

> Jiho: Let's play some music. What kind of music do you want to listen to?
> Minho: Why don't we listen to *trot* songs?
> ----
> Q: What kind of music does Minho want to listen to?
> A: He _____.

[14~15] Read the following and answer each question.

> **Happy Valentine's Day**
>
> Dear Sabin,
>
> ⓐTo meet you was my destiny. (A) <u>I don't know how to explain my feelings.</u> My dream is ⓑto marry a man like you. I love you so much. I want ⓒto be your valentine.
>
> Love,
>
> Young
>
> *destiny: 운명 **valentine: 사랑하는 사람, 연인

14 Match the underlined ⓐ~ⓒ with (A)~(C) according to the usage. 각 2점 서술형

> (A) I don't wish <u>to be</u> rude.
> (B) It's easy <u>to make</u> a mistake.
> (C) My plan is <u>to retire</u> in Florida.

(A) _____ (B) _____

(C) _____

15 Rewrite the underlined sentence (A) in <u>9 words</u> without changing its meaning. 6점 서술형

→ _____

_____

24 형용사적 용법, 부사적 용법

■ 아래 표의 빈칸에 알맞은 내용을 써 넣으세요. ›› 정답 29쪽

개념이해책
113쪽 함께 보기

① to부정사의 형용사적 용법

명사+to부정사	I have lots of homework to do. (해석: 1))
대명사+to부정사	I want something to drink. (해석: 2))
명사+to부정사+전치사	He has no chair to sit on. (해석: 3))
It's time+to부정사	It's time to leave. (해석: 4))

② to부정사의 부사적 용법

목적(뜻: 5))	I went to the library to study. (해석: 6))
원인(뜻: 7))	She was happy to meet him. (해석: 8))
형용사 수식(뜻: 9))	The question is hard to answer. (해석: 10))
결과(뜻: 11))	He lived to be 100 years old. (해석: 12))

③ 부사적 용법의 too ~ to와 enough to

| too+형용사/부사+to부정사
= 13)　　　+형용사/부사+14)　　　+주어+15)　　　~ | 뜻: 16) |
| 형용사/부사+enough+to부정사
= 17)　　　+형용사/부사+18)　　　+주어+19)　　　~ | 뜻: 20) |

Level 1 Test

›› 정답 29쪽

A 밑줄 친 부분을 바르게 해석하시오.

1 I don't have any money to lend him.

→ 나는 그에게 _____이 하나도 없다.

2 It's time to finish the class.

→ 수업을 _____ 시간이다.

3 Did he have a friend to help him?

→ 그는 그를 _____ 친구가 있었니?

4 The old lady doesn't have anyone to live with.

→ 그 할머니는 _____ 사람이 아무도 없다.

5 She has some errands to run today.

→ 그녀는 오늘 _____이 있다.

VOCA　run errands 심부름을 하다 | miss 놓치다 | nervous 초조한 |
calmly 침착하게

B to부정사의 부사적 용법의 '목적', '원인', '결과' 중에서 밑줄 친 부분에 해당하는 것을 쓰시오.

1 He was sad to miss the concert.　→ _____

2 I saved money to move to Rome.　→ _____

3 He lived to be 80 years old.　→ _____

C 다음 빈칸에 알맞은 말을 써 넣으시오.

1 She is so nervous that she can't talk calmly.

→ She is _____ _____

_____ _____ calmly.

2 I was so tired that I slept until noon.

→ I was _____ _____

_____ _____ until noon.

01 다음 빈칸 중 어느 것에도 들어갈 수 <u>없는</u> 것은?

> • He needs a house _____.
> • It's _____ have lunch.
> • He had _____ his real son.
> • He doesn't have a bike _____.
> • Give me _____.

① to meet a chance 　② to live in

③ time to 　④ something to drink

⑤ to ride

02 밑줄 친 to부정사의 의미가 나머지 넷과 <u>다른</u> 것은?

① Kate was disappointed <u>to make</u> a mistake.

② The girl felt sad <u>to lose</u> her lovely puppy.

③ I was glad <u>to have</u> a mini airplane.

④ We left early <u>to catch</u> the first train.

⑤ They were happy <u>to get</u> the prize.

03 밑줄 친 to부정사가 [보기]와 같은 의미로 쓰인 것은?

> 보기　 We had no chance <u>to respond</u>.

① This math question is hard <u>to solve</u>.

② She and her husband are hard <u>to treat</u>.

③ I have no energy <u>to run</u>.

④ Her class is easy <u>to understand</u>.

⑤ It is impossible <u>to fix</u>.

04 다음 중 어법상 어색한 문장의 개수는?

> ⓐ I called Emily to say sorry.
> ⓑ They need more money to build a house.
> ⓒ I'm not ready to start.
> ⓓ He has nothing to lose.

① 0개 　② 1개

③ 2개 　④ 3개

⑤ 4개

05 우리말과 같은 뜻이 되도록 단어들을 바르게 배열하시오.

> 저에게 따뜻한 마실 것을 좀 주세요.
> give, me, drink, to, warm, something

→ _____

06 다음과 같은 의미가 되도록 한 문장으로 바꿔 쓰시오.

> He was so tired that he couldn't cook.

→ _____

07 다음 문장을 조건에 맞게 같은 의미로 바꾸시오.

> He woke up and heard the rain outside.
>
> • 조건1　위 문장의 단어를 활용할 것
> • 조건2　새로운 단어는 하나만 추가할 것
> • 조건3　모두 8단어로 쓸 것

→ _____

08 그림과 조건에 맞게 같은 의미의 두 문장을 쓰시오.

> • 어휘　enough, so, small
> • 조건　(1)에는 3단어를, (2)에는 5단어를 쓸 것

(1) My smartphone is _____

　　 fit in my pocket.

(2) My smartphone is _____

_____ fit in my pocket.

VOCA　disappointed 실망한 | lovely 사랑스러운 | puppy 강아지 | prize 상 | respond 응답하다 | solve 풀다 | treat 대우하다 | fix 고치다 | be ready to ~할 준비가 되다 | fit in ~에 들어가다

01 Which translation is correct? 2점

> 맛있는 먹을 것 좀 있니?

① Is there to eat delicious anything?
② Is there anything delicious to eat?
③ Is there delicious anything to eat?
④ Is there to eat anything delicious?
⑤ Is there anything to eat delicious?

02 How many sentences are incorrect? 2점

> ⓐ We decided to not go abroad.
> ⓑ The question is hard to answer.
> ⓒ He is old enough to watch that movie.
> ⓓ There is no food to eat on the table.

① zero   ② one
③ two   ④ three
⑤ four

03 Which of the following is correct for the blank? 2점

> He needs a piece of paper _____.

① to write   ② to write on
③ on to write   ④ in the write
⑤ to write of

04 Which underlined word is used differently than the others? 2점

① It's time to have lunch.
② I need some water to drink.
③ She doesn't have a bike to ride.
④ She hopes to become an engineer.
⑤ We have a promise to keep.

05 Which underlined phrase is used in the same way as the given sentence? (Up to 3 answers) 3점

> I came to bring a sword.

① We need time to think about it.
② Are there many places to visit there?
③ They left early to catch the plane.
④ I always do my best to understand him.
⑤ There is nothing to change now.

06 Which translation is correct? 2점

> 나는 살아갈 이유를 발견했다.

① I found to live a reason.
② I found a reason to live.
③ I found for live a reason.
④ I found to live me a reason.
⑤ I found to a reason to live.

07 Which of the underlined words is used differently than the others? 2점

① I'm really sorry to hear that.
② You come to school to study, not to play.
③ He must be a genius to pass this level.
④ Santa carried lots of gifts to give the children.
⑤ The word is not easy to pronounce.

08 Which of the underlined words are used in the same way? 3점

> ⓐ I sang to make them happy.
> ⓑ Love and coughs are hard to hide.
> ⓒ Few people live to be 100 years old.
> ⓓ We need one more person to play with.
> ⓔ The book is difficult to read.
> ⓕ John tried hard, only to fail.

① ⓐ, ⓑ   ② ⓑ, ⓔ, ⓕ
③ ⓒ, ⓓ   ④ ⓓ, ⓔ
⑤ ⓒ, ⓕ

VOCA · delicious 맛있는 | decide 결심하다 | sword 검 | reason 이유 | genius 천재 | level 수준, 레벨 | carry 나르다 | pronounce 발음하다 | cough 기침

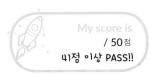
09 Find the error and correct it. 4점

서술형

> Can you give me a chair to sit?

_____ → _____

10 Complete the sentence with the given words to make the dialog natural. (5 words) 4점

서술형

> Roy:　I can't go to the meeting today.
> Willy: Why not?
> Roy:　My mom is sick. I have to go home early.
> Willy: _____.
> 　　　　(sorry, hear)

11 Complete the sentence describing the picture according to the conditions. 5점

서술형

> · Condition 1　words – late, get on the bus, too, to
> · Condition 2　Fill in the blank with 7 words.

→ He is _____.

12 Rearrange the given words to translate the Korean sentence. 4점

서술형

> 사람들에게 나쁜 말을 쓰지 않도록 조심해라.
> be, to, careful, not, use, bad language, with people

→ _____

13 Rewrite the sentences without changing their meanings. 각 3점

서술형

(1) I was so nervous that I couldn't sleep.

→ I _____.

(2) She is so kind that she can help me.

→ She is _____ me.

[14~15] The following is the beginning of the tale "Jack and the Beanstalk." Read it and answer each question.

Jack and the Beanstalk

Jack and his mom had nothing ⓐto eat. So Jack went to the market ⓑto sell the cow. (A)The cow was too weak to work. On the way to the market, an old man wanted ⓒto buy the cow. He gave Jack some magic beans ⓓto buy the cow. Jack's mom was upset ⓔto see the beans.

14 Among the underlined ⓐ~ⓔ, which set groups the ones of the same usage? 3점

① ⓐ, ⓑ　　　　　② ⓑ, ⓓ
③ ⓒ, ⓔ　　　　　④ ⓒ, ⓓ, ⓔ
⑤ ⓓ, ⓔ

15 Rewrite the underlined part (A) without changing its meaning. 6점

서술형

> · Condition 1　Use the words "that" and "it."
> · Condition 2　Write in 9 words.

(A) _____
_____

VOCA　meeting 모임, 회의 | get on ~을 타다 | nervous 초조한 | on the way to ~로 가는 길에 | upset 속상한

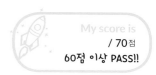
U23_2

01 Which sentence is grammatically correct? 2점

① Get up early is hard.
② He doesn't like talk about his private life.
③ It is wonderful to swim in the ocean.
④ What did she want be?
⑤ My hobby is play computer games.

U23_2+U24_1+2

02 밑줄 친 부분의 쓰임이 [보기]와 같은 것은? 2점

> [보기] My grandfather likes to play *janggi*.

① My brother has lots of toys to play with.
② She is too sick to stand.
③ He is rich enough to be a millionaire.
④ Were you happy to join the army?
⑤ It is helpful to use the navigation system in the car.

U23_GP

03 밑줄 친 'It[it]'의 쓰임이 나머지와 다른 하나는? 2점

① It is very difficult to teach him.
② It's too hot to eat. Please cool it down.
③ It's not easy to install this program.
④ Is it good to have a robot vacuum cleaner?
⑤ It is important to recycle things.

U23_3+U24_1+GP

04 Which sentences are incorrect? 3점

고난도

> ⓐ She told me when leave.
> ⓑ Can you tell me where going.
> ⓒ Give me something interesting to read.
> ⓓ Do you have a pen to write?
> ⓔ It's time to rest.

① ⓐ   ② ⓐ, ⓑ, ⓓ
③ ⓐ, ⓑ, ⓔ   ④ ⓑ, ⓓ
⑤ ⓒ, ⓓ

U23_2+U24_2

05 밑줄 친 부분의 쓰임이 나머지와 다른 하나는? 2점

한눈에 쏙

① I went there to make a video.
② I brought the key to lock the door.
③ She got up early not to be late.
④ Everybody likes to talk with him.
⑤ He turned on the TV to watch a drama.

U24_1

06 [보기]와 같은 의미의 문장을 고르시오. 2점

> [보기] It is time for a bath.

① It is time to a bath.
② It is time for take a bath.
③ It is to bath time.
④ It is time to take a bath.
⑤ It is time taking a bath.

U24_1+2

07 다음 중 밑줄 친 to부정사가 같은 용법인 것끼리 묶인 것을 고르시오. 3점

고난도

> ⓐ It's time to go to bed.
> ⓑ I don't have time to play.
> ⓒ He has nothing to say.
> ⓓ She went to Paris to study French.
> ⓔ I'm happy to meet you.

① ⓐ, ⓑ   ② ⓐ, ⓑ, ⓒ
③ ⓑ, ⓒ, ⓓ   ④ ⓒ, ⓓ
⑤ ⓐ, ⓔ

U24_3+U23_2+GP

08 다음 각 빈칸에 들어갈 말로 짝지어진 것을 고르시오. 2점

> • Is it too cold _____ the window?
> • He wants _____ the window.

① open – open   ② to open – to open
③ to open – opening   ④ opening – to open
⑤ open – to open

09 U23_2+U24_2

다음 우리말과 일치하는 문장을 고르시오. 2점

나는 작별 인사를 하기 위해 그녀에게 전화하기로 했다.

① I decided to call her to say goodbye.
② I decided to say goodbye to call her.
③ I decided to call her and say goodbye.
④ I decided to call her and said goodbye.
⑤ I called her to say goodbye to decide.

10 U23_2+U24_2+3+GP

밑줄 친 부분의 용법이 [보기]와 같은 것을 고르시오. 2점

[보기] This machine is easy to use.

① Josh is comfortable to work with.
② It is important to win the game.
③ She broke the eggs to make an omelet.
④ They were so disappointed to lose the game.
⑤ The brothers grew up to be famous soccer players.

11 U23_GP+3

빈칸에 알맞은 말을 써서 주어진 문장과 같은 의미의 문장을 완성하시오. 각 2점

(1) To cross this bridge is dangerous.
→ _____ is dangerous _____ _____ this bridge.

(2) They know what to choose.
→ They know _____ _____ _____ _____.

12 U24_GP

조건에 맞게 우리말을 영작하시오. 4점

그 아이는 함께 놀 친구가 없다.

· 조건 1 the kid, play, any friends를 포함할 것
· 조건 2 관사 포함해서 9단어로 쓸 것

→ _____

13 U24_3

Fill in the blanks to complete the sentence. 4점

I was very shy. I could not talk to him.

→ I was _____ _____ to
_____ _____
_____.

14 U23_2

다음 조건에 맞게 영작하시오. 4점

그녀의 꿈은 수의사가 되는 것이다.

· 조건 1 become, a vet을 포함할 것
· 조건 2 7단어로 쓸 것

→ _____

15 U23_GP

주어진 단어를 포함해서 그림을 묘사하는 문장을 쓰시오. 4점

hard, fix, the car, it, to

→ _____

16 U24_GP

주어진 단어를 배열하여 우리말을 영작하시오. 4점

교생 선생님께 질문할 재미난 것 있니?
is, anything, to, funny, ask, a student-teacher, there

→ _____

17 다음 우리말을 조건에 맞게 영작하시오. 5점

> 우리는 가지고 놀 야구 방망이가 없다.
>
> ・조건1 a baseball bat, play를 포함할 것
> ・조건2 전치사를 추가할 것
> ・조건3 9단어로 쓸것

→ _____

18 Rearrange the given words and fill in the blank. 4점

> He decided _____.
> (to, not, play, the game, again).

19 다음 문장을 조건에 맞게 같은 의미로 바꾸시오. 4점

> He grew up and became a boxing champion.
>
> ・조건1 위 문장의 단어를 활용하고 필요하면 형태를 바꿀 것
> ・조건2 새로운 단어는 하나만 추가할 것
> ・조건3 모두 8단어로 쓸 것

→ _____

20 그림을 보고 아이에게 할 말을 조건에 맞게 쓰시오. 각 2점

> ・조건1 too, young, wear를 쓸 것
> ・조건2 같은 의미의 두 문장을 쓸 것
> ・조건3 (1)의 빈칸에 4단어를 쓸 것

(1) You are _____
high heels.

(2) You are _____
wear high heels.

[21~22] 다음 글을 읽고 물음에 답하시오.

It is unimaginable ⓐto live without soap. We all want ⓑto be clean. Today, you can get soap everywhere. However, a long time ago, people did not have ⓒthem. They just washed with water. The water just washed away dirt. Who first invented soap? Egyptians made soap from animal and vegetable oils with alkaline salt. (A)[their / to / clean / bodies / They / used / soap]. But soap was ⓓan expensive item at that time. Most people ⓔcould not buy it.

*alkaline: 알칼리성의

21 윗글의 밑줄 친 ⓐ~ⓔ에 대한 설명이 잘못된 것은?
(정답 최대 3개) 4점

① ⓐ 가주어로 쓰인 명사적 용법이다.
② ⓑ want의 목적어로 쓰였다.
③ ⓒ 불가산명사를 가리키므로 it으로 고쳐야 한다.
④ ⓓ 단수이면서 모음으로 시작하므로 an이 쓰였다.
⑤ ⓔ was not able to로 바꿔 쓸 수 있다.

22 윗글의 밑줄 친 (A)에 주어진 단어를 조건에 맞게 바르게 배열하시오. 4점

> ・조건 주어진 단어를 변형하지 말 것

(A) _____

CHAPTER 09
동명사

25 동명사

개념이해책
120쪽 함께 보기

■ 아래 표의 빈칸에 알맞은 내용을 써 넣으세요. ›› 정답 30쪽

1 동명사의 의미와 형태

형태	의미
동사원형+-ing	1)

2 동명사의 역할

문장 성분	위치	예문
2)	3) ___ 앞	Sleeping well is important.
4)	5) ___ 뒤	His hobby is doing yoga.
6)	7) ___ 뒤	He enjoys swimming in the rain.
	8) ___ 뒤	Anita is good at speaking Korean.

3 동명사와 현재분사

9) ___	My hobby is collecting rocks. (해석: 10) ___)
11) ___	I am collecting rocks now. (해석: 12) ___)

4 동명사의 관용 표현

go+-ing: 13)	How[What] about+-ing ~?: 14)
be busy+-ing: 15)	spend+시간/돈+-ing: 16)
feel like+-ing: 17)	look forward to+-ing: 18)

Level 1 Test

›› 정답 31쪽

A 밑줄 친 것이 '동명사'인지, '현재분사'인지 구분하시오.

1 Rex, what are you doing here?

➡ _____

2 We don't mind waiting for her.

➡ _____

3 The strange man was standing by me.

➡ _____

4 Thank you for helping me with my work.

➡ _____

B 우리말과 일치하도록 빈칸을 채우시오.

1 엄마는 드라마를 보시느라 바쁘셔.

➡ Mom _____ _____ _____ a soap opera.

2 저는 당신을 만나는 것을 고대하고 있습니다.

➡ I'm _____ _____ _____ _____ you.

3 캠핑 가는 게 어때?

➡ How about _____ _____ ?

VOCA strange 낯선, 이상한 | soap opera 드라마, 연속극

01 다음 빈칸에 알맞은 것은? 2점

> The boy kept _____ a ball to me.

① kick   ② kicked

③ to kick   ④ kicking

⑤ to kicking

02 다음 중 밑줄 친 부분의 쓰임이 옳은 것은? 2점

① I will go to fish this Friday.

② I'm looking forward to see her.

③ She is busy to write her report.

④ Do you feel like eating something?

⑤ She spent ₩1,500 buy the hotdog.

03 다음 중 밑줄 친 부분의 쓰임이 다른 하나는? 2점

① Teaching children is so hard.

② He likes watching late-night movies.

③ She is finishing the job now.

④ He stopped writing a letter to her.

⑤ Going to the market is fun for me.

04 어법상 어색한 부분을 찾아 바르게 고친 것은? 2점

> Being polite to old people are important.

① Being → Be   ② polite → politely

③ old → oldest   ④ people → peoples

⑤ are → is

05 다음 중 어법상 어색한 문장의 개수는? 2점

> ⓐ Mina, I'm sorry for dropping your phone.
> ⓑ Listening to his music was nice.
> ⓒ Do you mind to smoke here?
> ⓓ Editing the articles were a lot of work.
> ⓔ Thank you, Aaron, for being with us.
> ⓕ Wait for the bus is really boring.

① 1개   ② 2개

③ 3개   ④ 4개

⑤ 5개

06 어법상 어색한 것을 찾아 바르게 고치시오. 4점

서술형

> She finally gave up on lose weight.

_____ → _____

07 우리말과 일치하도록 주어진 단어들을 배열하시오. 4점

서술형

> 새로운 사람을 만나는 것은 항상 흥미진진하다.
> always, exciting, is, people, meeting, new

→ _____

08 다음을 조건에 맞게 영작하시오. 4점

서술형

> 그는 숙제를 하느라 늘 바쁘다.
>
> · 조건1   전치사를 사용하지 말 것
> · 조건2   어휘 – be, always, his

→ _____

09 그림을 보고 빈칸에 공통으로 들어갈 말을 쓰시오. 4점

서술형

> My dad's hobby is _____. I am going to go _____ with him tomorrow. I want to catch a lot of fish.

→ _____

10 주어진 문장과 같은 의미가 되도록 빈칸에 알맞은 말을 쓰시오. 4점

서술형

> Thank you for your help.

→ Thank you for _____ me.

VOCA   kick 차다 | late-night movie 심야 영화 | polite 예의 바른 | edit 편집하다 | article 기사 | finally 마침내 | give up (on) ~을 포기하다 | lose weight 살을 빼다

01 Which of the following is correct for the blank? 2점

> My hobby is _____ the ukulele.

① play ② played
③ playing ④ to playing
⑤ plays

02 Whose translation is correct? 2점

> 가장 나쁜 습관 중 하나는 늦게 일어나는 것이다.

① 성수: One of the bad habits is getting up late.
② 동민: One of the bad habit is get up late.
③ 혜민: One of the worst habit is getting up late.
④ 세연: One of the worst habits are getting up late.
⑤ 영주: One of the worst habits is getting up late.

03 Which TWO of the following expressions are NOT correct for the blank? 2점

> We all enjoyed _____.

① the shrimp
② our holiday
③ to see the rainbow
④ riding the roller coaster
⑤ watched the old movie

04 Who analyzes the sentence correctly? 2점

> Some people don't like watching movies at home.

① 현우: people이 아니라 persons로 써야 해.
② 수희: don't가 아니라 doesn't로 써야 해.
③ 민구: like는 주어가 복수니까 likes로 써야 해.
④ 혜란: watching은 문장에서 보어로 쓰였어.
⑤ 학준: 완벽한 문장이야. 틀린 게 없어.

05 Which correction is incorrect? 2점

> Send an email to he will a best choice than call him.

① Send → Sent ② he → him
③ will → will be ④ best → better
⑤ call → calling

06 Which is grammatically correct? (2 answers) 2점

① I am sorry for to invite him.
② They talked about sold their old car.
③ Chatting on the Internet is fun.
④ The master started teaching his skills.
⑤ Making good friends take a lot of time.

07 Which of the underlined words is used differently than the others? 2점

① Driving in Manhattan is a bad idea.
② She dislikes waking up in the morning.
③ How about going for a ride tonight?
④ She likes shopping online too much.
⑤ The animal trainer is training a leopard.

08 Which part of the dialog is grammatically incorrect? 3점

> A: ① What country do you want to visit?
> B: ② I really look forward to visit France some day.
> A: ③ Why is that?
> B: ④ You know, France is famous for fashion.
> A: ⑤ I agree with you.

VOCA ukulele 우쿨렐레(악기 이름) | shrimp 새우 | roller coaster 롤러코스터 | chat 잡담하다 | go for a ride 드라이브하다 | train 훈련시키다 |
leopard 표범

09 How many sentences are grammatically <u>incorrect</u>? 3점

> ⓐ I don't feel like having dinner now.
> ⓑ She spent $100 paint the bike.
> ⓒ He started singing in 2009.
> ⓓ Koreans are good at shoot arrows.
> ⓔ He enjoyed running at the park.

① one　　　② two
③ three　　④ four
⑤ five

10 Which is NOT necessary when translating the sentence? 2점

> 그녀는 점심을 사먹는 데 보통 8,000원을 쓴다.

① usually　　② spends
③ buying　　④ to
⑤ lunch

11 Find the sentence that has an error and correct it. 4점
서술형

> ⓐ Did you finish packing your things?
> ⓑ I am not afraid of ask her out.

( ) ＿＿＿＿＿＿ → ＿＿＿＿＿＿

12 Choose three words and fill in the blanks to complete the sentence. 4점
서술형

> usually, either, skates, skating, enjoying, enjoys

→ He ＿＿＿＿＿ ＿＿＿＿＿
＿＿＿＿＿ in winter.

13 Rearrange the given words to translate the sentence. 4점
서술형

> 그녀는 이를 닦지 않고 잤다.
> her, bed, she, without, went, brushing, to, teeth

→ ＿＿＿＿＿＿＿＿＿＿＿＿＿＿

14 Look at the picture and complete the sentence. 4점
서술형

> Boy: How come you're so late?
> Girl: I'm sorry. I ＿＿＿＿＿＿＿＿
> 　　　the floor. (busy, sweep)

15 Find ALL of the errors and rewrite the whole sentence correctly. 6점
서술형

> Washing your hand before eating are a good habit.

→ ＿＿＿＿＿＿＿＿＿＿＿＿＿
＿＿＿＿＿＿＿＿＿＿＿＿＿

16 Translate the sentence according to the conditions. 6점
서술형

배달 시켜 먹고 싶니?	
· Words	feel, order in
· Condition 1	동명사를 반드시 포함할 것
· Condition 2	총 6단어로 쓸 것
	*order in: 음식을 배달 주문하다

→ ＿＿＿＿＿＿＿＿＿＿＿＿＿

VOCA　shoot 쏘다 | arrow 화살 | pack 짐을 싸다 | ask ~ out ~에게 데이트 신청하다 | how come 어째서 | sweep 쓸다

■ 아래 표의 빈칸에 알맞은 내용을 써 넣으세요. ▷▷ 정답 31쪽

개념이해책
123쪽 함께 보기

1 동명사만 목적어로 취하는 동사

1) _____ (즐기다),	2) _____ (꺼리다),	3) _____ (포기하다),
4) _____ (끝내다),	5) _____ (연습하다),	6) s_____ (멈추다, 그만두다),
7) _____ (계속 ~하다),	8) q_____ (그만두다),	9) _____ (싫어하다)

2 to부정사만 목적어로 취하는 동사

10) _____ (원하다),	11) w_____ (바라다),	12) h_____ (바라다),
13) _____ (기대하다),	14) _____ (계획하다),	15) _____ (약속하다),
16) _____ (결정하다),	17) w_____ (~하고 싶다),	18) _____ (배우다)

3 둘 다 목적어로 취하는 동사

A 의미 차이가 거의 없는 경우

start[19) _____](시작하다),	20) _____ (좋아하다),	21) _____ (사랑하다),
22) _____ (계속하다),	23) _____ (싫어하다)	

B 의미 차이가 있는 경우

remember	동명사	24)	try	동명사	28)
	to부정사	25)		to부정사	29)
forget	동명사	26)	stop	동명사	30)
	to부정사	27)		to부정사	31)

Level 1 Test

▷▷ 정답 31쪽

A 괄호 안의 단어를 빈칸에 알맞은 형태로 쓰시오.

1 He gave up _____ rugby. (play)

2 My daughter wants _____ an astronaut. (be)

3 He expected _____ a gold medal. (win)

4 She continued _____ her husband. (support)

5 What does she hope _____? (sell)

B 빈칸에 알맞은 말을 쓰시오.

1 여자친구한테 문자 보내는 걸 잊었네.

→ I forgot _____ my girlfriend.

2 그들은 별을 보기 위해 멈춰 섰다.

→ They stopped _____ at the stars.

3 빗속에서 버스 기다렸던 거 기억나니?

→ Do you remember _____ for the bus in the rain?

VOCA rugby 럭비 | astronaut 우주 비행사 | expect 기대하다 | support 지지하다 | text 문자를 보내다

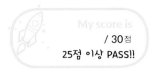
01 다음 빈칸에 알맞지 <u>않은</u> 것은?

> My daughter _____ reading comic books.

① likes   ② enjoyed

③ finished   ④ loves

⑤ hopes

02 다음 빈칸에 가장 적절한 것은?

> I tried _____ you, but the line was busy.

① call   ② calls

③ called   ④ to call

⑤ to calling

03 각 빈칸에 알맞은 것으로 짝지어진 것은?

> Yongchan decided _____ on _____ the
> test.

① to give up – taking   ② giving up – taking

③ giving up – to take   ④ giving up – take

⑤ to give up – to take

04 다음 중 어법상 <u>어색한</u> 것은?

① They stopped fighting each other.

② Do you plan going by train?

③ He hopes to go to New Zealand.

④ They finished doing their homework.

⑤ She really likes writing poems.

05 다음 중 어법상 올바른 것으로 묶인 것은?

> ⓐ Would you mind to close the door?
> ⓑ I enjoy watching the reality show on TV.
> ⓒ They wanted to find their missing dog.
> ⓓ Did you finish to read this book?
> ⓔ You should stop wasting your talent.

① ⓐ, ⓑ   ② ⓑ, ⓒ

③ ⓓ, ⓔ   ④ ⓐ, ⓑ, ⓔ

⑤ ⓑ, ⓒ, ⓔ

06 다음 문장에서 어법상 어색한 부분을 찾아 바르게 고치시오.

서술형

> They dislike to study in the library.

_____ → _____

07 다음 대화의 빈칸에 알맞은 말을 조건에 맞게 쓰시오.

서술형

You stole these computers, cell phones, and bus cards, didn't you?

No, I didn't. I really _____(A)_____ things, Officer.

· 조건1	대화 속의 단어를 활용할 것
· 조건2	어휘 – quit
· 조건3	2단어로 쓸 것

(A) _____

08 그림을 보고 아이가 엄마에게 할 수 있는 말을 쓰시오.

서술형

Happy birthday, my dear son!

| · 조건1 | (A)는 forget, bring을 이용할 것 |
| · 조건2 | (B)는 부가의문문으로 쓸 것 |

→ Mom, you didn't (A) _____

_____ any gifts,

(B) _____ _____ ?

VOCA comic book 만화책 | each other 서로 | poem 시 | reality show 리얼리티 쇼 | missing 잃어버린 | waste 낭비하다 | talent 재능

01 Find ALL of the correct words for the blank. 2점

> When did you begin _____ ?

① drawing the picture
② the project
③ help the children
④ to shave your mustache
⑤ to keep a diary in English

02 Which words are correct for the blanks? 2점

> • Do you mind _____ the movie again?
> • She feels like _____ in the pool.
> • He hoped _____ a singer.

① watch – to swim – to become
② watch – swimming – becoming
③ watching – swimming – becoming
④ watching – swimming – to become
⑤ watching – to swim – to become

03 Which translation is incorrect? 2점

① My father stopped singing and looked at me.
  → 아빠는 노래를 멈추고 나를 바라보셨다.
② I just tried putting on the pink cap. Why?
  → 난 그냥 핑크색 모자를 써본 거야. 왜?
③ I remembered to fold 1,000 paper swans.
  → 나는 종이 학 천 마리를 접었던 것을 기억했다.
④ He forgot to send a parcel to his son.
  → 그는 그의 아들에게 택배 보낼 것을 잊었다.
⑤ I started to run 10km yesterday.
  → 나는 어제 10km 달리기를 시작했다.

04 Which one is correct for the blank? 2점

> I forget _____ him at the cafeteria once.

① to see   ② seeing
③ see   ④ saw
⑤ to seeing

05 Which dialog is unnatural? 2점

① A: Do you know the girl in jeans?
  B: Yes. I remember meeting her several times.
② A: I tried bungee jumping yesterday.
  B: Really? How was it?
③ A: Stop to make noise. I can't hear the teacher.
  B: Oh, I'm sorry.
④ A: I saw a UFO last night.
  B: Come on! Stop telling lies.
⑤ A: Jack, I'm leaving now.
  B: Don't forget to turn off the lights.

06 Who finds the incorrect sentence and rewrites it correctly? 2점

> ⓐ I would like having some coffee.
> ⓑ Everybody likes going on picnics.

① 제현: ⓐ I would like to having some coffee.
② 우성: ⓐ I would like to have some coffee.
③ 현희: ⓑ Everybody likes to go in picnics.
④ 남용: ⓑ Everybody like going on picnics.
⑤ 주리: ⓑ Everybody likes to going on picnics.

07 How many sentences are grammatically correct? 3점

> ⓐ We enjoyed playing cards.
> ⓑ She didn't expect getting an A.
> ⓒ How about going with me?
> ⓓ He doesn't want to wear the coat.
> ⓔ I don't want to remember seeing you there.

① one   ② two
③ three   ④ four
⑤ five

VOCA shave 면도하다 | mustache 콧수염 | keep a diary 일기를 쓰다 | fold 접다 | cafeteria 구내식당 | bungee jump 번지 점프를 하다

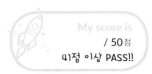

08 Who analyzes the sentence correctly?

> She kept practicing to ride her bike.

① 찬성: practicing을 practice로 바꾸면 돼.
② 미영: to가 없어야 올바른 문장이 돼.
③ 혜련: to ride를 riding으로 써야 해.
④ 연주: to ride를 and ride로 써도 돼.
⑤ 혜진: 잘못된 곳이 없는 완벽한 문장이야.

09 Which one is grammatically <u>incorrect</u>?

① I hope to see you soon.
② He quit doing his work.
③ Let's keep going forward.
④ What did you promise doing?
⑤ Please continue to use the front door.

10 Which of following CANNOT make a correct sentence? (2 answers)

① alone / be / disliked / . / to / she
② about / kept / they / me / to / . / talk
③ early / ? / hate / he / waking / does / up
④ writing / writer / loves / the / . / a / with / pencil
⑤ there / remember / you / meeting / him / don't / ?

11 Correct the error in the translation.

서술형

> 이제야 아기가 재채기를 멈췄어요.
> = Now, the baby stopped to sneeze.

_____ → _____

12 Rearrange the given words to make a question.

서술형

> did, give, dancing, why, you, up

→ _____

13 Look at the picture below and complete the sentence.

서술형

→ The girl _____ her

umbrella. (forget, bring)

14 Find TWO errors and correct them.

서술형

> I love ⓐ <u>watching</u> nature. My house has a small yard. I want ⓑ <u>to grow</u> strawberries in it. When they become red, I won't mind ⓒ <u>to share</u> them with my neighbors. I hope ⓓ <u>being</u> a good gardener.

( ) → _____

( ) → _____

15 Translate the sentence according to the conditions.

서술형

1달러를 기부하고 싶으십니까?	
·Words	like, a dollar
·Condition 1	would를 꼭 사용할 것
·Condition 2	한 단어는 아래 영영풀이를 참고할 것
	d_____ : to give money or goods to help a person or organization
·Condition 3	7단어로 쓸 것

→ _____

U25_2

01 다음 빈칸에 들어갈 말로 가장 적절한 것은? 2점

> His hobby is _____ action figures.

① collect ② collects
③ collected ④ collecting
⑤ to collecting

U26_1+2+3

02 Which is NOT suitable for the blank? 2점

> The lady _____ growing lettuce in her yard.

① enjoyed ② gave up
③ decided ④ likes
⑤ continued

U25_2

03 밑줄 친 부분의 쓰임이 나머지와 다른 것은? 2점

① He kept <u>calling</u> her at night.
② He quit <u>drinking</u> coffee.
③ She likes <u>being</u> with people.
④ I can't stop <u>thinking</u> about you.
⑤ <u>Talking</u> with him was so boring.

U25_2+4+GP

04 Which of following CANNOT make a correct sentence? (2 answers) 3점

고난도

① camp / . / lake / we / the / went / at
② your / . / for / is / running / health / good
③ visit / looking / forward / . / to / I'm / your
④ night / all / driving / we / after / . / arrived / ,
⑤ are / teeth / important / brushing / . / your

U26_3A+3B

05 다음 중 우리말을 영어로 바르게 옮기지 <u>못한</u> 학생은? 2점

함정

① 비가 세차게 내리기 시작했다.
→ 현준: It started raining heavily.
② 약 먹는 것을 잊지 마.
→ 종식: Don't forget to take the medicine.
③ 그는 그녀를 만난 것을 기억했다.
→ 초연: He remembered to meet her.
④ 일단, 이거 한번 먹어봐.
→ 용수: First, try eating this.
⑤ 그는 그녀에게 말을 걸기 위해 멈춰 섰다.
→ 성준: He stopped to talk to her.

U26_1+2

06 각 빈칸에 들어갈 말이 바르게 짝지어진 것은? 2점

> • I didn't expect _____ you here.
> • Isaac had to give up on _____ to Korea.

① to see – come
② to see – to come
③ to see – coming
④ seeing – to come
⑤ seeing – coming

U25_2+U18_2

07 다음 우리말과 같은 뜻이 되도록 영어 문장을 완성할 때 빈칸에 알맞은 것은? (답 2개) 2점

> 많은 돈을 버는 것 또한 중요하다.
> → _____ is also important.

① Make much money
② Make plenty of money
③ To make lots of money
④ To make many money
⑤ Making a lot of money

08 다음 우리말을 영어로 가장 바르게 옮긴 것은?

> 우리 이번 주말에 쇼핑 가지 말자.

① Not let's go shopping this weekend.
② Let's not go shopping this weekend.
③ Let's not go to shop this weekend.
④ Let's do not go shopping this weekend.
⑤ Let's not going shopping this weekend.

09 How many words are NOT proper for the blank?

> Little Yuna _____ practicing skating.
>
> | 보기 | enjoys | wanted | stopped |
> | --- | --- | --- | --- |
> | | hated | finished | continued |

① 1개　　　　　② 2개
③ 3개　　　　　④ 4개
⑤ 없음

10 다음 중 어법상 어색한 문장의 개수는?

> ⓐ She doesn't mind working all night.
> ⓑ He felt like to take a picture of me.
> ⓒ I am looking forward to the next meeting.
> ⓓ How much time do Mexicans spend in food?
> ⓔ We didn't want to go fishing again.
> ⓕ Were you really busy to do your homework?

① 1개　　　　　② 2개
③ 3개　　　　　④ 4개
⑤ 5개

11 괄호 안의 단어를 빈칸에 알맞은 형태로 쓰시오.

> She is terrible at _____ pictures.
> (take)

12 Find the sentence that has an error and correct it.

> ⓐ They wished to go on a cruise trip.
> ⓑ I always looked forward to be 19 years old.

(　　) _____ → _____

13 우리말과 일치하도록 주어진 단어를 배열하시오.

> 아침 6시에 일어나는 것은 쉽지 않다.
> in the morning, is, getting up, easy, at 6, not

→ _____

14 다음 단체 채팅방을 보고 빈칸에 알맞은 말을 쓰시오.

→ Oh, I _____ her.

15 다음 대화에서 어법상 어색한 것을 모두 찾아 바르게 고치시오.

> A: I enjoy runing up the hill. How about you?
> B: I enjoy skiing in winter and swim in summer.

→ _____
_____

16 주어진 단어를 활용하여 영작을 완성하시오. 4점

> 우표를 모으는 것은 오래된 취미이다. (collect, be)

→ _____ stamps _____ an

old hobby.

17 그림의 상황을 묘사하는 문장을 조건에 맞게 완성하시오. 5점

> · 조건 1   과거 시제로 쓸 것
> · 조건 2   어휘 – keep, laugh, try, start

→ The announcer _____

calm but _____ .

18 Find TWO incorrect sentences and correct the errors. 7점

> ⓐ Wendy enjoys to knit. ⓑ She likes to knit
> in the living room. ⓒ She even likes to knit
> in the bathroom. ⓓ She sometimes knits on
> the bus on her way to school. ⓔ Knit is an
> important part of her life.
>
> *knit: 뜨개질하다

(   ) _____ → _____

(   ) _____ → _____

[19~20] 다음 글을 읽고 물음에 답하시오.

　(A)롤러 코스터를 타는 것은 재미있다. Christina and her friends went to an amusement park. ⓐStanding in line was boring. However, Christina and her friends decided to keep ⓑto wait. Christina tried to find some ways ⓒto pass time. She took pictures, tapped her foot, and ⓓtalked with her friends. Then, she played games on her smartphone. Later, she went to the restroom. Two hours passed. They were still in line. Now they wanted ⓔgoing home.

19 윗글의 밑줄 친 (A)와 같은 뜻이 되도록 다음 어휘를 이용하여 6단어로 영작하시오. 7점

> ride, a roller coaster, fun

→ _____

20 윗글의 밑줄 친 ⓐ~ⓔ 중 어법상 틀린 것의 개수는? 4점

① 1개   ② 2개

③ 3개   ④ 4개

⑤ 5개

CHAPTER 10
문장의 형식

There is 구문, 2형식(감각동사)

개념이해책
130쪽 함께 보기

■ 아래 표의 빈칸에 알맞은 내용을 써 넣으세요. ›› 정답 33쪽

1 There is/are 구문

긍정문	There is+ 1)　　　　주어 ~. / There are+ 2)　　　　주어 ~.		
부정문	There is 3)　　　　+단수 주어 ~. / There are 4)　　　　+복수 주어 ~.		
의문문	Is there+단수 주어 ~? – Yes, there 5)　　　　. / No, there 6)　　　　. Are there+복수 주어 ~? – Yes, there 7)　　　　. / No, there 8)　　　　.		
과거형	There 9)　　　　+단수 주어 ~. / There 10)　　　　+복수 주어 ~.		

2 2형식: 감각동사+형용사(주격 보어)

look	~하게 보이다		You look tall.
feel	11)	+형용사	I feel sad.
sound	12)		It sounds good.
smell	13)		It smells delicious.
taste	14)		The snack tastes salty.

Level 1 Test

›› 정답 33쪽

A [ ]에서 알맞은 것을 고르시오.

1 There [is / are] a little juice.

2 [Is / Are] there lots of homework?

3 There [isn't / aren't] any jam in the jar.

4 There [was / were] some mistakes.

5 There [wasn't / weren't] any toys for the kid.

B 우리말과 일치하도록 빈칸에 알맞은 말을 쓰시오.

1 A: _____ _____ many students?

   (학생들이 많이 있어?)

   B: No, _____ _____. (아니, 없어.)

2 A: _____ _____ many

   passengers on the plane?

   (비행기에 많은 승객들이 있었나요?)

   B: Yes, _____ _____. (네, 그랬어요.)

C 우리말과 일치하도록 빈칸에 알맞은 말을 쓰시오.

1 그것은 유령처럼 보인다.

   → It _____ _____ a ghost.

2 그 우유는 신맛이 난다.

   → The milk tastes _____.

3 고양이 털은 부드러운 느낌이다.

   → The cat's fur _____ _____.

D 밑줄 친 부분을 어법에 맞게 고치시오.

1 The chocolate cake tastes greatly.

   → _____

2 What are you baking? It smells a pie.

   → _____

3 It sounds like amazing.

   → _____

VOCA jar 병 | mistake 실수 | passenger 승객 | plane 비행기 | ghost 유령 | sour 신 | fur 털 | amazing 굉장한

01 다음 각 빈칸에 들어갈 말이 바르게 짝지어진 것은? 2점

> • There _____ few people at the mall.
> • There _____ some food on the table.

① are – are ② are – is
③ is – is ④ is – are
⑤ was – was

02 다음 대화의 빈칸에 알맞은 것은? 2점

> A: Are there any ducks in the pond?
> B: _____. But there are many frogs in it.

① Yes, there is ② Yes, it is
③ No, it isn't ④ No, there aren't
⑤ No, there isn't

[03~04] 빈칸에 들어갈 말로 알맞지 <u>않은</u> 것을 고르시오. 각 2점

03

> Does she look _____?

① friend ② friendly
③ angry ④ sad
⑤ pretty

04

> It _____ wonderful.

① looks ② smells
③ tastes ④ sounds
⑤ sends

05 다음 중 어법상 <u>어색한</u> 문장을 고른 것은? 2점

> ⓐ Does it sound good?
> ⓑ The medicine tasted very bitter.
> ⓒ The soap looks a real rose.
> ⓓ The blanket felt softly.

① ⓐ ② ⓑ, ⓒ, ⓓ
③ ⓑ, ⓒ ④ ⓒ, ⓓ
⑤ ⓓ

06 주어진 단어 중 **필요한** 것만 골라 우리말을 영작하시오. 6점
서술형

> 그 향수는 달콤한 솜사탕 같은 향이 난다.
> smell, cotton candy, the perfume, smells, like,
> sweetly, sweet

→ _____

07 어법상 <u>어색한</u> 부분을 찾아 바르게 고치시오. 4점
서술형

> There is a lot of trash in the kitchen. Please
> take it out. It smells terribly.

_____ → _____

08 주어진 단어를 이용해서 그림을 묘사하는 문장을 완성하시오. 4점
서술형

> there, boy, two

→ _____ in the pool.

09 다음 대화에서 어법상 <u>어색한</u> 문장에 밑줄을 치고 바르게 고쳐 쓰시오. 6점
서술형

> A: There is a lot of snow outside. It looks like
>   a huge mountain.
> B: Really? There aren't any snow last night.

→ _____

VOCA pond 연못 | frog 개구리 | bitter 쓴 | blanket 담요 | cotton candy 솜사탕 | perfume 향수 | trash 쓰레기 | terribly 끔찍하게 | huge 커다란

01 Which words are correct for the blanks? 2점

> • _____ there lots of trash in the bin?
> • There _____ any sheep on the hill.

① Were – are ② Is – aren't
③ Is – are ④ Are – isn't
⑤ Was – was

02 Which of the underlined words is used <u>differently</u> than the others? 3점

① We went <u>there</u>.
② <u>There</u> is a lot of dust on the bench.
③ Is <u>there</u> lots of sugar in juice?
④ Were <u>there</u> many cars on the road?
⑤ <u>There</u> aren't any cards in my wallet.

03 Which one is correct for the blank? 2점

> A: Are there any mice in the kitchen?
> B: _____ several.

① Yes, there are ② Yes, it is
③ No, there isn't ④ No, they aren't
⑤ Yes, there is

04 Which does NOT agree with the information in the picture? 2점

① There is a bank on the corner.
② There are two supermarkets.
③ There is a bookstore across from Dr. Kim's office.
④ There is a bank next to the flower shop.
⑤ There isn't a library.

05 Which CANNOT make a grammatically correct sentence? 4점

① chicken / tastes / It / . / like
② smell / What / does / it / like / ?
③ an / The / baby / angel / . / looks
④ often / sad / do / you / How / ? / feel
⑤ sound / not / does / very / . / That / nice

06 How many sentences are grammatically correct? 3점

> ⓐ Was there a sign about that?
> ⓑ There aren't a lot of apples.
> ⓒ How many mistakes are there in the report?
> ⓓ There wasn't much traffic.
> ⓔ Are there lots of rain in Hawaii?
> ⓕ There weren't a pen and a book.

① one ② two
③ three ④ four
⑤ five

07 Which translation is correct? 2점

> 그녀는 사랑스러워 보인다.

① She looks lovely.
② She looks like love.
③ She looks lovelily.
④ She looks like lovely.
⑤ She looks like a love.

08 Which is NOT correct for the blank? 2점

> It _____ very good.

① was ② looks
③ tasted ④ didn't smell
⑤ didn't hear

VOCA **bin** 쓰레기통 | **dust** 먼지 | **across from** ~의 건너편에 | **next to** ~ 옆에 | **sign** 표지판 | **traffic** 교통량

09 Choose the grammatically incorrect word. 2점

> The noodles ① look ② delicious but ③ taste ④ too ⑤ spice.

10 Which correction of the underlined word is correct? 3점

① There is no time to lose. → are
② Are there tigers in Korea? → Is
③ A: Is there a pond in your town?
   B: No, it isn't. → there
④ There were no clouds in the sky. → was
⑤ There is a small church on the hill. → are

11 Which CANNOT make a grammatically correct sentence? 4점

① feels / . / scarf / soft / Your
② great / soup / tasted / . / The
③ shoes / smell / ? / my / Do / bad
④ good / a / sounds / . / idea / That
⑤ The / cookie / moon / looks / a / . / like

12 Which is NOT proper for the blank? (Up to 3 answers) 2점

> It tastes _____.

① well   ② salty
③ less good   ④ like mud
⑤ a lot better

13 Which sentence is correct? (Up to 3 answers) 3점

① The milk smells worse than garbage.
② I often feel lonely at night.
③ The cookies taste sweet.
④ It smells a flower.
⑤ His voice sounded funnily.

14 서술형 Complete the sentence describing the picture. 5점

> there, goldfish, two

→ _____ in the plastic bag.

15 서술형 Write the correct answer in the dialog. 5점

> A: Were there any calls for me?
> B: _____. Nobody called you.

16 서술형 Find the grammatically incorrect sentence in the dialog and underline it. Then, rewrite the sentence correctly. 6점

> A: Your dog looks scare.
> B: Don't worry. It's very friendly.

→ _____

VOCA noodle 국수 | spice 양념, 향신료 | garbage 음식물 쓰레기 | lonely 외로운 | goldfish 금붕어 | plastic bag 비닐봉지 | call 전화하다; 전화, 통화

4형식(수여동사), 5형식

개념이해책
133쪽 함께 보기

■ 아래 표의 빈칸에 알맞은 내용을 써 넣으세요. 〉〉 정답 34쪽

① 4형식(수여동사)

1)	2)	3)	4)
I	showed	him	a picture.

② 수여동사의 문장 변환

4형식: 수여동사+간접 목적어(~에게)+직접 목적어(…을)
→ 3형식: 수여동사+ 5)   + 6)   + 7)

to를 사용하는 동사	8) (주다), 9) (가져오다), 10) (빌려주다), 11) (보내주다), 12) (팔다), 13) (보여주다), 14) (가르쳐주다), 15) (써주다), 16) (건네주다)
for를 사용하는 동사	17) (만들어 주다), 18) (사주다), 19) (요리해주다), 20) (갖게 해주다), 21) (찾아주다)
of를 사용하는 동사	22) (물어보다)

③ 5형식

주어+동사+목적어+목적격 보어(23)   /24)   /25)   )

 Level 1 Test

〉〉 정답 34쪽

A 문장이 '4형식'인지 '5형식'인지 구분하시오.

1 The horror movie made us scared. → _____

2 We made him a robot for his birthday. → _____

3 Grandma told us an old story. → _____

4 She asked me to leave immediately. → _____

B [ ]에서 알맞은 것을 고르시오.

1 She bought a shirt [to / for / of] me.

2 Will you show the way [to / for / of] me?

3 He didn't ask the reason [to / for / of] me.

4 This will keep you [warm / warmly].

5 What makes you so [special / specially]?

C 4형식은 3형식으로, 3형식은 4형식으로 바꾸시오.

1 Mr. King made his daughter a tree house.

→ _____

2 Did he find a nice hotel for her?

→ _____

D 괄호 안의 어휘를 바르게 배열하시오.

1 그 소식은 우리를 화나게 만들었다. (angry, us, made, the news)

→ _____

2 아빠는 내가 아빠 전화기를 사용하지 못하게 하신다. (Dad, use, his phone, doesn't, allow, to, me)

→ _____

VOCA horror movie 공포 영화 | scared 겁에 질린 | immediately 즉시 | reason 이유 | tree house 나무 위의 집

>> 정답 34쪽

01 다음 빈칸에 알맞지 않은 것은? 2점

> I _____ her to carry my bag.

① wanted ② didn't help
③ will ask ④ don't find
⑤ am going to tell

02 빈칸에 들어갈 말이 나머지와 <u>다른</u> 하나는? 2점

① She showed the picture _____ her family.
② Please lend the book _____ me.
③ Do you teach art _____ children?
④ Kate made salad _____ everybody.
⑤ Girls gave some chocolate _____ boys.

03 주어진 문장과 바꾸어 쓸 수 있는 것은? 2점

> Can I ask you a question?

① Can I ask a question of you?
② Can I ask of you a question?
③ Can I ask a question to you?
④ Can I ask a question for you?
⑤ Can I ask for you a question?

04 다음 두 빈칸 중 어느 것에도 알맞지 <u>않은</u> 것은? 2점

> · She _____ a thank-you card for me.
> · The patient _____ some questions of the doctor.

① made ② didn't get
③ asked ④ gave
⑤ bought

05 다음 중 어법상 <u>어색한</u> 문장을 <u>모두</u> 고르시오. 2점

① Can you show me the menu?
② Will you hand me the salt?
③ Can you bring my bag me?
④ I bought new socks for her.
⑤ The chef cooked a delicious dinner to us.

06 주어진 문장과 의미가 같도록 빈칸을 채우시오. 4점

서술형

> Grandma got me a violin.

→ Grandma got _____ me.

07 우리말과 같은 뜻의 영어 문장을 <u>2개</u> 쓰시오. 각 2점

서술형

> 나는 Harley에게 이메일을 쓸 것이다. (write, an email)

(1) _____
(2) _____

08 다음 중 <u>어색한</u> 부분을 고쳐 문장을 다시 쓰시오. 4점

서술형

> Mr. Gong advised me continuing with my studies.

→ _____

09 조건에 맞게 우리말을 영작하시오. 4점

서술형

> 저에게 일자리를 구해줄 수 있어요?
>
> · 조건1 어휘 – could, find, a job
> · 조건2 3형식 문장으로 쓸 것
> · 조건3 7단어로 쓸 것

→ _____

10 주어진 어휘를 배열하여 그림을 묘사하는 문장을 쓰시오. 4점

서술형

> my brother, cookies, made, his friends, for

→ _____

VOCA patient 환자 | chef 요리사, 주방장 | job 직업, 일자리

01 Which words are correct for the blanks? 2점

> • I'll cook a nice brunch _____ my wife.
> • Can you lend your camera _____ me?

① for – for　　　② for – of
③ to – to　　　　④ to – of
⑤ for – to

02 Which translation is correct? 2점

> 그는 우리에게 좋은 소식을 가져왔다.

① He brought us some good news.
② He brought some good news us.
③ He brought to us some good news.
④ He brought some good news of us.
⑤ He brought us for some good news.

03 Find ALL of the possible words for the blank. 2점

> Tallulah _____ a text message to me.

① sent　　　　② showed
③ asked　　　④ found
⑤ got

04 Which word is NOT suitable for the blank? 2점

> Please _____ the comic book to her.

① pass　　　② bring
③ give　　　④ get
⑤ send

05 Which words are correct for the blanks? 2점

> • Don't give too many snacks _____ the children.
> • May I ask a favor _____ you?

① to – of　　　② for – to
③ of – to　　　④ with – for
⑤ to – for

06 Who finds the error and corrects it? 2점

> Semi and I have the same birthday. Semi gave to me some perfume. I bought some lipstick for her.

① 미나: to me → for me
② 현영: some perfume → to some perfume
③ 민서: for her → her
④ 승훈: to me → me
⑤ 현서: for her → to her

07 How many sentences are grammatically incorrect? 3점

> ⓐ Could you pass me the pepper?
> ⓑ Give me that candy.
> ⓒ Mom got a bicycle to me.
> ⓓ He often makes Lego buildings for me.
> ⓔ We found the bed very comfortably.
> ⓕ Would you like me to help you?

① one　　　② two
③ three　　④ four
⑤ five

08 Which sentences do NOT have the same meaning? 2점

① She made me a delicious cake.
　= She made a delicious cake for me.
② He gave his mom flowers.
　= He gave flowers to his mom.
③ Don't send him an invitation.
　= Don't send an invitation for him.
④ Would you show me the note?
　= Would you show the note to me?
⑤ Can I ask you a favor?
　= Can I ask a favor of you?

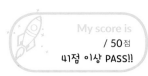

09 Which is the common word for the blanks?

> • I _____ a pumpkin pie.
> • Susan _____ a doll for me.
> • They _____ us some nice sandwiches.

① had ② gave
③ made ④ did
⑤ got

10 Which CANNOT make a grammatically correct sentence? (2 answers)

① it / lend / didn't / . / Mr. Ahn / me
② Please / two / hand / . / eggs / me
③ door / the / They / open / . / found
④ . / She / coffee / for / will / us / make
⑤ can / ? / vegetables / I / How / freshly / keep

11 Complete the sentence so that it has the same meaning as the underlined sentence.
서술형

> Minju won first prize in a science contest. <u>We gave Minju a big hand.</u>

→ We gave a big hand _____ Minju.

12 Complete the sentence according to the picture.
서술형

→ Mom bought _____ me.

13 Rewrite the sentence without changing its meaning.
서술형

> He cooked me an amazing meal.

→ _____

14 Find the sentence that has an error and correct it.
서술형

> ⓐ I told you being home before 11:00.
> ⓑ She made me a better person.

(_____) _____ → _____

15 Complete the translation according to the conditions.
서술형

> 약간의 치즈를 추가하세요. 그것은 여러분의 수프를 더 맛있게 만들어줄 거예요.
>
> ·Condition 1 어휘 – make, soup, tasty
> ·Condition 2 빈칸에 6단어로 쓸 것

→ Add some cheese. _____ .

16 Translate the sentence according to the conditions.
서술형

> 우리는 그가 약간 이상하다고 생각했다.
>
> ·Words a little, strange
> ·Condition 1 필요 시 어형 변화할 것
> ·Condition 2 주어진 어휘를 포함하여 6단어로 쓸 것
> ·Condition 3 아래 영영풀이를 참조하여 f로 시작하는 단어를 쓸 것
>
> f_____ : to become aware of; to discover to be the case
>
> *aware: 인식하는

→ _____

VOCA pumpkin 호박 | first prize 1등상 | give a big hand 큰 박수를 쳐주다 | amazing 놀라운 | meal 식사 | add 첨가하다 | discover 발견하다

Review Test

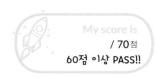

U27_1+GP

01 각 빈칸에 들어갈 말이 순서대로 짝지어진 것은? 2점

> • There _____ two glasses of wine.
> • There _____ lots of Koreans on the flight.

① were – was   ② were – were

③ are – was   ④ is – are

⑤ is – is

U28_1

02 다음 두 빈칸에 공통으로 들어갈 말은? 2점

> • Please _____ her a call.
> • I'll _____ you a ride.

① have   ② do

③ get   ④ give

⑤ bring

[03~04] 대화의 빈칸에 알맞은 것을 고르시오. 각 2점

U27_2+GP

03

> A: How does Joy look today?
> B: She looks _____.
> A: Do you know why?
> B: Yes, I do. She studied hard at the city library all day long.

① tired   ② happily

③ pretty   ④ sweet

⑤ sadly

U27_1

04

> A: How many children are there in the car?
> B: _____ only one child.

① They are   ② There is

③ It is   ④ There are

⑤ That is

[05~07] 빈칸에 알맞은 것을 고르시오. 각 2점

U27_2+GP

05

> Jasmine was very happy yesterday. The world looked _____. The sky was clear, and the birds were singing.

① bad   ② badly

③ beautiful   ④ beautifully

⑤ nicely

U27_GP

06 한눈에 쏙

> My marble looks like _____. It's round and blue.

① clear   ② brightly

③ the Earth   ④ lovely

⑤ expensive

U28_3+GP

07

> What would you like me _____?

① to do   ② did

③ do   ④ doing

⑤ for doing

U28_3

08 어법상 빈칸에 들어갈 수 없는 것은? 2점

> My dog makes me _____.

① sadly   ② happy

③ angry   ④ upset

⑤ tired

U28_2

09 Which word is NOT necessary when translating the sentence? 2점

함정

> 수학 선생님은 나에게 자주 어려운 질문을 하신다.

① math teacher   ② to me

③ a difficult question   ④ of

⑤ often

10 다음 중 수여동사 구문을 바르게 바꾸지 <u>못한</u> 것은 몇 개 인가? 3점

고난도

ⓐ He sent her a rose every day.
→ He sent a rose to her every day.
ⓑ May I ask you something?
→ May I ask something of you?
ⓒ We gave Brad a big hand.
→ We gave a big hand for Brad.
ⓓ He bought me a model car.
→ He bought a model car for me.

① zero ② one
③ two ④ three
⑤ four

11 다음 우리말을 조건에 맞게 영작하시오. 4점

그 마을에는 일곱 명의 아이들이 있었다.

· 조건 1 어휘 – children, the village
· 조건 2 세 번째 단어는 seven으로 쓸 것

→ _____

12 Complete the sentence according to the picture. 4점

그녀의 머리 스타일은 토마토처럼 보인다.

→ Her hairstyle _____ a
tomato.

13 대화의 밑줄 친 우리말을 조건에 맞게 영작하시오.

함정

Q: I didn't see Insu last week.
A: He didn't come to school last week. He was ill.
Q: How does he look today?
A: <u>그는 건강해 보여.</u>

· 조건 well을 포함하여 3단어로 쓸 것

→ _____

14 다음은 여러분의 부모님이 여러분에게 허락해 주시거나 허락하시지 않는 것들이다. 말이 자연스럽게 이어지도록 빈칸에 공통으로 들어갈 단어를 쓰시오. 4점

· They don't _____ me to stay out late.
· They _____ me to have parties.
· They don't _____ me to listen to heavy metal.

→ _____

15 다음 문장에서 어법상 <u>어색한</u> 부분을 찾아 바르게 고쳐 문장을 다시 쓰시오. 4점

It may sound fool.

→ _____

16 다음 단어들을 바르게 배열하여 <u>의문문</u>을 만드시오. 4점

함정

may, favor, I, of, you, a, ask

→ _____

17 다음 각 문장을 같은 뜻의 문장으로 바꾸어 쓸 때 각각의 빈칸에 알맞은 전치사를 쓰시오. 4점

(1) Ms. Kim teaches us Korean.

→ Ms. Kim teaches Korean _____ us.

(2) He bought me a game console.

→ He bought a game console _____ me.

18 Find the error in the dialog and correct it. 4점

> A: (*phone rings*) Sarah, what's up?
> B: Wow! Your voice sounds so softly.

_____ → _____

19 Translate the Korean into English according to the conditions. 6점

> 신문에 무슨 재미있는 뉴스라도 있어요?
>
> · Condition 1 어휘 – interesting, newspaper, there, news
> · Condition 2 8단어로 쓸 것

→ _____

20 그림을 보고 조건에 맞게 우리말을 영작하시오. 4점

> 엄마는 나에게 웃긴 점심 도시락을 만들어주셨다.
>
> · 조건 1 어휘 – a funny boxed lunch
> · 조건 2 전치사를 쓰지 말 것

→ _____

[21~22] 다음 글을 읽고 물음에 답하시오.

In Lebanon, people ⓐlike to have guests at their homes. They show ⓑtheir kindness to their guests with food. They invite people to their houses and (A)그들에게 맛있는 식사를 제공한다. In their meals, they use ⓒa lot of vegetables such as cucumbers, eggplant, and tomatoes. In addition, bread is ⓓextreme important in their culture. If the bread starts to ⓔtaste like bad, they kiss the bread and throw it away.

21 윗글의 밑줄 친 부분 ⓐ~ⓔ 중 어법상 어색한 것의 개수는? 3점

① one　　　　② two
③ three　　　④ four
⑤ five

22 밑줄 친 우리말과 같은 뜻이 되도록 주어진 단어를 배열하시오. (한 단어를 반드시 추가할 것) 4점

> a, nice, them, meal, give

(A) _____

CHAPTER 11
전치사와 접속사

시간 전치사, 장소 전치사

■ 아래 표의 빈칸에 알맞은 내용을 써 넣으세요. ›› 정답 36쪽

개념이해책
140쪽 함께 보기

1 시간 전치사

1)	(~에)	시각, 정오, 일출, 일몰과 같은 때의 한 시점
2)	(~에)	날짜, 요일, 특정한 날
3)	(~에)	월, 연도, 계절, 오전, 오후
4)	(~까지)	동작, 상태의 계속 (= till)
5)	(~까지)	동작의 완료
6)	(~ 동안)	구체적인 지속 기간 – 수사, 시간 명사(시간, 날, 주, 달, 연도)와 함께 씀
7)	(~ 중에, 동안)	사건, 특정한 기간과 함께 씀

2 장소 전치사

8)	(~에)	비교적 좁은 장소	12)	(~ 위에)	수직으로 바로 위
9)	(~에)	넓은 지역, ~ 안에	13)	(~ 밑에)	수직으로 바로 밑
10)	(~ 위에)	접촉되어	14)	(~ 뒤에)	(↔ in front of)
11)	(~ 옆에)	(= next to = beside)			

3 기타 전치사

교통수단	15)	(~을 타고)			
방향	16)	(~ 안으로), 17)	(~ 밖으로), 18)	(~을 따라서),	
	19)	(~의 맞은편에), 20)	(~을 통과하여)		

Level 1 Test

›› 정답 36쪽

A 빈칸에 알맞은 말을 [보기]에서 골라 쓰시오.

보기	in	until	on	during	for

1 They live _____ a small house.

2 I read a book on the plane _____ the flight.

3 My children don't sleep _____ midnight.

4 He ran _____ two hours last night.

5 Final exams will finish _____ April 27.

B 우리말과 같은 뜻이 되도록 빈칸을 채우시오.

1 그녀는 그 회사에서 5년 동안 근무했다.

→ She worked for the company _____ five years.

2 Tony 뒤에 있는 소녀는 누구니?

→ Who is the girl _____ Tony?

3 울타리를 따라 아름다운 꽃들이 있었다.

→ There were beautiful flowers _____ the fence.

VOCA flight 비행 | midnight 자정 | final exam 기말시험 | fence 울타리

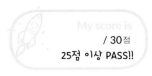

>> 정답 36쪽

01 다음 글에서 'in'이 들어가기에 알맞은 곳은?

> I (①) visited (②) China (③) 2019. I (④) visited (⑤) the Great Wall.

02 다음 중 'between'이 들어가기에 알맞은 곳은?

> Ladies and gentlemen, the concert will start (①) soon. Please turn (②) your cell phones (③) off. In addition, please do not clap (④) movements. Thank you and enjoy (⑤) the concert.

03 대화의 빈칸에 알맞은 것을 <u>모두</u> 고르시오.

> A: When is your birthday?
> B: My birthday is _____.

① at winter   ② in 2011

③ on December 1   ④ on January

⑤ in March

04 대화의 각 빈칸에 알맞은 말이 바르게 짝지어진 것은?

> A: Do you work out every day?
> B: Yes, I go for a run _____ 20 minutes _____ night.

① for – in   ② by – at

③ for – at   ④ by – in

⑤ during – until

05 다음 중 어법상 <u>어색한</u> 문장으로 묶인 것은?

> ⓐ I was born in February 11.
> ⓑ Winter begins in December.
> ⓒ He will arrive at noon.
> ⓓ Dana will be there until 7:30 p.m.
> ⓔ Roun took a walk during 30 minutes.

① ⓐ, ⓑ   ② ⓑ, ⓔ

③ ⓓ   ④ ⓐ, ⓓ, ⓔ

⑤ ⓐ, ⓔ

06 주어진 문장과 같은 의미가 되도록 빈칸에 알맞은 말을 쓰시오.

서술형

> Flora is standing behind Philip.

→ Philip is standing _____ _____ _____ Flora.

07 다음 그림을 보고 조건에 맞게 빈칸을 채우시오.

서술형

> 그는 길을 따라 자전거를 타고 있다.
>
> | 어휘 | the road |

→ He is riding a bike _____.

08 우리말에 맞게 각 빈칸에 알맞은 말을 쓰시오.

서술형

(1) We can read books _____ the subway.

    (우리는 지하철에서 책을 읽을 수 있다.)

(2) She was _____ the post office.

    (그녀는 우체국에 있었다.)

09 다음 중 어법상 <u>어색한</u> 부분을 찾아 바르게 고치시오.

서술형

> I usually go camping on weekends. I will go to the mountain on this weekend. I will make a campfire at night.

_____ → _____

VOCA   the Great Wall 만리장성 | in addition 또한 | clap 박수 치다 | movement 악장 | work out 운동하다 | campfire 모닥불

01 Which is the common word for the blanks? 2점

> • My mother was born _____ 1987.
> • A lot of flowers bloom _____ spring.

① at　　　　　　② on
③ in　　　　　　④ during
⑤ by

[02~03] Choose the corrects words for the blanks.
각 2점

02
> • We will stay here _____ tomorrow.
> • They will be here _____ the holiday.

① until – by　　　　② until – during
③ by – during　　　④ by – for
⑤ on – on

03
> A: What did you do _____ your vacation?
> B: I stayed _____ San Francisco with my family.
> A: Sounds like fun. How long did you stay there?
> B: We were there _____ a week.

① during – in – for　　② for – to – during
③ during – to – for　　④ for – in – during
⑤ on – to – in

04 According to the picture, which is the correct word for the blank? 2점

> A: Where is Archie?
> B: I think he's in your room. He likes to hide _____ your bed.

① behind　　　　② under
③ next to　　　　④ in front of
⑤ over

05 Which words are proper for the blanks? 2점

> • I lost my credit card _____ the gas station.
> • There are many clouds _____ the sky.
> • Finish writing your essay _____ four o'clock.

① at – at – until　　② in – on – by
③ on – in – by　　　④ at – in – by
⑤ in– on – until

06 How many sentences are incorrect? 4점

> ⓐ Let's have lunch at noon.
> ⓑ Many birds flew on the mountain.
> ⓒ The houses along the road all looked the same.
> ⓓ We have social studies in Thursday.
> ⓔ There is some money on the floor.
> ⓕ There is a map in the wall.

① one　　　　　② two
③ three　　　　④ four
⑤ five

07 Which is incorrect according to the picture? 3점

① The bakery is across from the post office.
② The bank is between the post office and the dentist.
③ The post office is across from the library.
④ There is a library next to the convenience store.
⑤ There are several stores along the road.

VOCA　bloom (꽃이) 피다 | holiday 휴가, 휴일 | hide 숨다 | essay 글 | credit card 신용 카드 | floor 바닥 | convenience store 편의점

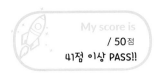

08 Which one needs a <u>different</u> word for the blank? 3점

① I went to sleep _____ midnight.

② My birthday is _____ May 4.

③ My father cooks lunch _____ Sundays.

④ They went to the movies _____ Friday.

⑤ Americans eat turkey _____ Thanksgiving Day.

09 Write the common word for the blanks. 4점

서술형

- You should finish your homework _____ 8 p.m.
- There is a lamp _____ the bed.

→ _____

10 Complete the sentence describing the picture. 4점

서술형

→ The bulls ran _____ the crowd in a bull festival in Spain.

11 Rewrite the <u>incorrect</u> sentence correctly. 4점

서술형

ⓐ This is the recipe for my favorite dish.

ⓑ First, boil the water in the pot.

ⓒ Then, put the noodles and the sauce into the water.

ⓓ Boil the noodles by 10 minutes.

( ) _____ → _____

12 Complete the sentence so that it has the same meaning as the given sentence. 4점

서술형

I studied from 6 o'clock to 9 o'clock.

→ I studied _____ three hours.

13 Which is NOT necessary for any of the blanks? (Write ALL.) 6점

서술형

보기	until	on	at
	during	between	under

ⓐ She is sitting _____ a chair.

ⓓ There should be no secrets _____ you and me.

ⓔ Some people were sleeping _____ a tree.

→ _____

14 Translate the sentence into English according to the conditions. 8점

서술형

네 옆에 앉아도 되니?

·Condition 1 어휘 – can

·Condition 2 '옆에'는 2단어로 쓸 것

·Condition 3 모두 6단어로 쓸 것

→ _____

VOCA turkey 칠면조 | Thanksgiving Day 추수 감사절 | lamp 램프, 등 | bull 황소 | crowd 군중 | recipe 요리법 | dish 음식 | boil 끓이다 | pot 냄비 | noodle 면 | sauce 소스

UNIT **29**　167

30 등위 접속사, 종속 접속사

■ 아래 표의 빈칸에 알맞은 내용을 써 넣으세요. ››› 정답 36쪽

개념이해책
143쪽 함께 보기

① 등위 접속사

	2)	와 2)	I want a banana and a strawberry.
and(1))	3)	와 3)	My hobbies are gardening and singing songs.
	4)	과 4)	I am in the room, and she is in the kitchen.
but(5))	6)	와 6)	He is poor but happy.
	7)	과 7)	It was not my fault, but it was God's will.
or(8))	9)	와 9)	You or your friend must go there.
	10)	와 10)	He went there by bus or on foot.
	11)	과 11)	Let's play games, or let's go shopping.
so(12))	13)	과 13)	He got up late, so he was late for school.

② 종속 접속사

	15)	역할	That Bora likes Seho is true.
that(14))	16)	역할	My hope is that Bin asks me out.
	17)	역할	I don't believe (that) he is a millionaire.
when(18))			When I was young, I lived in the country.
because(19))			We didn't go out because it was raining.
if(20))			If the weather is fine, I will go on a picnic.

 Level 1 Test

››› 정답 36쪽

A 빈칸에 알맞은 접속사를 쓰시오.

1 She may be three _____ four years old.

2 I went to the museum, _____ it was closed.

3 We went to Paris _____ London. They were beautiful.

4 I borrowed some money from my friend, _____ I bought some milk.

5 He got angry _____ he lost the game.

B 빈칸에 'that'과 'when' 중에서 알맞은 말을 쓰시오.

1 _____ I came back, no one was home.

2 I think _____ he will succeed.

3 It is certain _____ Mary will join us.

C 우리말과 같은 뜻이 되도록 빈칸을 채우시오.

1 그는 그녀가 나갔다고 생각했다.

→ He thought _____ she had gone out.

2 문을 닫아라, 그렇지 않으면 모기가 들어올 것이다.

→ Close the door, _____ mosquitoes will come inside.

VOCA **borrow** 빌리다 | **succeed** 성공하다 | **certain** 확실한 | **join** 함께하다 | **mosquito** 모기

01 다음 각 빈칸에 들어갈 말이 순서대로 짝지어진 것은? 2점

> • I like fruit, _____ my brother doesn't.
> • She _____ I are cousins.

① and – and   ② but – and

③ so – but   ④ and – but

⑤ but – so

02 밑줄 친 'When[when]'의 쓰임이 나머지와 다른 것은? 2점

① When do you have lunch at school?

② I was sleeping when the earthquake hit.

③ Please send me a text message when you get there.

④ She was surprised when I visited her.

⑤ When I was young, I never needed anyone.

03 다음 중 자연스럽지 않은 문장은? (답 2개) 2점

① The guests were hungry but tired.

② Which do you like better, pork or beef?

③ She got a lot of gifts, so she was happy.

④ Hurry up, and you will be sorry.

⑤ He opened his eyes, but he didn't get up.

04 다음 밑줄 친 부분 중 어법상 어색한 것은? 2점

> ① After I ② will finish my class, I ③ am going to ④ go ⑤ to the dentist.

05 우리말 뜻과 같도록 빈칸에 알맞은 것을 고르시오. 2점

> 네 여동생을 돌봐줘. 그렇지 않으면 그 아이는 울 거야.
> = Take care of your sister, _____ she will cry.

① or   ② and

③ but   ④ unless

⑤ so

06 다음 우리말을 조건에 맞게 영작하시오. 4점

서술형

> 우리는 에버랜드에서 재미있게 놀 수 있길 바란다.
>
> • 어휘   hope, at Everland, can, have fun
> • 조건 1   생략될 수 있는 단어에 괄호로 표시하시오.
> • 조건 2   생략 가능한 것을 포함하여 9단어로 쓸 것

→ _____

07 빈칸에 들어갈 알맞은 말을 쓰시오. 4점

서술형

> Do the right thing _____ it is right.

08 두 문장을 'When'을 이용해 한 문장으로 연결하시오. 4점

서술형

> She falls asleep. She listens to classical music.

→ _____,

_____.

09 주어진 문장과 같은 의미가 되도록 빈칸에 알맞은 말을 쓰시오. 4점

서술형

> If you take the subway, you will not be late.

→ Take the subway, _____ you will not be late.

10 'if'를 사용해서 다음 두 문장을 자연스러운 의미가 되도록 연결하시오. (문장을 'if'로 시작할 것) 4점

서술형

> It will rain tomorrow. I will wear my new rubber boots.

→ _____

_____

VOCA   earthquake 지진 | text message 문자 | pork 돼지고기 | beef 쇠고기 | gift 선물 | sorry 후회하는 | dentist 치과 의사 | have fun 재미있게 놀다 | rubber boots 고무 장화

01 Which correction is right? 2점

> If you buy one, you will get one for free.

① buy → bought
② buy → will buy
③ will get → get
④ will get → got
⑤ There are no errors.

02 Which is correct for the blank? 2점

> I will be happy _____.

① and they are my friends
② because I'm tired
③ when I saw him
④ if I get a good score
⑤ after I met my old friends

03 Which words are correct for the blanks? 2점

> • He cannot hear well, _____ someone needs to help him at school.
> • She wanted to help the poor student, _____ the school agreed.

① and – so
② so – because
③ so – and
④ and – but
⑤ because – and

04 Choose the possible word for the blank. 2점

> I touched the stone _____ I was curious.

① because
② if
③ but
④ so
⑤ that

05 Which underlined word is NOT necessary? 2점

① I know that old man is French.
② Can you pass me that bowl of sugar, please?
③ I think that English is a useful language.
④ That accident changed a lot of things.
⑤ My hope is that everybody will like me.

06 Which is the correct word for the blank to make one sentence with the following two sentences? 2점

> The children go home. The sun goes down then.
> → The children go home _____ the sun goes down.

① if
② why
③ where
④ that
⑤ when

07 Which words are correct for the blanks? 2점

> • I can't remember the spelling of the word, _____ I know its meaning.
> • She had a fever, _____ she stayed in bed all day.

① but – so
② but – but
③ so – but
④ so – and
⑤ and – so

08 Who finds the error and corrects it? 2점

> When he'll grow up, he wants to be an architect.

① 희석: When을 If로 바꾸어야 해.
② 승훈: he'll을 he로 바꾸어야 해.
③ 영애: wants를 will want로 바꾸어야 해.
④ 민서: he'll grow를 he grows로 바꾸어야 해.
⑤ 환기: 이 문장은 틀린 게 없어.

VOCA curious 궁금한 | useful 유용한 | language 언어 | go down (해가) 지다 | spelling 철자 | meaning 의미 | fever 열 | architect 건축가

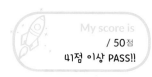
09 Which word for the blank is different from the others?

① Turn right, _____ you'll see the building.

② It cost a hundred _____ twenty dollars.

③ She _____ I could cross the river last night.

④ He was my bother, _____ I looked after him.

⑤ Run faster, _____ you'll be late for the show.

10 Write the correct word for the blank according to the picture.

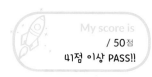

(1) I was busy, _____ I couldn't finish my work.

(2) I couldn't finish my work _____ I was busy.

11 Complete the sentence so that it has the same meaning as the given sentence.

If you do your best, you will not regret it.

→ Do your best, _____ you will regret it.

12 Rewrite the sentence by correcting the error.

When she will come to my house again, I will light the candles for her.

→ _____

_____

13 Write the common word for the blanks.

• The truth is _____ she is very attractive.
• It is necessary _____ you exercise regularly.

→ _____

14 Translate the sentence according to the conditions.

만약 내일 눈이 오면, 나는 눈사람을 만들 것이다.

· Condition 1   it, snow, build, a snowman을 활용할 것
· Condition 2   조건절을 문장 앞에 쓸 것
· Condition 3   9단어

→ _____

_____

15 Choose the necessary words and rearrange the given words translate the sentence.

이 약을 먹어. 그러면 넌 기분이 더 좋아질 거야.
and / Take / better / pill, / feel / . / or / this / will / you / ,

→ _____

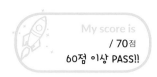
01 U29_1
빈칸에 공통으로 들어갈 수 있는 것은? 2점

- The school festival starts _____ noon.
- The KTX will leave _____ 9:30.
- I can study well _____ night.

① in   ② at
③ by   ④ until
⑤ on

02 U29_1+GP
Which is correct for the blank? 2점

A: How long do you practice swimming every day?
B: _____.

① By tomorrow   ② For two hours
③ During three hours   ④ At night
⑤ In the evening

[03~04] 각 빈칸에 들어갈 말이 올바르게 짝지어진 것을 고르시오. 각 2점

03 U29_1

함정

- I read the book _____ midnight.
- I have to go back home _____ 5 o'clock.

① until – by   ② for – till
③ by – until   ④ around – for
⑤ for – until

04 U29_1+GP
함정

A: My family will stay on a mountain _____ one week. Will you join us?
B: I'd like to, but I should stay home. My uncle will be here _____ summer vacation.

① for – during   ② in – during
③ during – during   ④ for – for
⑤ in – for

05 U30_1+2+GP

한눈에 쏙
다음 문장과 같은 의미인 것을 고르시오. 2점

I will go to work, and then I will go to church.

① After I go to work, I will go to church.
② I will go to church after I will go to work.
③ Before I go to work, I will go to church.
④ I go to work before I will go to church.
⑤ After I go to work, I go to church.

06 U30_2
다음 문장에서 'that'이 들어갈 위치로 알맞은 것은? 2점

(①) I don't (②) think (③) it (④) is (⑤) a good plan.

07 U30_2
다음 빈칸에 알맞은 것은? 2점

I feel down _____ you are down.

① that   ② which
③ when   ④ how
⑤ what

08 U29_GP+U30_2
고난도
How many sentences are <u>incorrect</u>? 2점

ⓐ When all men speak, no man hears.
ⓑ If you have any problems, please call me.
ⓒ After you eat food, you should brush your teeth.
ⓓ I like fruit a lot, but I'm allergic to strawberries.
ⓔ She couldn't go out because she had a cold.
ⓕ I went to bed early so I was tired.

① one   ② two
③ three   ④ four
⑤ five

09 다음 빈칸에 들어갈 말로 알맞은 것은?

U30_1

| I got home, ate something, _____ watched TV. |

① and ② or
③ so ④ but
⑤ because

10 각 빈칸에 들어갈 말이 순서대로 나열된 것을 고르시오.

U29_1+2

- She came to see me _____ October seventeenth.
- Giho hurried _____ the telephone.
- The players are already _____ the field.
- I scored those goals thanks _____ your help today.

① on – to – on – to ② in – in – in – for
③ on – to – to – in ④ in – in – for – for
⑤ at – at – on – for

11 다음 중 어법상 어색한 것을 모두 찾아 바르게 고치시오.

U29_1+GP

ⓐ You waited during three hours.
ⓑ We had a costume party on Halloween.
ⓒ I will study for the test on this weekend.

→ _____
_____

12 우리말과 같은 의미가 되도록 빈칸에 알맞은 단어를 쓰시오.

U29_3

우리는 시골을 통과하여 오랫동안 버스를 타고 갔다.

→ We had a long bus ride _____ the countryside.

13 두 문장의 빈칸에 공통으로 들어갈 전치사를 쓰시오.

U29_1+U28_2

- He didn't say anything _____ the next thirty minutes. (그는 다음 30분 동안 아무 말도 하지 않았다.)
- His mother made some delicious food _____ us. (그의 어머니는 우리에게 맛있는 음식을 만들어 주셨다.)

→ _____

14 우리말과 일치하지 않는 부분을 찾아 바르게 고치시오.

U29_3

그들은 라스베이거스로 비행기를 타고 갔다.
= They went to Las Vegas for the airplane.

_____ → _____

15 Complete the sentence describing the picture.

U29_2

→ The boy is hiding _____ the curtains.

16 주어진 문장과 같은 의미가 되도록 빈칸에 알맞은 말을 쓰시오.

U29_GP+U30_2

Before he started the class, he gave everyone a gift.

→ _____ he gave everyone a gift, he started the class.

17 빈칸에 공통으로 들어갈 말을 쓰시오. 4점

> • Wake up now, _____ you can eat a delicious breakfast.
> • She has a dog _____ two cats.

➡ _____

18 Write the common word for the blanks. 4점

> • I was so scared _____ I couldn't open my eyes.
> • I think _____ we should care about our own and others' safety.

➡ _____

19 다음 우리말을 조건에 맞게 영작하시오. 6점

고난도

> 네가 나의 등을 긁어주면, 나는 너의 것을 긁어줄 것이다.
> ┄┄┄┄┄┄┄┄┄┄┄┄┄┄┄┄┄┄┄┄
> · 어휘   scratch, back
> · 조건1   접속사를 먼저 쓸 것
> · 조건2   8단어로 쓸 것

➡ _____

20 다음 두 문장을 자연스러운 의미가 되도록 연결하시오.

한눈에 쏙

(답 2개) 각 3점

> She bought her ticket early. She could get a good seat.

(A) _____

_____

(B) _____

_____

[21~22] 다음 글을 읽고 물음에 답하시오.

BRAILLE NUMBERS AND ENGLISH ALPHABET

Louis Braille became ⓐblind when he was three years old. However, he was a ⓑgreatly kid inventor. He ⓒused raised dots for his own writing system, Braille. He finally finished ⓓto make the system for blind people when he was fifteen. He became a teacher ⓔin Paris and taught Braille to blind children. Today, blind people all over the world use the system (A)그들이 읽고 쓸 때.

*Braille: 점자(點字)

21 윗글의 밑줄 친 부분 ⓐ~ⓔ 중 어법상 옳은 것으로 짝지어진 것은? 3점

① ⓑ, ⓓ
② ⓒ, ⓔ
③ ⓐ, ⓒ, ⓓ
④ ⓐ, ⓒ, ⓔ
⑤ ⓒ, ⓓ, ⓔ

22 밑줄 친 우리말 (A)를 5단어로 영작하시오. 4점

(A) _____

불규칙 동사 변화표

불규칙 동사도
외우는 방법이 있다!

1 A – A – A 형태 동일

★표시는 필수 기본 동사들

원형	뜻	과거
broadcast	방송하다	broadcast
bet	돈을 걸다	bet
burst	파열하다	burst
cast	던지다	cast
cost	비용이 들다	cost
★cut	자르다	cut
forecast	예고하다	forecast
★hit	치다	hit
hurt	아프게 하다	hurt
let	~하게 하다	let
★put	놓다	put
quit	~을 그만두다	quit
★read	읽다	read [red]
rid	~을 제거하다	rid
set	놓다	set
shed	흘리다	shed
shut	닫다	shut
spit	침을 뱉다	spit
split	쪼개다	split
spread	펴다	spread
thrust	찌르다	thrust
upset	뒤엎다	upset

2 A – A – A' 과거분사만 살짝 바뀜

원형	뜻	과거
beat	때리다, 이기다	beat

3 A – B – A 과거형에서 모음만 바뀜

원형	뜻	과거
★come	오다	came
★become	되다	became
★run	달리다	ran

A – B – A' 과거형은 모음 변화, 과거분사형은 원형에 –n 붙임

원형	뜻	과거
arise [əráiz]	(일이) 일어나다	arose [əróuz]
＊be (am, is, are)	～이다	was, were
blow	불다	blew [blu:]
＊do, does	하다	did
draw	당기다, 그리다	drew [dru:]
＊drive	운전하다	drove [drouv]
＊eat	먹다	ate
fall	떨어지다	fell
forbid	금지하다	forbade
forgive	용서하다	forgave
forsake	그만두다, 저버리다	forsook
＊give	주다	gave [ɡeiv]
＊go	가다	went [went]
＊grow	자라다	grew [ɡru:]
＊know	알다	knew [nju:]
ride	(차, 말 등을) 타다	rode [roud]
rise	일어서다	rose [rouz]
＊see	보다	saw [sɔ:]
shake	흔들다	shook [ʃuk]
show	보여주다, 보이다	showed
sow [sou]	(씨를) 뿌리다	sowed [soud]
strive	노력하다	strove [strouv]
＊take	잡다	took [tuk]
thrive	번영하다	throve [θrouv], thrived
＊throw	던지다	threw [θru:]
withdraw	물러나다	withdrew [wiðdrú:]
＊write	쓰다	wrote [rout]

A – B – B 원형에 –t 붙임

원형	뜻	과거
bend	구부리다	bent
＊build	세우다	built
burn	태우다	burnt, burned
deal	다루다	dealt [delt]
dwell	거주하다, 살다	dwelt, dwelled
lend	빌려주다	lent
mean	의미하다	meant [ment]
＊send	보내다	sent
smell	냄새 맡다, 냄새가 나다	smelt, smelled

spend	소비하다	spent
spoil	망쳐놓다	spoilt, spoiled

6 A – B – B 원형의 자음 + ought/aught

원형	뜻	과거
*bring	가져오다	brought [brɔːt]
*buy	사다	bought [bɔːt]
*catch	잡다	caught [kɔːt]
*fight	싸우다	fought [fɔːt]
seek	찾다	sought [sɔːt]
*teach	가르치다	taught [tɔːt]
*think	생각하다	thought [θɔːt]

7 A – B – B 원형의 자음 + ound

원형	뜻	과거
bind	묶다	bound [baund]
*find	발견하다	found [faund]

8 A – B – B 원형의 모음이 하나로 줄고 + t

원형	뜻	과거
creep	기다, 포복하다	crept [krept]
*feel	느끼다	felt
*keep	유지하다	kept
kneel [niːl]	무릎 꿇다, 굴복하다	knelt [nelt]
*leave	떠나다	left
*lose [luːz]	잃다	lost [lɔːst]
*sleep	자다	slept
sweep	쓸다	swept [swept]

9 A – B – B 원형의 모음이 하나로 줄어듦

원형	뜻	과거
feed	먹이다	fed [fed]
*meet	만나다	met [met]
shoot [ʃuːt]	쏘다	shot [ʃat]

원형	뜻	과거
lay	두다	laid [leid]
*pay	지불하다	paid [peid]
*say	말하다	said [sed]

원형	뜻	과거
behold	~를 보다	beheld
bleed	피를 흘리다	bled
breed	기르다	bred
cling	달라붙다	clung
dig	파다	dug [dʌg]
fling	내던지다	flung
hang	걸다	hung
*hold	잡다, 손에 들다	held
lead	이끌다	led
shine	빛나다	shone [ʃoun]
*sit	앉다	sat [sæt]
spin	(실을) 잣다	spun [spʌn]
*stand	서다	stood [stud]
stick	찌르다	stuck
sting	쏘다	stung
strike	때리다	struck [strʌk]
*win	이기다	won [wʌn]
wind [waind]	감다	wound [waund]
withhold	보류하다	withheld

원형	뜻	과거
flee	도망치다	fled [fled]
*have, has	가지다	had
*hear [hiər]	듣다	heard [həːrd]
*make	만들다	made
*sell	팔다	sold
slide	미끄러지다	slid
*tell	말하다	told

178

원형	뜻	과거
awake [əwéik]	깨다	awoke [əwóuk]
*bear [bɛər]	낳다	bore [bɔər]
bite	물다	bit [bit]
*break	깨뜨리다	broke [brouk]
*choose	고르다	chose [tʃouz]
*forget	잊다	forgot [fərgát]
freeze	얼음이 얼다	froze [frouz]
*get	얻다	got [gɑt]
*hide	감추다	hid [hid]
*speak	말하다	spoke [spouk]
steal	훔치다	stole [stoul]
swear	맹세하다	swore [swɔər]
tear [tɛər]	찢다	tore [tɔər]
tread [tred]	걷다, 짓밟다	trod [trɑd]
wake	깨다	woke
*wear	입다	wore [wɔər]

14 A – B – C

원형	뜻	과거
*begin	시작하다	began [bigǽn]
*drink	마시다	drank [dræŋk]
*fly	날다	flew [fluː]
lie	가로눕다	lay [lei]
cf. lie (규칙 변화)	거짓말하다	lied
*ring	울리다	rang [ræŋ]
shrink	줄어들다	shrank [ʃræŋk]
*sing	노래하다	sang [sæŋ]
sink	가라앉다	sank [sæŋk]
spring	튀다	sprang [spræŋ]
*swim	수영하다	swam [swæm]

15 조동사

원형	뜻	과거
*must	~해야 한다	(had to)
*can	~할 수 있다	could [cud]
*may	~해도 좋다	might [mait]
shall	~할 것이다	should [ʃud]
*will	~할 것이다	would [wud]

16 뜻에 따라 활용이 달라지는 불규칙 동사

원형	뜻	과거
bear	참다	bore
	낳다	bore
bid	명령하다	bade
	말하다	bid
hang	걸다	hung
	교수형에 처하다	hanged

17 혼동하기 쉬운 불규칙 동사와 규칙 동사

원형	뜻	과거
bind	묶다	bound [baund]
bound [baund]	되튀다	bounded
fall	떨어지다, 쓰러지다	fell
fell	쓰러뜨리다	felled
find	발견하다	found [faund]
found [faund]	세우다, 창립하다	founded
fly	날다	flew [fluː]
flow	흐르다	flowed
lie	눕다	lay
lay	눕히다, 낳다	laid
see	보다	saw
saw [sɔː]	톱질하다	sawed [sɔːd]
sew [sou]	바느질하다	sewed [soud]
sit	앉다	sat
set	두다	set
wind	감다	wound [waund]
wound [wuːnd]	상처를 입히다	wounded
welcome	환영하다	welcomed
overcome	이겨내다, 극복하다	overcame

신영주

2급 외국어 정교사 자격증, UCSD TESOL 취득(국제영어교사 교육자격증, University of California)
(전) EBSi 온라인 강사, 대치 시대인재, 이강학원 강사
(현) 프라우드 세븐 어학원 원장, 리딩타운 원장
저서: 체크체크, 올백(천재교육), 투탑 영어(디딤돌), Grammar 콕, VOCA콕(꿈을담는틀), 중학 영문법 클리어(동아) 등 다수의 교재 공저

이건희

쥬기스(http://jugis.co.kr) 대표
저서: 맨처음 수능 시리즈 – 맨처음 수능 영문법, 맨처음 수능 영어(기본, 실력, 독해, 완성)
　　　내공 시리즈 – 내공 중학영문법, 내공 중학 영어구문, 내공 중학영어듣기 모의고사 20회
　　　체크체크(천재교육), Grammar In(비상교육) 외 다수
instagram@gunee27

최신개정판

내신공략 중학영문법 1 문제풀이책

지은이 신영주, 이건희
펴낸이 정규도
펴낸곳 (주)다락원

개정판 1쇄 발행 2021년 3월 15일
개정판 5쇄 발행 2024년 1월 25일

편집 김민주
디자인 구수정
조판 블랙엔화이트
영문 감수 Michael A. Putlack
삽화 김진용

다락원 경기도 파주시 문발로 211
내용문의: (02)736-2031 내선 532
구입문의: (02)736-2031 내선 250~252
Fax: (02)732-2037
출판등록 1977년 9월 16일 제406-2008-000007호

ISBN 978-89-277-0890-2 54740
　　　978-89-277-0888-9 54740(set)

http://www.darakwon.co.kr
다락원 홈페이지를 방문하시면 상세한 출판 정보와 함께 동영상 강좌, MP3 자료 등 다양한 어학 정보를 얻으실 수 있습니다.

내공 중학영문법

신영주 ✦ 이건희 지음

최신개정판

문제풀이책

정답 및 해설

1

DARAKWON

내신공략 중학영문법

문제풀이책 1
정답 및 해설

UNIT 01 인칭대명사와 be동사

1) my
2) me
3) mine
4) your
5) you
6) yours
7) his
8) him
9) his
10) her
11) her
12) hers
13) its
14) it
15) our
16) us
17) ours
18) your
19) you
20) yours
21) their
22) them
23) theirs
24) am
25) I'm
26) are
27) we're
28) are
29) you're
30) are
31) they're
32) is
33) he's
34) is
35) she's
36) is
37) it's
38) is
39) is
40) that's

Level 1 Test
p. 12

A 1 is
2 are
3 are
4 are
5 is

B 1 are
2 is
3 is
4 are
5 are

C 1 She's a good singer.
2 They're on the subway.
3 He's a great gamer.
4 It's a good idea.
5 I'm a very simple person.

Level 2 Test
p. 13

01 ② ⑤
02 ③
03 ③
04 ⑤
05 ③ ④
06 They are my enemies.
07 ⓐ Their dog is very smart. (또는 Their dogs are very smart.)
08 favorite drink is coke
09 is / is
10 are / airplane

>>> 해설
01 be동사가 are이므로 주어는 you 또는 복수가 와야 한다.
02 • 주어가 3인칭 복수이므로 are를 쓴다.
• 주어가 3인칭 단수이므로 is를 쓴다.
03 ③은 are, 나머지는 is이다.

04 It is의 줄임말은 It's이다.
05 ③ are → is ④ am → are
06 '그들은(They)'이 주어이고 be동사는 복수라 are를 쓰고 나머지 보어를 쓰면 된다.
07 '그들의'는 theirs가 아니라 their이며, Their dog은 3인칭 단수이므로 is로 쓰거나 are에 맞도록 dog을 복수형으로 쓴다.
08 「주어+be동사+보어」 순으로 쓴다.
09 둘 다 주어가 3인칭 단수이므로 is를 쓴다.
10 주어가 they이므로 be동사는 are이고, 비행기에 있으므로 airplane 또는 plane인데 두 단어의 첫 글자가 같아야 하므로 airplane을 쓴다.

Level 3 Test
p. 14

01 ②
02 ④
03 ①
04 ③ ④
05 ③ ④
06 ④
07 ③ ④ ⑤
08 ④
09 ⑤
10 ⑤
11 ① ④
12 They're my distant cousins.
13 (1) are (2) is (3) is
14 ⓑ Its → It's
15 (E) are
16 He is a firefighter
17 My dad am → My dad is / my mom are → my mom is / They is → They are / I'am → I'm[I am]

>>> 해설
01 ②에서 be동사는 '~이다'의 의미이고, 나머지에서는 '(~에) 있다'의 뜻이다.
02 • 주어가 3인칭 단수이므로 is
• 주어가 3인칭 복수이므로 are
• 주어가 3인칭 단수이므로 is
03 ①에는 is를, 나머지에는 are를 써야 한다.
04 ③ This is는 줄여 쓸 수 없다. ④ It is의 줄임말은 It's이다.
05 ③, ④는 3인칭 단수이므로 is로 써야 한다.
06 My grandparents are very generous to me.가 바른 영작이므로 ④가 옳다.
07 동사가 are이므로 복수인 ③, ④, ⑤ 모두 맞다.
08 주어가 3인칭 단수인 My Canadian friend Myles이므로 be동사를 is로 써야 한다.
09 ① am → is ② ③ is → are ④ yours → your ⑤의 *Ali Baba and the Forty Thieves*는 책 제목이므로 단수 취급한다.
10 ⓐ ⓑ ⓒ are → is ⓔ am → is ⓕ are → is
11 ① Liam's hands are big. ④ My best friends are crazy. ② The party are tonight. (are → is) ③ Jack are in the bathroom. (are → is) ⑤ The food are on the table. (are → is)
12 단어 수에 맞게 They're로 쓰고 사촌들이므로 cousins로 쓰면 된다.
13 (1) 주어가 3인칭 복수이므로 are를 쓴다.
(2) (3) 주어가 3인칭 단수이므로 is를 쓴다.
14 It is의 줄임말은 It's이다.
15 (A)~(D)는 is, (E)는 are가 들어간다.

16 uncle이라고 했으므로 주어는 He로 써야 하며, 직업을 나타내는 말을 사용해야 하므로 firefighter를 쓰면 된다.

17 주어가 3인칭 단수이면 is, 복수이면 are를 쓰며, I am의 줄임말은 I'm이다.

02 be동사의 부정문과 의문문

1) I'm not
2) you're not[you aren't]
3) he's not[he isn't]
4) she's not[she isn't]
5) it's not[it isn't]
6) we're not[we aren't]
7) you're not[you aren't]
8) they're not[they aren't]
9) be동사＋주어 ~?
10) Yes, 주어＋be동사.
11) No, 주어＋be동사＋not.

Level 1 Test
p. 16

A 1. am
2. is not
3. She's not
4. aren't
5. isn't

B 1. We are not[We're not, We aren't] the champions.
2. My girlfriend is not[isn't] a musician.
3. It's not[It is not, It isn't] back on the menu.
4. This is not[isn't] a coin from the Joseon Dynasty.

C 1. Is this online broadcast fun?
2. Is that his new nickname?
3. Are Sunny and Russell in the same class?

D 1. I am
2. it's not 또는 it isn't
3. he is
4. they're not 또는 they aren't

Level 2 Test
p. 17

01 ③
02 ⑤
03 ④
04 ②
05 ② ③
06 They're not broken. 또는 They aren't broken.
07 Are the girls in the restroom?
08 No, we're not. 또는 No, we aren't.
09 No, she is not. 또는 No, she isn't. 또는 No, she's not. (She is[She's] a vet.)
10 (1) It is not[It's not, It isn't] his new laptop computer.
(2) Is it his new laptop computer?
(3) Yes, it is.

≫ 해설

01 주어가 복수이므로 are를 쓰고 not은 be동사 뒤에 쓴다.
02 aren't로 써야 한다.
03 B가 화성(Mars)이 아니라 금성(Venus)에서 왔다고 했으므로 부정의 답을 선택해야 하며, you는 I로 답하고 am not은 줄여 쓰지 않는다.
04 주어진 대화를 영작하면 A: Is her husband a police officer? B: Yes, he is.이므로 she는 필요 없다.

05 ② Is → Are ③ Are → Is
06 These buttons는 3인칭 복수 대명사 They로 받으므로 be동사 are를 써서 부정문을 만든다.
07 주어가 복수이므로 be동사 are를 사용하여 의문문을 만든다.
08 you는 복수로 사용되었고, 빈칸 뒤의 문장을 읽어보면 빈칸에 부정의 답이 와야 한다는 것을 알 수 있다.
09 여자는 치과 의사(dentist)가 아니라 수의사(vet)이므로 부정으로 답해야 한다.
10 부정문은 be동사 뒤에 not을 쓰고, 의문문은 be동사를 주어 앞에 쓴다.

Level 3 Test
p. 18

01 ③
02 ③ ④
03 ⑤
04 ③
05 ④ ⑤
06 ④
07 ②
08 ④
09 ④
10 ③
11 (A) is not 또는 isn't (B) am not
12 they're / They are
13 Are → Is / Yes → No
14 Is she / No, she isn't. 또는 No, she's not.
15 (1) Those are not[aren't] fresh from the farm.
(2) Are those fresh from the farm?
(3) Yes, they are.
16 둘째 줄: No, she is. → No, she isn't. 또는 No, she's not.
셋째 줄: hers → her
넷째 줄: that → it

≫ 해설

01 상반되는 내용이 나오므로 뒤의 문장이 긍정이면 부정, 부정이면 긍정이 와야 한다.
02 be동사 뒤에 not을 써야 한다. ③ → Its cover is not very old. ④ → The ramen is not tasty.
03 ① amn't → am not ② n't → not ③ not is → is not ④ not → are not
04 Yes, you are. You are not wrong.으로 답해야 한다.
05 ①~③은 Are, ④, ⑤는 Is가 들어간다. Romeo and Juliet은 영화 제목으로 단수 취급해야 한다.
06 바른 영식은 His rules are not strict.이므로 ④가 맞다.
07 This is not your fault but mine.이 옳으므로 바르게 분석한 학생은 ② 기태이다. (not A but B: A가 아니라 B)
08 not을 are not 또는 aren't로 써야 한다.
09 Are Yuki and Maki your friends?로 쓰면 된다.
10 ⓐ Is → Are ⓑ Am → Is ⓒ Are → Is
11 두 번째 문장을 보면 Sandy는 중학생이므로 (A)에는 부정형인 is not 또는 isn't가 와야 한다. (B)에는 상반되는 내용이 와야 하므로 am not으로 써야 한다.
12 those는 they로 답하며 빈칸이 하나이므로 they're, 다음은 빈칸이 두 개이므로 They are로 쓴다.
13 your brother는 Is를 쓰고, 오빠[형, 남동생]가 짓궂냐는 질문에 착하다고 했으므로 Yes를 No로 바꿔야 한다.
14 be동사의 의문문은 be동사를 먼저 쓰고, 그림을 보니 부지런하지 않으므로 부정으로 답한다.

15 부정문은 be동사 뒤에 not을 쓴다. 의문문은 be동사를 앞에 쓴다. 긍정의 대답에서 those는 they로 받아 쓴다.

16 둘째 줄: No라고 답했으므로 isn't로 써야 한다.
   셋째 줄: 명사 (car)를 수식하는 소유격인 her로 써야 한다.
   넷째 줄: that은 it으로 받는다.

UNIT 03 일반동사

1) go
2) come
3) sit
4) walk
5) run
6) eat
7) have
8) like
9) love
10) think
11) comes
12) plays
13) walks
14) eats
15) passes
16) washes
17) teaches
18) does
19) studies
20) flies
21) cries
22) has

Level 1 Test
p. 20

A
1 teach
2 take
3 stay
4 play
5 wear
6 draw

B
1 dances
2 eats
3 has
4 wears
5 misses

C
1 놀다 / plays
2 걷다 / walks
3 통과하다 / passes
4 하다 / does
5 가지고 있다 / has
6 가르치다 / teaches
7 공부하다 / studies

D
1 eats
2 goes
3 enjoys
4 cooks
5 has

Level 2 Test
p. 21

01 ④
02 ③
03 ②
04 ②
05 ③
06 have / has
07 They go to the library every day.
08 flies in the sky
09 ⓐ I brush my teeth after meals.
10 opens / closes

》》해설

01 play의 뜻은 다음과 같다. ① (운동) 경기하다 ② 놀다 ③ (악기를) 연주하다 ④ (게임을) 하다

02 ① '자음+y'로 끝나는 동사 → '자음+ies' (cry → cries) ② have → has ④⑤ '모음+y'로 끝나는 동사+s (stay → stays / play → plays)

03 ① The queen이 3인칭 단수이므로 have → has ③ They가 3인칭

복수이므로 writes → write ④ studys → studies ('자음+y' → '자음+ies') ⑤ gos → goes (-o로 끝나는 동사+-es)

04 ① are have busy → are busy (have동사 필요 없음) ③ I가 1인칭이므로 has → have ④ has를 지워야 한다. ⑤ Her students가 3인칭 복수이므로 does → do

05 ⓑ be busy(바쁘다)이므로 has → is가 되어야 한다. ⓔ he가 3인칭 단수이므로 carry → carries ('자음+y' → '자음+ies')

06 주어 I는 1인칭이므로 have, my sister는 3인칭 단수이므로 has를 쓴다.

07 They는 3인칭 복수이므로 일반동사 go를 그대로 쓴다.

08 An airplane은 3인칭 단수이므로 fly → flies로 바꾼다.

09 주어가 1인칭일 때는 동사원형이 와야 한다.

10 주어가 3인칭 단수이므로 open과 close에 -(e)s를 붙인다.

Level 3 Test
p. 22

01 ②
02 ④
03 ⑤
04 ③
05 ④
06 ①
07 ①
08 ② ④
09 ③ ④ ⑤
10 ② ④
11 ① ③
12 takes
13 Cathy does her homework at school.
14 Everybody understands me.
15 (1) is   (2) comes
16 swims 또는 goes swimming
17 wakes → wake / exercises → exercise / study → studies

》》해설

01 rise(오르다, 뜨다)의 3인칭 단수형 rises가 알맞다.

02 주어 Little Alex는 3인칭 단수이므로 wants가 알맞고, People은 3인칭 복수이므로 spend가 와야 한다.

03 ⑤는 '가지고 있다'는 의미의 have이고 나머지는 play가 알맞다. play의 의미는 다음과 같다. ① 놀다 ② (운동) 경기하다 ③ (게임을) 하다 ④ (악기를) 연주하다

04 • have동사가 '먹다'라는 의미로 사용되었다.
   • have동사가 '(신체 특징을) 가지다'라는 의미로 사용되었다.
   • have동사가 '(질병) 가지다'라는 의미로 사용되었다. 모두 주어가 3인칭 단수이므로 has가 들어가야 한다.

05 동사가 3인칭 단수형 stays이므로 We, You, Ryan and John은 주어로 올 수 없다.

06 ① 주어가 3인칭 단수이고 water는 '물을 주다'라는 동사의 뜻을 가지고 있으므로 waters가 알맞다. ② water는 타동사로 water the plant 하면 '식물에게 물을 주다'라는 의미가 되므로 전치사 to는 필요 없다. ④ water = give water to로 바꾸어 쓸 수 있지만 give에 -s를 붙여 gives로 써야 한다. ⑤ grandma는 grandmother의 애칭으로 틀린 표현이 아니다.

07 ① each(각각의)는 3인칭 단수 취급하므로 have → has가 되어야 한다.

08 ②④ 주어가 3인칭 복수이므로 takes → take, comes → come이 되어야 알맞다.

09 ③ pickes → picks ④ haves → has ⑤ washs → washes

10 ① have → has ③ respects → respect ⑤ He trust → He trusts

11 ① weares → wears ③ catchs → catches

12 • take동사가 '(사진을) 찍다'라는 의미로 사용되었다.
   • take동사가 '(시간이) 걸리다'라는 의미로 사용되었다.
   • take care of: ~을 돌보다

13 '숙제를 하다'는 do one's homework이고 주어가 3인칭 단수이므로 does를 이용하여 쓴다.

14 everybody(모든 사람)는 3인칭 단수 취급한다.

15 (1) '겨울은 한 해의 마지막 계절이다'라는 뜻이 되기 위한 be동사 is가 필요하다.
   (2) '겨울은 봄 전에 온다'라는 뜻이 되도록 comes가 와야 알맞다.

16 주어 My mom은 3인칭 단수이므로 swims 또는 goes swimming이 된다.

17 wakes의 주어는 I이므로 wake로 쓴다. 주어가 my friends로 3인칭 복수이므로 동사원형을 쓰고, my best friend Leo는 나의 제일 친한 친구인 Leo 한 명이므로 3인칭 단수이다.

UNIT 04 일반동사의 부정문과 의문문

1) does not[doesn't]
2) do not[don't]
3) you do
4) you don't
5) I do
6) I don't
7) he/she/it does
8) he/she/it doesn't
9) we[you] do
10) we[you] don't
11) we do
12) we don't
13) they do
14) they don't

Level 1 Test
p. 24

A 1 don't
2 doesn't
3 Are
4 Does
5 Does / draw
6 isn't
7 doesn't like
8 watch

B 1 My father doesn't[does not] read the newspaper.
2 We don't[do not] swim in the pool.
3 Danny doesn't[does not] like webtoons.

C 1 Do you have a cool smartphone?
2 Is your favorite subject music?
3 Does he come from Argentina?
4 Does your sister have a tablet computer?

D 1 Do / I[we] do
2 Does / she doesn't
3 Do / they do

Level 2 Test
p. 25

01 ④
02 ②
03 ③
04 ②
05 ③
06 No, he doesn't.
07 The children don't[do not] use the Internet.
08 Do you like / I don't

09 Does he have a funny nickname?
10 good / cooks / poor / doesn't sing

》》해설

01 My boyfriend(3인칭 단수)+does not[doesn't]+동사원형

02 Do they ~?로 물었으므로 Yes, they do.나 No, they don't.로 답해야 한다.

03 ①, ②, ④, ⑤에는 Do가 들어가지만 ③에는 Does가 들어간다.

04 의미상 be동사는 올 수 없다. (take a lot of pictures: 많은 사진을 찍다)

05 주어가 3인칭 단수인 일반동사의 의문문은 「Does+주어+동사원형 ~?」의 형태이다. Does she have ~?가 되어야 한다.

06 주어가 3인칭 단수인 일반동사의 의문문에 대한 부정의 대답은 「No, 주어+doesn't.」로 한다.

07 children은 '어린이들'이라는 의미의 3인칭 복수이므로 「주어+don't[do not]+동사원형 ~.」의 순서로 부정문을 만든다.

08 2인칭 단수 주어 you의 일반동사 의문문은 「Do+주어+동사원형 ~?」으로 만들고 대답은 I로 한다.

09 주어가 3인칭 단수일 때 의문문의 어순은 「Does+주어+동사원형 ~?」이다.

10 be good at은 '~을 잘하다', be poor at은 '~을 못하다'라는 뜻이다. 그림에서 Sally는 요리를 잘하므로 긍정문의 cooks로 쓰고, Mike는 노래를 못하므로 부정문의 doesn't sing으로 써야 한다.

Level 3 Test
p. 26

01 ③
02 ②
03 ④
04 ①
05 ②
06 ②
07 ① ③
08 ③
09 ③ ⑤
10 ③
11 ① ⑤
12 tell
13 Does she get[wake] up early?
14 Yes, it does. / No, it doesn't.
15 (My) Mom doesn't post pictures on her blog.
16 Does / have / doesn't / has
17 (A) Does Hannah sing well
   (B) She is a terrible singer

》》해설

01 주어가 3인칭 단수일 때 일반동사의 의문문은 「Does+주어+동사원형 ~?」의 형태로 쓴다. ③의 sounds를 sound로 고쳐야 한다.

02 버스를 타고 학교에 가는지 묻는 말에 자전거를 타고 간다고 했으므로 빈칸에는 부정의 대답이 와야 하고, 주어는 I이므로 ②가 알맞다.

03 ④ Ms. Kim은 3인칭 단수이므로 부정문을 만들 때 「doesn't+동사원형」이 와야 한다.

04 ② B: Yes, he doesn't. → Yes, he does. 또는 No, he doesn't.
   ③ B: No, you don't. → No, I[we] don't. ④ B: No, he don't. → No, he doesn't. ⑤ B: Yes, he do. → Yes, he does.

05 ② 주어가 3인칭 단수이며 일반동사 원형이 온 것으로 보아 Does이다. ① afraid와 어울리는 be동사 Is를 쓴다. ③ ④ ⑤ 주어가 3인칭 단수가 아니며 일반동사 원형이 온 것으로 보아 Do가 들어가야 알맞다.

06 일반동사 study의 의문문으로, 주어 you 앞에 Do를 쓴다.

07 ① 의문문에서 주어 뒤의 일반동사는 동사원형으로 써야 하므로 has

→ have ③ Alan이 3인칭 단수이므로 don't → doesn't가 되어야 알맞다.

08 ⓐ go 일반동사의 부정문은 aren't가 아니라 don't가 와야 한다. ⓑ does not 다음에 동사원형 throw가 와야 한다.

09 ① 주어가 1인칭 단수이므로 'don't+동사원형'을 쓴다. (doesn't like → don't like) ② ④ 주어가 3인칭 단수이므로 「doesn't+동사원형」을 쓴다. (don't → doesn't)

10 주어가 1·2인칭일 때 일반동사 부정문은 「주어+do not[don't]+동사원형」이므로 ⓐ don't likes → don't like ⓑ aren't have → don't have가 되어야 한다. ⓒ는 올바른 문장이다.

11 ① He doesn't needs help. (needs → need) ⑤ Jenna doesn't has time for me. (has → have) ② Does she go to the gym? ③ Flowers don't grow without rain. ④ Do they celebrate Christmas?

12 주어가 3인칭 단수일 때 일반동사의 의문문은 「Does+주어+동사원형 ~?이므로 Does he tell great stories about his childhood?가 알맞다.

13 주어가 3인칭 단수인 일반동사 의문문은 「Does+주어+동사원형 ~?」으로 쓴다.

14 your school은 3인칭 단수이므로 대답할 때 it으로 대답하고 Does로 물어보면 does로 대답한다.

15 주어 (My) Mom은 3인칭 단수이므로 doesn't post로 써야 한다.

16 주어가 3인칭 단수일 때 일반동사 의문문은 「Does+주어+동사원형 ~?」이고 이에 대한 부정의 대답은 「No, 주어+doesn't.」로 한다.

17 (A) 일반동사의 의문문이므로 Does Hannah sing well?
(B) 아니라고 했으므로 She is a terrible singer.로 쓰면 된다.

Review Test

p. 28

01 ①
02 ②
03 ②
04 ②
05 ④
06 ④
07 ⑤
08 ④
09 ②
10 ①
11 ② ⑤
12 his
13 No, he isn't.
14 ⓒ their → them[theirs] ⓓ It's → Its
15 are not[aren't]
16 3. lives → live
4. rides → ride
5. doesn't → doesn't do
17 catches frogs by hand
18 Victor doesn't use chopsticks very well.
19 (A) Does Emma have breakfast every morning?
(B) Yes, she does.
20 has → have / flys → flies / call hers → call her
21 ① ③ ④
22 She is not very loud

》》 해설

01 be동사가 are이므로 We, They, The girls, He and I가 알맞고, Billy와 His cousin은 is가 와야 한다.

02 ②는 are, 나머지는 is이다.

03 상반되는 내용이 나오고 mine은 단수이므로 ②가 알맞다.

04 주어가 Lucy's hair이므로 Yes, it is.로 써야 한다.

05 각각 주어가 3인칭 단수이므로 has, drinks로 써야 한다.

06 My brother doesn't watch a lot of TV.가 맞는 문장으로 ④가 정답이다.

07 ①~④는 일반동사의 의문문으로 Do가, ⑤는 be동사의 의문문으로 Are가 필요하다.

08 대답이 she이므로 ④가 적절하다. ①은 be동사 의문문으로 대답이 적절하지 않다.

09 studies를 study로 써야 한다. ⑤의 you는 복수도 될 수 있으므로 대답은 이상하지 않다.

10 ⓑ Are → Is ⓒ Yes, I am. → Yes, you are. ⓓ He → He is

11 ② those는 they로 답하고 ⑤ Paul Walker는 한 명이므로 Are를 Is로 써야 한다.

12 his는 소유격도 되지만 소유대명사도 된다.

13 영화 감독이 아니라 만화 캐릭터이므로 부정으로 답해야 한다.

14 ⓒ 목적격으로 them 또는 theirs로 쓴다. ⓓ it의 소유격은 its이다.

15 주어가 복수이고 be동사가 들어가야 하므로 are not 또는 aren't로 써야 한다.

16 3. 주어가 복수이므로 live 그대로 쓴다.
4. 의문문에서 본동사는 원형으로 쓰므로 ride로 쓴다.
5. doesn't 다음에 본동사가 없으므로 do를 써야 한다.

17 주어가 3인칭 단수이므로 일반동사에 -(e)s를 붙여야 한다.

18 「주어+doesn't+동사원형 ~」 순으로 쓰면 된다.

19 주어가 3인칭 단수이므로 「Does+주어+동사원형 ~?」으로 물으며, 대답은 대명사로 한다.

20 has는 doesn't 뒤이므로 원형을 써야 하며, fly의 3인칭 단수형은 flies이고, hers는 '그녀의 것'이므로 목적격인 her로 써야 한다.

21 ⓐ 주어가 복수이므로 are ⓒ 주어가 3인칭 단수이므로 talks
ⓓ doesn't 다음에는 동사원형을 쓰므로 doesn't like

22 내용상 Daisy는 Anna와 상반되므로 '그녀는 매우 시끄럽지 않다'가 되어야 하며, 일반동사가 없으므로, She is not very loud.로 쓰면 된다.

[21~22]

Anna와 Daisy는 쌍둥이이다. 그들은 똑같아 보인다. 하지만 그들은 다르게 행동한다. Anna는 스포츠를 좋아한다. 그녀는 축구를 잘한다. 그녀는 매우 활발하다. 그녀는 말을 많이 한다. Daisy는 독서를 좋아한다. 그녀는 하루에 책 한 권을 읽는다. 그녀는 매우 시끄럽지 않다. 그녀는 이야기하는 것을 좋아하지 않는다. 하지만, 그들은 서로 사랑한다.

• 어휘 • look ~처럼 보이다 | act 행동하다 | differently 다르게 | be good at ~을 잘하다 | active 활발한 | a lot 많이 | a day 하루에 | however 하지만 | each other 서로

CHAPTER 02

UNIT 05 명사의 종류와 수량 표현

1) lakes	2) dogs	3) houses
4) buses	5) benches	6) boxes
7) pianos	8) photos	9) babies
10) cities	11) parties	12) knives
13) leaves	14) roofs	15) men
16) women	17) teeth	18) feet
19) children	20) mice	21) deer
22) fish	23) sheep	24) 복수
25) 많은	26) many	27) much
28) lots of	29) plenty of	30) a few
31) a little	32) few	33) little
34) piece	35) loaf	36) bottle
37) cup	38) bar	39) pound
40) glass	41) slice	42) bowl

Level 1 Test
p. 32

A 1 ① cars ② ×
  2 ① children ② apples
  3 ① fish ② ×
  4 ① × ② ×
  5 ① bikes ② babies
  6 ① toys ② photos
  7 ① shelves ② libraries
  8 ① sheep ② ×

B 1 little
  2 a few
  3 few

Level 2 Test
p. 33

01 ①   02 ④
03 ⑤   04 ⑤
05 ①
06 (1) a pair of (2) three glasses of
07 It has eight arms.
08 a piece[slice] / a glass
09 There are few monkeys in this zoo.
10 are → is / cheeses → cheese

》》 해설
01 ② tooth → teeth ③ potatos → potatoes / foot → feet
④ oxes → oxen ⑤ knifes → knives
02 a lot of 뒤에는 셀 수 있는 명사와 셀 수 없는 명사 둘 다 올 수 있지만 두 번째 문장에 many가 있으므로 셀 수 있는 명사의 복수형이 와야 한다.
03 truck의 복수형은 trucks이다.
04 단위 명사는 셀 수 있지만 물질 명사는 셀 수 없다. 종이는 piece 또는 sheet로, pizza는 piece 또는 slice로 센다.

05 ① friends는 셀 수 있는 명사이므로 little이 아니라 few를 써야 한다.
06 jeans는 pair를, juice류는 glass를 사용하여 표현한다.
07 대명사를 사용해야 하므로 문어(an octopus)는 it으로 쓰고, arm의 복수형인 arms로 써야 한다.
08 피자는 a piece[slice] of로, 물은 a glass of를 사용하여 수량을 표현한다.
09 '거의 없는'이라고 했으므로 few가 오며, 복수 명사(monkeys) 및 복수 동사(are)를 써야 한다.
10 네덜란드는 나라 이름으로 단수 취급하며, cheese는 셀 수 없는 명사로 복수형이 없다.

Level 3 Test
p. 34

01 ②   02 ④
03 ④   04 ④
05 ③   06 ⑤
07 ① ② ③ ④   08 ④
09 ②   10 ② ③
11 ⓑ sugars → sugar
12 Ryan has a lot of personalities.
13 Few
14 brushes / teeth
15 few gentlemen
16 a few → a little / oils → oil

》》 해설
01 ice cream은 셀 수 없는 명사이다.
02 geese가 goose의 복수형이다.
03 tomatoes, children으로 써야 한다.
04 dish의 복수형은 dishes이며, 주어가 복수이므로 동사는 are로 써야 한다.
05 plenty of는 셀 수 있는 명사와 셀 수 없는 명사 앞에 모두 사용되는데, 셀 수 있는 명사는 복수로 써야 한다. ③은 song이 단수이므로 plenty of가 들어가기에 적절하지 않다.
06 ① → much[a lot of, lots of, plenty of] ② → much[a lot of, lots of, plenty of] ③ → a little ④ → few
07 notebooks은 셀 수 있는 명사이므로 ⑤를 제외하고는 다 들어갈 수 있다.
08 ① loaf → cup ② sheet → sheets ③ pairs → pair ⑤ milks → milk
09 ⓐ childrens → children ⓒ chair → chairs ⓔ coffees → coffee
10 ② He drinks a lots of coffee. (→ a 삭제 또는 lots → lot)
③ She puts few salt in her soup. (few → little) ① Do fish like swimming? ④ Irene calls me a few times a day. ⑤ He has two safes in his basement.
11 sugar는 셀 수 없으므로 sugar로 써야 한다.
12 주어(Ryan)와 동사(has)를 쓰고 a lot of personalities라는 목적어를 쓰면 된다. personality는 셀 수 있는 명사이다.
13 '요즘은 한복을 입는 사람들이 거의 없다. 하지만 특별한 날에는 그것을 입는 사람들이 있다.'라는 의미가 되어야 자연스럽다. people이 셀 수 있는 명사이므로 부정의 의미로 few를 쓰면 된다.
14 '점심을 먹고 이를 닦는다'라는 내용으로 주어가 3인칭 단수 현재이므

로 brush를 brushes로 쓰고, tooth의 복수인 teeth로 쓰면 된다.

15 gentleman의 복수는 gentlemen이다. 셀 수 있는 명사가 '거의 없는'이란 뜻으로 few를 쓰면 된다.

16 참기름은 셀 수 없으므로 a little과 oil로 써야 한다.

06 부정관사와 정관사

1) a
2) an
3) a
4) an
5) 명사
6) The
7) the
8) 유일
9) The[the]
10) 악기
11) the
12) 수식어구
13) The
14) 운동
15) 교통수단
16) 소유
17) 목적

Level 1 Test
p. 36

A 1 ① an ② a   2 ① × ② ×
  3 ① × ② ×   4 ① a ② an

B 1 the   2 The
  3 an   4 The
  5 The

C 1 an   2 ×
  3 ×   4 the

D 1 the   2 The
  3 an   4 ×

Level 2 Test
p. 37

01 ③   02 ⑤
03 ⑤   04 ③
05 ④
06 an / a
07 The / ×
08 an pen-mouse → a pen-mouse / a mouse → the mouse
09 A year is[has] twelve months.
10 a old → an old / the breakfast → the 삭제

≫ 해설

01 물(water)은 셀 수 없는 명사로 a를 쓸 수 없다.

02 uniform의 발음은 [júːnəfɔ̀ːrm]으로 첫 소리가 모음이 아니라 a를 쓰고 나머지는 an을 쓴다.

03 세상에서 유일한 것 앞에는 정관사를 쓴다.

04 서로 알고 있는 경우에는 정관사 the를 쓴다.

05 yellow[jélou]는 발음이 모음으로 시작하지 않으므로 a를 써야 한다.

06 online이 모음으로 시작하므로 an을 쓴다. useful의 발음이 [júːsfəl]이므로 a를 써야 한다.

07 coach는 수식어구 of our team의 꾸밈을 받으므로 정관사가 필요하다. Istanbul은 고유명사로, 고유명사에는 관사를 쓰지 않는다.

08 pen-mouse는 자음으로 시작하므로 a를 써야 하고, but 뒤에서는 앞서 말한 것을 다시 말하므로 the를 써야 한다.

09 year는 셀 수 있는 단수 명사이고 자음으로 시작하므로 A year로 쓰고, month는 12개이므로 복수형으로 써야 한다.

10 모음 앞에는 an을 쓰며, 식사명에는 관사를 쓰지 않는다.

Level 3 Test
p. 38

01 ④   02 ①
03 ② ③ 04 ②
05 ② ⑤ 06 ②
07 ⑤   08 ②
09 ④   10 ②
11 ①
12 ⓐ a → the
13 The / the
14 a / an / a
15 × / an / the
16 ⓐ gray hair ⓓ an hourglass ⓔ the hourglass
17 isn't an artist / a UFC

≫ 해설

01 rice는 셀 수 없는 명사로 a를 쓰지 않는다.

02 ⓐ ⓒ 모음으로 시작하는 단수 명사라 an이 필요하다. ⓑ engineers가 복수이므로 부정관사를 쓰지 않는다. ⓓ 인칭대명사의 소유격과 관사는 함께 쓰지 않는다.

03 ② 악기 이름 앞에 정관사 the를 쓴다. ③ 수식받는 명사 앞에는 정관사 the를 쓴다.

04 • roses가 복수 명사이므로 불필요
   • expensive bag이 셀 수 있는 단수 명사이면서 모음으로 시작하므로 an
   • umbrella가 셀 수 있는 단수 명사이면서 모음으로 시작하므로 an
   • 악기 이름 앞에는 the를 쓴다.

05 ② 고유명사 앞에는 부정관사를 쓰지 않는다. (a John → John)
   ⑤ toys가 복수이므로 a를 빼야 한다.

06 hour는 셀 수 있는 단수 명사이면서 모음으로 시작하므로 an이 들어간다.

07 관사가 an이므로 모음으로 시작하는 단수 명사만 쓸 수 있다.

08 ⓐ The ⓓ a가 필요하다. 나머지는 관사가 필요 없다.

09 university는 발음이 모음으로 시작하는 단어가 아니기 때문에 a를 써야 한다.

10 ① a 삭제 ③ a 삭제 ④ a 삭제 ⑤ a → the

11 모두 문법적으로 틀린 부분이 없다.

12 악기 이름 앞에는 the를 쓴다.

13 수식을 받는 명사나 서로 알고 있는 경우에는 the를 쓴다.

14 pen과 ruler는 셀 수 있는 단수 명사이면서 자음이므로 a를 쓰고, eraser는 모음이므로 an을 쓴다.

15 운동 경기에는 관사를 쓰지 않는다. / 모음으로 시작하는 단수 명사이므로 an을 쓴다. / 서로 알고 있는 것이라 the를 쓴다.

16 ⓐ 머리카락은 셀 수 없는 명사이므로 부정관사를 쓰지 않는다. ⓓ hourglass는 발음이 모음으로 시작하므로 an으로 쓴다. ⓔ 앞에 나온 명사를 다시 쓰므로 the로 써야 한다.

17 be동사의 부정문인데 빈칸이 하나이므로 isn't를, artist는 모음으로 시작하므로 an을, UFC에서 U는 발음이 모음이 아니므로 a로 쓰면 된다.

지시 · 재귀대명사, 비인칭 주어

1) this 2) these 3) that
4) those 5) myself 6) yourself
7) himself 8) herself 9) itself
10) ourselves 11) yourselves 12) themselves
13) 날씨 14) 시간 15) 날짜
16) 요일 17) 계절 18) 명암
19) 거리

Level 1 Test

p. 40

A 1 These 2 that
  3 It 4 they

B 1 yourselves 2 ourselves
  3 themselves 4 themselves

C 1 = 2 ≠
  3 ≠ 4 =
  5 =

Level 2 Test

p. 41

01 ② 02 ②
03 ③ 04 ④
05 ① ② ④ ⑤ 06 Those are pictures of me.
07 It 08 sets the table for himself
09 (1) 달까지 얼마나 멀어? (2) 비인칭 주어
10 herself

》》 해설

01 ②는 지시형용사이고 나머지는 지시대명사이다.
02 ②는 강조 용법이고 [보기]와 나머지는 재귀적 용법이다.
03 ③은 인칭대명사이고 나머지는 비인칭 주어이다.
04 alone은 '홀로'이므로 by oneself와 바꿔 쓸 수 있다.
05 ① umbrella → umbrellas (주어가 복수이므로 umbrella도 복수로 써야 한다.) ② themselves → ourselves ④ himself → herself ⑤ this → it
06 That의 복수형은 Those이며 동사도 are로 써야 한다.
07 • 인칭대명사 It
   • 날씨를 나타내는 비인칭 주어 It
   • 날짜를 나타내는 비인칭 주어 It
08 set the table이 '상을 차리다'이고 '스스로'는 for oneself로 쓴다.
09 it은 거리를 나타내는 비인칭 주어로, 해석하지 않는다.
10 주어와 목적어가 같으면 재귀대명사를 쓴다.

Level 3 Test

p. 42

01 ② 02 ③
03 ② 04 ④
05 ④ 06 ③
07 ⑤ 08 ①
09 ④ 10 ⑤

11 ③
12 that / it isn't 또는 it's not
13 herself → her (myself도 가능)
14 It[it]
15 rains
16 It snows
17 Do you make these cakes yourselves?

》》 해설

01 this는 단수이므로 보어도 단수가 와야 한다.
02 복수 those가 아니라 단수 that이 되어야 한다.
03 ⓐ those → they ⓑ himself → itself ⓓ theirselves → themselves
04 ④는 인칭대명사이고 나머지는 비인칭 주어이다.
05 ④는 인칭대명사이고 [보기]와 나머지는 비인칭 주어이다.
06 She often speaks to herself in the bathroom.으로 영작할 수 있다.
07 ⑤는 강조적 용법이라 생략할 수 있다.
08 A: Is this your house? – B: No, it isn't.로 영작할 수 있다. this로 물으면 it으로 답한다.
09 us → ourselves로 써야 한다.
10 날씨를 표현하는 비인칭 주어이다.
11 주어가 단수(neighbor)이므로 themselves가 아니라 himself[herself]가 필요하다. (→ My neighbor lives by himself[herself].) ① He himself trains dogs. ② She loves herself very much. ④ The children cook for themselves. ⑤ I myself walk my dog every evening.
12 멀리 있는 단수는 that으로 쓰고, that으로 물으면 it으로 답한다.
13 소개하는 대상이 '그녀'이면 '소개하다'의 주체(me)와 목적어가 다르므로 재귀대명사를 쓰면 안 된다. 소개하는 대상이 '나'이면 myself를 쓴다.
14 • 비인칭 주어(시간)
   • 비인칭 주어(명암)
   • 인칭대명사
15 비인칭 주어로 날씨를 표현할 수 있다.
16 날씨를 나타내는 비인칭 주어 it을 쓴다.
17 you가 '여러분'이고 이를 강조하는 표현은 재귀대명사로 yourselves를 마지막에 쓰면 된다.

Review Test

p. 44

01 ④ 02 ②
03 ② 04 ⑤
05 ⑤ 06 ④
07 ③ 08 ④ ⑤
09 ② 10 ③
11 Are these your puppies?
12 ⓐ monkeis → monkeys
13 two bowls of rice
14 mice are
15 He drinks two bottles of coke
16 goes → go / by an bus → by bus
17 The 18 draws herself
19 × / an / ×

20 play badminton / breakfast / Sundays

21 ② ④

22 We go out and play ball together.

01 potato – potatoes, toy – toys로 써야 한다.

02 friends는 셀 수 있는 명사이므로 many가 필요하고, money는 셀 수 없는 명사이므로 much가 들어간다. a lot of는 둘 다 쓸 수 있다.

03 child의 복수형은 children이다.

04 ① times → time ② homeworks → homework ③ salts → salt ④ tooth → teeth

05 '종이 세 장'은 three pieces[sheets] of paper, '가위 하나'는 a pair of scissors로 쓴다.

06 ④는 강조적 용법이고 나머지는 재귀적 용법이다.

07 bananas가 왔으므로 복수형인 These가 와야 한다.

08 ④ 복수이므로 dress → dresses로 써야 한다. ⑤ 셀 수 없는 명사이므로 milks → milk로 바꿔야 한다.

09 학과목 앞에는 관사를 쓰지 않는다.

10 ⓒ와 ⓕ는 인칭대명사이고 나머지는 비인칭 주어이다.

11 this의 복수형은 these, puppy의 복수형은 puppies이다.

12 '모음+y'로 끝나는 단어는 -s만 붙여서 복수형을 만든다.

13 '밥 두 공기'는 two bowls of rice로 쓴다.

14 mouse의 복수형은 mice이고, 주어가 복수이므로 be동사는 are를 쓴다.

15 주어(he)와 동사(drinks)를 쓰고 목적어는 two bottles of coke로 쓴다.

16 주어가 복수이므로 goes → go로 고쳐야 하며, 「by+무관사+교통수단」으로 쓰므로 an을 a로 쓰는 것이 아니라 빼야 한다.

17 • 앞서 말한 명사를 재언급할 때 정관사 the 사용
 • 수식받는 명사 앞에서 정관사 the 사용
 • 유일한 것 앞에 정관사 the 사용

18 주어가 3인칭 단수이므로 동사는 draws로 쓰고, 주어와 목적어가 같으므로 재귀대명사(herself)로 써야 한다.

19 나라 이름 앞에 관사를 쓰지 않는다. / English teacher가 셀 수 있는 단수 명사이면서 모음으로 시작하므로 an을 쓴다. / 언어 앞에는 관사를 쓰지 않는다.

20 운동 경기와 식사명 앞에는 관사를 쓰지 않으며, '일요일마다'는 on Sundays 또는 every Sunday라고 쓴다.

21 ⓑ by oneself는 '홀로'라는 뜻으로 herself로 고쳐야 한다. ⓓ 일반동사의 부정이므로 isn't가 아닌 doesn't로 고쳐야 한다.

22 주어는 We, '나가서 논다'는 go out and play로 쓰고, 운동(공놀이) 앞에는 관사를 쓰지 않으므로 a를 삭제하고 together를 쓰면 된다.

[17~18]

나는 학교에서 집으로 돌아와 문을 연다. Max가 나에게 달려들어 자신의 꼬리를 흔든다. Kitty는 소파 위에 홀로 있다. 그녀는 내려와서 자신의 얼굴을 나의 발에 비빈다. 나는 고양이 먹이 박스를 열어 약간의 먹이를 Kitty에게 준다. 하지만 Max는 어떤 먹이도 원하지 않는다. 그는 문으로 걸어간다. 그는 약간 짖고서는 자신의 코를 문에 갖다 댄다. 그는 "우리 나가요."라고 말한다. <u>우리는 밖으로 나가서 공놀이를 함께 한다.</u>

• 어휘 • jump at ~에게 달려들다 | tail 꼬리 | rub 비비다 | bark 짖다 | a bit 약간

CHAPTER 03

08 be동사의 과거형

1) was
2) was not
3) wasn't
4) was
5) was not
6) wasn't
7) were
8) were not
9) weren't
10) Was/Were
11) was/were
12) wasn't/weren't

Level 1 Test
p. 48

A 1 was
2 was
3 were
4 was

B 1 I wasn't very sick.
2 We weren't friends.
3 Jack and Tina weren't in my house.
4 The director wasn't very happy.
5 The rocks weren't from the moon.

C 1 Was she sad?
2 Was their dog quiet?
3 Was his father a computer expert?
4 Were you and Jimin very close?

D 1 were
2 was
3 어색한 곳 없음
4 어색한 곳 없음
5 어색한 곳 없음

Level 2 Test
p. 49

01 ④
02 ③
03 ②
04 ③

05 Were[were]

06 Was / is

07 ⓐ not was → were not[weren't]

08 Were those shoes over 50,000 won?

09 My great-grandfather was a freedom fighter.

01 주어가 단수이고 과거이므로 was를 써야 한다.

02 be동사의 과거형은 주어와 줄여 쓸 수 없다.

03 be동사 과거형의 의문문은 be동사를 앞에 쓰고 물음표를 하면 된다.

04 ⓒ were → are (또는 now → then) ⓔ Were → Was ⓕ wasn't → isn't으로 써야 한다.

05 주어가 복수이고 시제가 과거(last night, yesterday)이므로 were를 쓰면 된다.

06 첫 번째는 B의 대답이 Yes it was.로 되어 있는 것으로 보아 과거형으로 질문을 해야 하고, 두 번째는 현재(now)이기 때문에 현재형으로

써야 한다.

07 주어가 복수(children)이므로 were를 쓰고, 부정문은 were 다음에 not을 쓴다.

08 「be동사의 과거형＋주어 ～?」 순으로 의문문을 만들면 된다.

09 주어(My great-grandfather)가 단수이고 과거형이므로 was로 쓴다.

Level 3 Test

p. 50

01 ②   02 ①
03 ⑤   04 ④
05 ①   06 ① ④
07 ④   08 ④
09 ② ④   10 ④
11 ④ ⑤
12 The cat[kitten] was not
13 (A) was (B) is (C) is (D) were
14 He was not with me last night.
15 Were / No, they weren't / were
16 Were you at the party three days ago?

≫ 해설

01 과거 부사(last night, yesterday)가 있으므로 과거형으로 써야 한다.

02 주어가 단수면 was, 복수이면 were를 쓴다.

03 B의 응답이 남자(he)이며 과거(was)이므로 ⑤가 적절하다.

04 B에서 그들이 카메룬에 있었다는 것으로 보아 「No, 주어＋weren't.」로 부정으로 답해야 한다.

05 is의 과거형의 부정은 was not 또는 wasn't이다.

06 ① 주어(Harriet and her brother)가 복수이므로 was → were로 바꿔야 한다. ④ *Les Misérables*은 책 또는 영화 제목으로 단수 취급해야 한다. (were → was)

07 ⓑ에서 주어(these tables)가 복수라 Were로 써야 한다.

08 게임이 지루했다고 했으므로 만족하지 못했을 것이다. 그리고 시제가 과거(yesterday)라서 were not 또는 weren't가 답이다.

09 ① ③ ⑤ Were → Was

10 ⓑ was → were ⓓ Were → Are (또는 now → then)

11 ④ Physics were my favorite subject. (were → was) ⑤ The weather is really bad yesterday. (is → was) ① I was there last night. ② Your answer was not right. ③ Were his sons baseball players?

12 고양이가 커다란 개를 무서워하지 않고 있으므로 부정문으로 써야 하며, 4단어이므로 was not으로 쓰면 된다.

13 (A) 과거(yesterday)이므로 was로 써야 한다.
   (B) 출신은 현재 시제로 쓴다.
   (C) 현재(now)이므로 is로 쓴다.
   (D) 과거(last year)이므로 were를 쓴다.

14 주어를 대명사로 쓰고, be동사의 현재형을 부정의 과거형으로 바꾸고, 시간 부사를 괄호 안의 과거 부사로 바꾸면 된다.

15 A: 주어가 복수이고 과거(yesterday)이므로 Were로 쓴다.
   B: 도서관이 아니라 피시방에 있었으므로 No, they weren't.로 답하고, 마지막 빈칸은 과거 시제이므로 were로 써야 한다.

16 be동사 과거형의 의문문이고, 당신들은 you이므로 Were you at the party three days ago?로 쓰면 된다.

UNIT 09 일반동사의 과거형

1) ＋-ed   2) ＋-d   3) y → i＋-ed
4) 자음＋자음＋-ed 5) came   6) went
7) did   8) had   9) hit
10) said   11) drank   12) met
13) taught   14) cut   15) got
16) spoke   17) thought   18) found
19) hurt   20) bought   21) brought
22) took   23) sat   24) read
25) did not   26) didn't   27) Did
28) did   29) did not   30) didn't

Level 1 Test

p. 52

A 1 studied   2 enjoyed
   3 took   4 saved
   5 met   6 played
   7 left

B 1 My son baked bread.
   2 They didn't collect cans and paper.
   3 She didn't lose her math textbook.
   4 Did they have a pet dog?
   5 Did somebody sleep in my bed?

Level 2 Test

p. 53

01 ⑤   02 ④ ⑤
03 ③   04 ④ ⑤
05 went / didn't buy
06 (A) Did (B) did (C) swam
07 He did not answer the phone.
08 (1) put (2) didn't put (3) Did / put

≫ 해설

01 과거 부사 yesterday가 있으므로 과거형을 쓴다. write의 과거형은 wrote이다.

02 동사(went)가 과거이므로 미래를 나타내는 어구는 적절하지 않다.

03 2020년이므로 과거이고, win의 과거형은 won이다.

04 ① understood → understand ② liked → like ③ doesn't → didn't

05 첫 번째는 과거(last weekend)이므로 went로 써야 한다. 두 번째는 직판점에서 빈손으로 나오고 있으므로 부정형인 didn't buy가 알맞다.

06 (A) 과거(yesterday)이고 일반동사(swim)가 있으므로 Did로 쓴다.
   (B) Did로 물었으므로 did로 답을 한다.
   (C) swim의 과거형은 swam이다.

07 주어는 He이고 일반동사 과거형의 부정문은 「did not＋동사원형」으로 쓴다.

08 put의 과거형은 put이고, 부정문은 「didn't＋동사원형」이며, 의문문은 「Did＋주어＋동사원형 ～?」으로 만든다.

01 ③   02 ④
03 ⑤   04 ① ②
05 ④   06 ③
07 ④   08 ④
09 ③ ⑤   10 ④
11 saw / see / didn't see
12 pick → picked / was gave → gave
13 drew / made / didn't know / saw / laughed
14 Mom called me, but I didn't get up.
15 A: Did
   B: Yes, she did / rode
   A: Did
   B: No, he didn't / had[ate]

≫ 해설

01 replyed → replied / huged → hugged / growed → grew
02 과거(yesterday)이므로 leave도 과거형으로 써야 한다.
03 과거(last night)이므로 현재형은 어울리지 않는다.
04 ① didn't 다음에 동사원형을 쓰므로 draw로 쓴다. ② 과거 (last night)이므로 didn't go로 써야 한다.
05 buy의 과거형은 bought이고, 과거형의 부정문은 「didn't+동사원형」이다.
06 didn't 다음에 동사원형을 써야 하므로 didn't have로 쓴다.
07 didn't 다음에는 동사원형을 써야 한다. (saw → see)
08 ⓒ reads → read ⓔ be 삭제
09 didn't 다음에는 동사원형이 와야 하는데 ③과 ⑤는 각각 과거형과 3인칭 단수 현재형이 왔다.
10 (A) ⓑ wrote → write (B) ⓐ plaied → played (C) ⓐ said → say (E) ⓐ cleaned → clean로 고쳐야 한다.
11 A는 내용상 과거이므로 saw와 일반동사의 과거형 의문문이므로 see, B는 내용상 아무것도 못 본 것이므로 didn't see를 쓰면 된다.
12 pick을 과거형으로 고치고 was gave는 '~이었다 주었다'라는 의미가 되어 '~이었다'가 불필요하다. 일반동사가 있으면 be동사를 빼야 한다.
13 시제가 과거(Last night)이므로 모두 과거형으로 쓰면 된다. 내용상 know는 부정문으로 써야 한다.
14 A, but B 구조로 쓰며 주어는 각각 Mom과 I이고 이에 맞는 동사는 called, didn't get up으로 쓰면 된다.
15 제목에서 그림 일기(picture diary)라고 했으므로 과거형으로 써야 하고 의문문은 「Did+주어+동사원형」으로, 대답은 「Yes, 주어+did.」 또는 「No, 주어+didn't.」로 한다. ride의 과거형은 rode, have의 과거형은 had, eat의 과거형은 ate이다.

UNIT 10 진행 시제

1) +-ing   2) -e를 빼고 +-ing
3) -ie → y+-ing   4) 자음+자음+-ing
5) am not   6) are not[aren't]
7) is not[isn't]   8) Am
9) Are   10) Is
11) am   12) am not
13) are   14) are not[aren't]
15) is   16) is not[isn't]
17) was not[wasn't]   18) were not[weren't]
19) Was   20) Were
21) was   22) was not[wasn't]
23) were   24) were not[weren't]

A 1 I am[I'm] working on a farm.
  2 My father is running in the park.
  3 Yumi is not[isn't] making coffee for me.
  4 She is not[She isn't, She's not] hitting the nail on the wall.

B 1 are watching   2 isn't raining
  3 wasn't driving

01 ④   02 ⑤
03 ④   04 ③
05 doing / She is catching
06 Somebody was watching me in the dark.
07 She is peeling a cucumber.
08 Foolishly, he was lying to his lawyer.
09 (A) Were   (B) wasn't   (C) was

≫ 해설

01 우리말이 현재 시제이므로 현재 진행형으로 쓰고, write의 -ing형은 writing이다.
02 eat의 -ing형은 eating으로 과거 진행형인 ⑤가 답이다.
03 ① isn't → doesn't ② began → begin ③ begining → beginning ⑤ 과거 진행형 의문문으로 바꿔야 하는데 현재 진행형 의문문으로 바꿨다. (Is → Was)
04 ⓑ swiming → swimming ⓒ aren't → don't 또는 speak → speaking ⓔ does → is
05 A는 진행형이므로 doing으로 쓴다. B도 진행형이므로 is catching을 쓴다.
06 주어를 쓰고 진행형(be+-ing)을 이어 써서 답을 완성해 나가면 된다.
07 「주어+be+-ing」 순으로 쓰면 되고, peel(껍질을 벗기다)의 -ing형은 peeling이다.
08 시제가 과거(lied)이므로 과거 진행형으로 써야 한다. lie의 -ing형은 lying이다.
09 (A) -ing형(jogging)과 과거(yesterday morning)이므로 과거 진행

형 의문문이다.

(B) 이에 대한 부정의 답이다.

(C)도 역시 과거 진행형으로 쓰면 된다.

Level 3 Test
p. 58

01 ②　　　　　　　　　　　02 ③
03 ①　　　　　　　　　　　04 ③
05 ② ④　　　　　　　　　　06 ④
07 ④　　　　　　　　　　　08 ③
09 ⑤　　　　　　　　　　　10 ③ ⑤

11 I am doing Pilates right now. 또는 I'm doing Pilates right now.

12 ⓑ is wanting → wants

13 (1) is watering　(2) are sleeping　(3) are playing
(4) is reading

14 wasn't speeding / weren't / ran

≫ 해설

01 eat의 -ing형은 eating이다.

02 B가 진행형으로 답한 것으로 보아 진행형으로 물어야 한다.

03 감정을 나타내는 말은 진행형으로 쓰지 못한다. ④에서 have동사는 동작을 나타내므로 진행형으로 쓸 수 있다.

04 ⓒ 현재 진행형이므로 are making으로 써야 한다. ⓓ are walking은 주어(Many people)가 복수라 맞는 답이다.

05 대답이 She이고 현재 진행형이므로 질문은 3인칭 단수 여자이면서 현재 진행형으로 물어야 한다. ③의 your friend는 she가 될 수 있기 때문에 어색하지 않다.

06 · 일반동사(feed)이므로 Did
· 주어가 3인칭 복수(they)인 진행형의 의문문
· 주어가 3인칭 복수(his brothers)인 진행형의 의문문

07 · 상태를 나타내는 동사는 진행형을 쓸 수 없으므로 현재형 know를 쓴다.
· now가 있으므로 현재 진행형으로 써야 한다.

08 ③ babys → babies, sleeping → sleeping, a → an: 3개 ① 틀린 것 없음 ② Is he having → Does he have: 2개 ④ cring → crying, don't → am not: 2개 ⑤ 틀린 것 없음

09 exciting은 진행형이 아니고 형용사이다.

10 과거 진행형으로 물었으므로 과거 진행형으로 답한다. ③ did watching → was watching ⑤ drank → was drinking

11 주어가 I이고 현재 진행형으로 I am doing을 기본으로 문장을 완성하면 된다.

12 소유를 나타내는 동사는 진행형으로 쓰지 않는다.

13 주어가 3인칭 단수이면 is, 복수이면 are를 쓰고 각 동사의 -ing형을 쓰면 된다.

14 Lily가 과속을 하지 않았으나 신호 위반을 했다는 내용으로 첫 번째 빈칸에는 과거 진행형의 부정형, 두 번째는 이에 대한 답, 세 번째는 단순 과거형으로 쓰면 된다.

Review Test
p. 60

01 ③　　　　　　　　　　　02 ②
03 ②　　　　　　　　　　　04 ⑤
05 ① ⑤　　　　　　　　　　06 ③
07 ⑤　　　　　　　　　　　08 ④

09 ④　　　　　　　　　　　10 ⑤
11 weren't / were
12 Was she okay now? → Is she okay now?
13 was / wasn't
14 Was Fred at the library / he wasn't
15 (1) fought　(2) drove　(3) made　(4) hit
16 sing → sang
17 (1) She is changing her mind.
(2) Was he cutting the red ribbon?
18 ⓒ → visited ⓔ → rain
19 (1) studied　(2) didn't study　(3) studied
20 answered, study
21 ① ⑤
22 I bought a hand fan for my friend in Canada.

≫ 해설

01 주어(it)가 단수이고 과거(yesterday)이므로 Was를 써야 한다.

02 둘 다 과거 부사(at that moment, yesterday)가 쓰였으므로 과거형을 써야 한다.

03 주어(Her pet dogs)가 복수이고 과거(a few years ago)이므로 was가 아닌 were로 써야 한다.

04 ⑤는 현재라 does가, 나머지는 과거 부사가 있어서 did가 들어간다.

05 ① fall의 과거형은 fell이다. ⑤ wash의 과거형은 washed이다.

06 didn't 다음에는 동사원형이 와야 한다. (felt → feel)

07 B의 대답으로 보아 과거형으로 물었고, sleep의 과거는 slept이다.

08 · 과거(last week)이고 일반동사(invite)가 있으므로 didn't
· 내용상 과거이고 일반동사(go off)가 있으므로 didn't

09 현재 진행형으로 물었으므로 현재 진행형으로 답해야 한다.

10 cry의 과거형은 cried, 현재분사형은 crying이다.

11 시제는 과거이고 마지막 문장에서 훈련을 끝냈다고 했으므로 두 번째에는 were가, 첫 번째에는 반대인 weren't가 와야 자연스럽다.

12 now라는 현재 부사가 있으므로 현재형(Is)으로 써야 한다.

13 현재 14살이고 중학생이므로 작년에 13살이었다고 과거형 was를 쓴다. / 그때[작년]는 초등학생이었고 중학생이 아니었으므로 was not이 들어가야 하는데 빈칸이 하나이므로 줄여 쓴다.

14 주어(Fred)가 단수이므로 「Was + 주어 ~?」로 의문문을 만들고, 답변은 No로 시작하므로 「주어 + wasn't」로 답한다.

15 각 동사의 과거형은 fight–fought, drive–drove, make–made, hit–hit이다.

16 sing을 과거형 sang으로 고쳐야 한다.

17 (1) 현재형이므로 is + -ing
(2) cut이 현재형이라면 주어가 3인칭 단수이므로 cuts로 써야 한다. 하지만 cut–cut에서 과거형이 쓰인 것으로 시제는 과거이다.

18 ⓒ 글의 내용이 과거이므로 과거형 visited로 쓴다. ⓔ didn't 다음에는 동사원형을 써야 한다.

19 (1)은 과거형으로, (2)는 내용상 부정형으로 써야 한다. (3)은 영어 말고 수학을 공부했다는 의미이므로 긍정형으로 써야 한다.

20 다음과 같이 영작 가능하다.
A: Hey! You didn't answer my call. What were you doing?
B: (I'm) Sorry. I was studying.

21 ⓐ take의 과거형은 took ⓔ didn't 다음에는 동사원형이 온다.
(→ didn't finish)

22 buy의 과거형은 bought이고 '~을 위해'는 for를 이용하여 쓴다.

엄마와 나는 북촌 한옥 마을에 갔다. 우리는 마을 주변을 걸어다녔다. 우리는 오래된 집과 골목의 사진을 찍었다. 그것은 특별한 경험이었다. 그리고 나서 우리는 인사동으로 이동했다. 우리는 길을 따라 있는 많은 전통 골동품 가게와 식당들을 봤다. 나는 캐나다에 있는 친구를 위해 부채를 하나 샀다. 우리는 길거리에서 떡볶이를 먹었다. 그것은 맛있었으나 매우 매워서, 나는 그것을 다 먹지 않았다. 곧 그것을 다음에 또 먹어보고 싶다.

• 어휘 • village 마을 | take a picture of ~의 사진을 찍다 | special 특별한 | experience 경험 | traditional 전통적인 | hand fan 부채 | spicy 매운 | finish (음식을) 다 먹다

CHAPTER 04

UNIT 11 can, may

1) 조동사
2) not
3) 동사원형
4) 동사원형
5) could
6) cannot[can't]
7) be able to
8) be not able to
9) ~일 리다 없다
10) may
11) may not
12) might
13) may not
14) ~일지도 모른다
15) can
16) cannot

Level 1 Test
p. 64

A 1 drive   2 may
  3 Can you

B 1 Can dolphins talk to each other?
  2 We couldn't[could not] make a snowman.

C 1 I am[I'm] able to   2 Are you able to
  3 were not[weren't] able to

Level 2 Test
p. 65

01 ③   02 ②
03 ③   04 ②
05 ③
06 are able to
07 may be harmful
08 (1) May I put off today's work until tomorrow?

(2) Can I put off today's work until tomorrow?
09 may not

》》 해설

01 [보기]와 ③은 '추측'이고 나머지는 '허락'의 의미이다.
02 [보기]와 ②는 '능력, 가능'이고 나머지는 '허락'의 의미이다.
03 주어진 문장은 여권을 봐도 되는지 '허락'을 구하고 있다. may 대신 허락의 의미로 쓰일 수 있는 조동사는 can이다.
04 Was Ashley able to save him?이 옳은 문장으로, 세 번째 올 단어는 able이다.
05 ① came → come ② washes → wash ④ use not → not use ⑤ happy → be happy
06 can을 be able to로 바꾸어 쓸 때에는 be동사를 주어의 인칭과 수에 일치시켜야 한다.
07 harmful은 형용사이므로 be동사가 필요하다.
08 '~해도 되나요?'라는 뜻의 허락을 구할 때는 may 또는 can을 쓸 수 있다.
09 '~ 아닐지도 모른다'라는 부정의 추측을 나타낼 때는 may not을 쓴다.

Level 3 Test
p. 66

01 ②   02 ③
03 ②   04 ②
05 ②   06 ⑤
07 ③   08 ⑤
09 ③   10 ③
11 ② ③ ④
12 ⓒ cans → can
13 weren't able to
14 cannot[can't]
15 He may not be wrong.
16 May[Can] I speak to
17 You can successful at work. → You can be successful at work.

》》 해설

01 ②는 '추측'이고 나머지는 '허락'의 의미이다.
02 You can't miss it.은 '너는 그것을 놓칠 수 없을 것이다.' 즉 '쉽게 찾을 것이다.'라는 뜻이다.
03 ⓒ 조동사 may 다음에 동사원형 go가 와야 한다. ⓓ 조동사는 나란히 쓸 수 없으므로 may나 can 둘 중에 하나를 쓰거나 may be able to로 바꿔야 한다.
04 '가능'을 나타내는 조동사 can이다. (여러분은 박물관에서 반 고흐의 일부 위대한 작품들을 볼 수 있습니다. 그리고 또한 오디오 플레이어로 설명을 들을 수 있습니다. 즐거운 관람 되시길 바랍니다.)
05 • 공손한 표현의 could
   • '~할 수 있었다'라는 의미이므로 can의 과거형인 could
06 ⓓ, ⓕ는 '허락'이고 나머지는 '능력'의 의미이다.
07 '추측'의 may가 문맥상 알맞다. (그가 옳을지도 모르지만 나는 그를 이해할 수 없다.)
08 허락을 묻는 질문인 May I ~?에 대한 대답으로 may와 can 둘 다 가능하다. 승낙의 표현인 ① Of course. ③ Go ahead.도 가능하다. ⑤는 의미상 No, you can't.가 되어야 한다.
09 ① can과 be able to는 같은 의미이다. ② 조동사 will과 can이 같이

쓰일 수 없다. ④ fixes → fix ⑤ will과 may가 같이 쓰일 수 없다.

10 내용상 럭비를 할 수 없으니 가르쳐 줄 수 있냐는 뜻이므로 부정의 대답 No, I can't.가 알맞다.

11 ② 조동사는 나란히 쓰일 수 없다. (→ Will humans be able to live forever?) ③ 조동사 뒤에는 동사원형을 쓴다. (is → be) ④ 조동사 다음에 동사가 없다. (can't → can't be)

12 주어가 3인칭 단수여도 조동사에는 -(e)s를 붙일 수 없다.

13 can't = be not able to이다. could는 과거형이므로 be동사의 과거형을 주어에 맞추어 쓴다.

14 '~하면 안 된다'는 의미로 1단어로 쓸 수 있는 말은 cannot[can't]이다.

15 「may not+동사원형」의 어순으로 쓴다. is의 동사원형은 be이다.

16 '허락'을 묻는 May는 Can으로 바꿔 쓸 수 있다. 전화상에서 '~와 통화할 수 있을까요?'라는 말은 조동사 May나 Can으로 물어볼 수 있다.

17 successful(성공한)이 형용사이므로 조동사 can 다음에 be동사가 필요하다. (당신은 자주 미소 지으시나요? 미소가 왜 그렇게 중요할까요? 당신의 미소 때문에, 당신은 멋진 남자친구 또는 여자친구를 찾을 수 있습니다. 당신은 일에서 성공할 수 있습니다. 당신은 당신의 꿈의 직업을 얻을 수 있습니다. 당신은 많은 친구를 가질 수 있습니다. 미소는 성공을 만들 수 있습니다. 당신의 미소를 아끼지 마십시오. 미소 지으세요.)

12 UNIT will, be going to

1) will not[won't]
2) will not[won't]
3) be not going to
4) going to
5) ~할 것이다
6) ~로 가고 있는 중이다
7) ~로 갈 것이다

Level 1 Test
p. 68

A 1 to take
   2 will
   3 leave
   4 this evening

B 1 Will
   2 not going to

C 1 They will not[won't] travel by boat.
   2 Are you going to cancel the meeting?
   3 Will Bob go hiking this weekend?

D 1 Yes, she is
   2 No, I won't

Level 2 Test
p. 69

01 ③
02 ②
03 ③
04 ⑤
05 ⑤
06 Will[will]
07 Divers will search the bottom of the lake.
08 is not going to
09 Will he visit us tomorrow?
10 They will not[won't] listen to me.

≫ 해설

01 미래 부사 tomorrow가 있으므로 미래 시제를 써야 한다.

02 • ago가 과거 부사이므로 was
    • now가 현재 부사이므로 is
    • in the future가 미래 부사이므로 「will+동사원형」

03 미래를 나타내는 this weekend가 있고 주어 you 뒤에 going to가 있는 것으로 보아 Are가 와야 한다. (미래 조동사 will = be going to)

04 [보기]와 ⑤는 현재 진행형(~로 가고 있는 중이다)이고 ①, ④는 미래(~할 것이다), ②, ③은 미래(~로 갈 것이다)이다.

05 ① to do → do ② will과 be going to는 같은 의미이므로 둘 중 하나만 쓴다. ③ to give → give ④ will can → will be able to 또는 can

06 미래 시제를 나타낼 때는 조동사 will을 쓴다. will로 물어보면 will로 답한다.

07 주어로 divers를 쓰고 조동사 will 뒤에 동사원형 search를 쓴 후, 목적어로 the bottom of the lake를 쓰면 된다. (잠수부들은 호수 바닥을 수색할 것이다.)

08 will not[won't] = be not going to

09 「조동사+주어+동사원형 ~?」의 순서로 한다. 5단어로 써야 하므로 be going to는 안 되고 will을 써야 한다.

10 will의 부정형은 will not[won't]이다. (그들은 내 말을 듣지 않을 것이다.)

Level 3 Test
p. 70

01 ③
02 ②
03 ④
04 ②
05 ②
06 ②
07 ③
08 ②
09 ④
10 ④
11 ⓑ Be → Is
12 (1) No, he isn't. 또는 No, he's not.
    (2) Yes, he will.
13 Are you going to skip lunch?
14 is going to have a potluck party with her friends
15 ① ④

≫ 해설

01 미래를 나타내는 soon이 있고, 주어 Betty가 3인칭 단수이며, 뒤에 going to가 있는 것으로 보아 Is가 와야 한다.

02 미래 조동사 will은 be going to와 바꿔 쓸 수 있으며, 의문문이고 주어가 you이므로 be동사 are가 주어 앞에 위치한다.

03 ⓑ will → will be ⓒ busy → be busy ⓓ will visited → will visit ⓔ you are → are you

04 • every day가 있으므로 현재 시제 drink
    • yesterday가 있으므로 과거 시제 drank
    • tomorrow가 있으므로 미래 will drink

05 • 음식을 권유하는 표현
    • 미래 부사(in the future)와 함께 쓰일 수 있는 조동사
    두 경우 모두 쓰일 수 있는 것은 will이다.

06 ⓐ ⓒ '~로 가고 있는 중이다' ⓑ ⓔ '~할 것이다' ⓓ '~로 갈 것이다'

07 조동사 will은 미래 부사와 함께 쓰일 수 있다. 과거 부사 before(전에)와는 쓰일 수 없다.

08 「be going to+동사원형」으로 물었으므로 「Yes, 주어+be동사.」 또는 「No, 주어+be동사+not.」으로 답한다.

09 Will it ~?으로 물어보면 부정의 대답은 No, it won't.로 답하는 것이 알맞다.

10 ④ hurry(서두르다)는 일반동사로, 앞에 be동사가 필요 없다. (won't be → won't)

11 주어가 3인칭 단수(Sally)이므로 Be는 Is로 바꾸어야 한다.

12 (1) 수학이 아니라 과학 숙제를 할 것이라고 했으므로 부정의 대답이 알맞다. 「be going to+동사원형」으로 물었으므로 「No, 주어+be동사+not.」으로 답한다.
   (2) Danny가 Sam을 도와주기로 했으므로 긍정의 대답이 알맞다. will로 물었으므로 will을 써서 답한다.

13 go를 going으로 바꾸어 미래 시제로 써야 알맞다.

14 Amy가 포트럭 파티를 열며 친구들에게 초대장을 보내는 내용이다. 주어 Amy에 알맞은 미래 동사형 is going to가 들어가야 알맞다.

15 ① 친구들이 시장에 가고 있는 내용은 알 수 없다. ② Amy가 친구들에게 파티에 오라고 초대장을 쓴 내용이므로 알맞다. ③ Amy는 자기 집에서 파티를 할 예정이다. ④ 친구들에게 좋아하는 음식을 가져오라고 했으므로 모든 음식을 만들지는 않을 것이다. ⑤ 파티가 끝나고 청소를 친구들과 같이 하자고 했다.

[14~15]

포트럭 파티 초대

친구들과 함께 포트럭 파티를 합시다.
좋아하는 음식을 가져와서 나눌 수 있습니다.
우리는 파티 후 함께 청소할 겁니다.

- 언제: 11월 11일 오후 6시
- 어디서: 하버드 거리 2577 Amy의 집에서
Amy에게 123-456-7890으로 회신 바람

UNIT 13 must, should

1) 의무
2) have/has to
3) must not
4) don't/doesn't have[need] to
5) need not
6) ~임에 틀림없다
7) cannot[can't]
8) Must
9) ought to
10) ought not to

Level 1 Test
p. 72

A
1 don't have[need] to
2 ought not
3 have to
4 must be
5 cannot[can't] be

B
1 have to
2 Does / have to
3 need not
4 ought to

01 ②
02 ①
03 ③
04 ②
05 ②
06 ought not to
07 cannot[can't] be
08 We had to study all day long.
09 doesn't → didn't

≫ 해설

01 의미상 '인스턴트 음식을 먹으면 안 된다'가 자연스러우므로 must not이 알맞다.

02 ①은 '강한 추측'이고 나머지는 '의무'이다.

03 '우리는 이기적이어서는 안 된다. 그 대신에, 우리는 베풀어야 한다.'가 의미상 자연스러우므로 빈칸에 들어갈 알맞은 말은 should not이다.

04 ⓐ, ⓑ, ⓓ는 불필요를 나타내는 '~할 필요 없다'이고, ⓒ, ⓔ, ⓕ는 금지를 나타내는 '~하면 안 된다'이다.

05 ② needs not은 조동사이므로 need not이 되어야 한다.

06 should not은 ought not to로 바꿔 쓸 수 있다.

07 cannot[can't] be는 '~일 리 없다'라는 뜻이다.

08 '~해야 한다'라는 의무를 나타내는 조동사의 과거형은 had to이다.

09 '~할 필요가 없다'는 don't/doesn't have to의 과거 표현은 didn't have to이다.

Level 3 Test
p. 74

01 ③
02 ②
03 ③
04 ②
05 ②
06 ①
07 ③
08 ④
09 ①
10 ② ③ ④
11 No, you don't have[need] to. 또는 No, you need not.
12 ought not to
13 Drivers ought to obey the speed limit. 또는 Drivers should obey the speed limit.
14 Tommy
15 (1) must[have to]   (2) had to   (3) have to
16 said to myself / cannot[can't] be alive

≫ 해설

01 don't/doesn't need to: ~할 필요 없다 (Philip은 방을 청소할 필요 없다. Susie가 오늘 아침에 청소했다.)

02 금지를 나타내는 must not(~하면 안 된다)은 may not과 비슷한 의미이다.

03 ⓑ have to → has to ⓒ will must → will have to 또는 must ⓓ must not to make → must not make

04 don't have to: ~할 필요 없다 / ought to: ~해야 한다

05 '~해야 한다'와 '~임에 틀림없다'라는 뜻으로 둘 다 쓸 수 있는 조동사는 must이다.

06 ⓐ ⓓ ⓔ '~임에 틀림없다' ⓑ ⓒ '~해야 한다'

07 심한 치통이 있다고 했으므로 치과에 가라고 충고를 해야 한다. 충고의 조동사는 should이다.

08 last week로 보아 과거 시제 문장이므로 had to가 알맞다.

09 몸이 좋아 보이지 않으므로 '아픈 것이 틀림없다'고 하는 것이 적절하다.

10 ② to do → do ③ to buy → buy ④ don't 삭제 (또는 don't → not)

11 '주말에는 문을 열지 않는다'는 말이 이어지므로 '토요일에는 일할 필요 없다'는 불필요의 답이 알맞다.

12 should not = ought not to: ~하면 안 된다

13 ought to+동사원형: ~해야 한다(= should)

14 Tommy가 must be(~임에 틀림없다)로 강한 긍정의 추측을 하고 있다.

15 must가 의무, 필요를 나타내는 과거나 미래 표현에는 쓰이지 않으므로 had to와 will have to 형태로 써야 한다.

16 첫 번째 빈칸에는 말하는 대상이 주어와 같으므로 재귀대명사를 사용하고, 두 번째 빈칸에는 '~일 리가 없다'는 cannot[can't]을 이용한다.

Review Test
p. 76

01 ②   02 ③
03 ③   04 ④
05 ②   06 ①
07 ⑤   08 ①
09 ④   10 ⑤
11 should wear
12 don't have[need] to
13 Were they able to
14 should 또는 must
15 Will[will]
16 Are you going to
17 You must not bring your pets.
18 No, I won't.
19 Did he have to go home?
20 may 또는 might
21 ① ③ ⑤
22 I am going to get a good night's sleep.

≫ 해설

01 허락의 may는 can과 바꿔 쓸 수 있으므로 대답도 can이 가능하다. ②는 '불필요'의 뜻으로 Must I ~?에 대한 대답이 될 수 있다.

02 be able to는 '~할 수 있다'는 의미로 can과 같은 뜻이다.

03 Will을 Are로 또는 going을 go로 고쳐야 한다.

04 ought to(~해야 한다)의 부정형은 ought not to이다.

05 ⓓ에서 must는 '추측'의 뜻으로 쓰였다.

06 the day before yesterday는 '그제'라는 뜻의 과거 부사이다. 조동사 will은 과거 부사와 함께 쓰일 수 없다.

07 ⑤는 「be going to+명사」(~로 가고 있는 중이다)라는 의미의 현재진행형이고, 나머지는 「be going to+동사원형」(~할 것이다)라는 뜻으로 미래의 예정된 일이나 계획을 나타내는 표현이다.

08 ② 조동사는 나란히 쓸 수 없다. (must can → must be able to 또는 can) ③ don't need not → don't need[have] to 또는 need not(~할 필요 없다) ④ have → have to ⑤ has → had to

09 '~하면 안 된다'라는 의미의 말에는 may not, must not, should not 등이 있다.

10 ①~④의 must는 '의무'를 나타내는 '~해야 한다'의 뜻이고, ⑤는 '~임에 틀림없다'는 '추측'의 의미이다.

11 should(~해야 한다) 다음에는 동사원형이 오므로 주어가 3인칭 단수라도 should wear를 써야 한다.

12 don't have to는 have to(~해야 한다)의 부정으로 '~할 필요가 없다'는 뜻이다. don't need to도 같은 의미의 표현이다. need not도 같은 의미이지만 빈칸 개수가 맞지 않는다.

13 could는 was/were able to와 바꿔 쓸 수 있고, 주어가 they이므로 Were가 문장 앞으로 가서 의문문을 만든다.

14 도덕적 의무, 경고를 나타내는 조동사 should 또는 의무를 나타내는 must가 알맞다.

15 • be going to = will(~할 것이다): 미래 표현
• Can you ~? = Will you ~?: '~해줄래?'의 요청 표현
두 경우에 같이 쓰이는 조동사는 will이다.

16 will은 be going to로 바꿔 쓸 수 있다. 이때 be동사는 주어 you에 맞는 Are를 주어 앞에 써야 한다.

17 금지를 나타내는 must not을 써야 한다.

18 전주에 운전해서 갈 것이냐는 질문에 KTX를 타고 갈 것이라고 답했으므로, 부정의 답을 해야 한다. Will you ~?에 대한 부정의 대답은 No, I won't.이다.

19 had to('의무'의 과거형)의 의문문은 「Did+주어+have to ~?」이다.

20 perhaps는 '아마도'라는 의미이므로 '추측'을 나타내는 조동사 may 또는 might가 알맞다.

21 ⓐ speak의 과거형은 spoke이고 ⓒ 과거 진행형이므로 walked를 walking으로 ⓔ 조동사 다음에는 동사원형을 쓰므로 moved → move로 고쳐야 한다.

22 '나는 ~할 것이다'이고 9단어이므로 be going to를 이용한다.

[21~22]

> 너는 이걸 믿을 수 없을 거야! 우리 학교 축구부의 주장인 최태풍이 오늘 나에게 말을 걸었어! 그는 3학년이고 나는 1학년이야. 그는 팬이 많아. 우리 학교의 모든 학생들은 그를 좋아해. 오늘, 나는 집으로 걸어가고 있었어. 나는 버스 정류장 옆에서 그를 봤어. 그리고 그거 알아? 그는 내 이름으로 나를 부르고 나한테 안녕이라고 말했어. 그는 내 이름을 알고 있었어. 나는 아주 놀랐고 행복했어. 내 얼굴은 빨개졌고, 난 한 걸음도 움직일 수가 없었어. 그는 정말 멋져! 나는 오늘 밤 푹 잘 거야.

• 어휘 • captain 주장 | grade 학년 | Do you know what? 그거 알아? 있잖아. | awesome 멋진 | get a good night's sleep 밤에 푹 자다

CHAPTER 05
문장의 변환

UNIT 14 의문사 의문문

1) who   2) 누가   3) what
4) 무엇; 어떤   5) when   6) 언제
7) where   8) 어디서   9) why

10) 왜		11) how		12) 어떻게, 얼마나	
13) whom		14) 누구를		15) whose	
16) 누구의 (것)		17) which		18) 어느[어떤] (것)	
19) how ~		20) 얼마나 ~		21) 의문사	
22) be동사		23) 주어		24) 의문사	
25) do/does/did		26) 주어		27) 동사원형	

Level 1 Test

p. 80

A 1 Where   2 What
   3 How   4 When

B 1 Why   2 Who(m)
   3 Whose   4 How

C 1 ⓒ   2 ⓓ
   3 ⓐ   4 ⓑ

D 1 Whose bag is that?
   2 When is your birthday?

Level 2 Test

p. 81

01 ①   02 ②
03 ④   04 ④
05 Where do you live now?
06 (A) What time   (B) What
07 Who
08 How old

≫ 해설

01 선택을 물을 때는 which를 사용한다.
02 '무엇'에 해당하므로 what이 답이다.
03 when은 시간이나 때를 묻는 의문사로 ④가 적절하다.
04 ④ How is she?는 그녀의 상태를 묻는 질문인데, 답변으로 나이를 말하고 있으므로 어색하다.
05 「의문사+do+주어+동사원형 ~?」의 순으로 배열하면 된다.
06 (A) 시간을 묻는 두 단어이므로 What time이 적절하다.
    (B) '무엇'을 하느냐는 말로 What이 들어가야 한다.
07 '내 조카'라는 사람을 말하고 있으므로 Who를 써야 한다.
08 나이를 물을 때는 How old ~를 사용한다.

Level 3 Test

p. 82

01 ⑤   02 ④
03 ①   04 ②
05 ② ④   06 ③
07 ②   08 ⑤
09 ④
10 What[Which] flavor of ice cream
11 What time
12 How does your father go to work
13 Why
14 (1) What (2) How old (3) Where (4) Which 또는 What

≫ 해설

01 • 장소를 묻는 '어디(Where)'
    • 시간을 묻는 '언제(When)'
02 이유를 물었는데 때로 대답했으므로 자연스럽지 않다.
03 질문이 사람의 수를 묻고 있으므로 '아빠, 엄마, 남동생, 나' 총 네 명이다.
04 ②는 의문대명사(어느 것)이고, 나머지는 의문형용사(어느)로 사용되었다.
05 대답이 출신을 말하고 있으므로 ②와 ④는 적절하지 않다.
06 좋아하는 계절을 묻고 있는데 싫어하는 계절을 말하므로 ③이 어색하다.
07 바이올린 수업을 가는 '때'를 묻고 있으므로 ②가 적절하다.
08 노인이 있는 가족에게 선물을 준다는 것은 나와 있지만 선물의 종류는 알 수 없다.
09 Whose ringtone is this?와 Who(m) are you waiting for?로 영작할 수 있다.
10 which와 what은 의문대명사뿐 아니라 의문형용사(어떤)로도 사용된다.
11 B가 오전 1시에 잔다고 했으므로 A에는 '시간'을 묻는 When이나 What time이 와야 하는데 2단어로 쓰라고 했으므로 What time을 쓰면 된다.
12 「의문사+do+주어+동사원형 ~?」 순으로 쓰면 된다.
13 첫 번째는 because로 대답한 것으로 보아 Why가 적절하며, 두 번째는 Why don't you ~?를 써서 '~하는 게 어때?'라는 의미의 권유문을 만든다.
14 (1), (2), (3)에는 각각 이름, 나이, 출신을 묻는 의문사를 쓰고, (4)에는 어떤 언어를 말하냐고 물어야 하므로 '어떤'에 해당하는 which나 what을 쓴다.

UNIT 15 명령문

1) 동사원형   2) ~해라.   3) Don't[Do not]
4) Never   5) Let's   6) ~하자.
7) Let's not   8) ~하지 말자.

Level 1 Test

p. 84

A 1 Have   2 pick
   3 talk   4 Let
   5 hide

B 1 Call me every thirty minutes.
   2 Let's not walk that way.
   3 Be careful.
   4 Don't[Do not] drive fast. 또는 Never drive fast.

C 1 Never   2 Keep
   3 Be   4 Let

D 1 Don't   2 Wear
   3 Let's paint   4 Let's not believe
   5 Never cross

Level 2 Test
p. 85

01 ②　　　　　　　　02 ③
03 ③　　　　　　　　04 ④
05 ②
06 Run fast!
07 Don't[Do not, Never] bring your pet.
08 Be
09 Don't[Do not, Never] be cruel to me.
10 ⓐ swims → swim

≫ 해설

01 명령문에는 동사원형을 쓴다.
02 '~하지 말자'는 Let's not ~로 표현한다.
03 치킨을 너무 많이 먹지 말라는 뜻으로 「Don't[Do not, Never]+동사원형」을 써야 한다.
04 다음 버스가 곧 오기 때문에 부정의 답으로 답해야 한다. Let's (not) ~에 대한 부정의 대답은 No, let's not.으로 한다.
05 일반동사가 있는 명령문은 be동사를 쓰지 않는다.
06 명령문은 동사원형으로 시작한다.
07 부정 명령문은 「Don't[Do not, Never]+동사원형」으로 쓴다.
08 소음을 내지 말라는 말은 조용히 하라는 말과 같은 의미이므로 Be quiet로 쓰면 된다.
09 be동사나 일반동사의 부정 명령문은 「Don't[Do not, Never]+동사원형」으로 쓴다.
10 Never를 사용한 부정 명령문은 「Never+동사원형」이다.

Level 3 Test
p. 86

01 ②　　　　　　　　02 ③
03 ③　　　　　　　　04 ④
05 ③　　　　　　　　06 ③
07 ④　　　　　　　　08 ②
09 ②　　　　　　　　10 ⑤
11 ③ ⑤
12 buy
13 Don't be → Don't
14 Forgive / never forget
15 don't call me "*jagi*"
16 Let's not say goodbye.
17 Don't[Never] park

≫ 해설

01 명령문에는 동사원형을 쓴다. 여기서 Kevin은 문장의 주어가 아니라 부르는 말이다.
02 부정 명령문은 Don't 또는 Never로 시작한다. (→ Don't be mean. 또는 Never be mean.)
03 명령문은 please의 위치와 관계 없이 동사원형으로 써야 한다.
04 부정 명령문은 don't[never] 다음에 동사원형을 쓴다.
05 'A가 ~하게 하다'는 「let+A+동사원형」의 형태로 쓴다.
06 Never로 시작하는 부정 명령문도 동사원형을 써야 한다. (→ Never say)
07 Let's not ~에 대한 부정의 답변은 No, let's not.으로 한다.
08 ⓒ talked → talk ⓔ spending → spend

09 Don't 다음에 동사원형을 써야 하는데 동사가 없다. Don't turn off the lights.로 써야 한다.
10 ① Wears → Wear ② Not → Don't[Never] ③ Uses → Use ④ Doesn't → Don't
11 ③ Please look at me once. ⑤ Let's not mention it anymore. ① Let me speaking first. (speaking → speak) ② First, boils some water. (boils → boil) ③ Don't be do stupid things. (→ be 삭제)
12 Let's not buy Christmas gifts this year.이므로 세 번째 올 단어는 buy이다.
13 일반동사가 있는 문장의 부정 명령문에서는 be를 뺀다.
14 긍정 명령문은 동사원형인 Forgive로, 그리고 부정 명령문에서 do를 사용하지 말아야 하므로 never forget으로 쓰면 된다.
15 부정 명령문은 Don't 다음에 동사원형이 온다.
16 Let's의 부정문은 Let's not이고 say goodbye의 동사 say가 있으므로 be는 필요 없다.
17 부정 명령문은 Don't 또는 Never 다음에 동사원형을 쓴다.

UNIT 16 부가의문문

1) 부정　　　　2) 긍정　　　　3) 그대로
4) do/does/did　　5) will you　　6) shall we

Level 1 Test
p. 88

A 1 isn't　　　　　　2 can't
　 3 will　　　　　　 4 shall
B 1 ⓐ　　　　　　　 2 ⓑ
　 3 ⓓ　　　　　　　 4 ⓒ
C 1 isn't he　　　　　2 doesn't she
D 1 is he　　　　　　2 don't you
　 3 doesn't she　　　4 will you
E 1 어색한 곳 없음　　2 어색한 곳 없음
　 3 aren't you → are you　4 will you → shall we

Level 2 Test
p. 89

01 ③　　　　　　　　02 ③
03 ⑤　　　　　　　　04 ③
05 ①
06 didn't she
07 aren't we → don't they
08 Sam learned taekwondo, didn't he?
09 doesn't he

≫ 해설

01 일반동사가 있는 긍정문의 부가의문문은 「don't/doesn't+주어(대명사)?」로 만든다.
02 be동사의 부가의문문은 그대로 be동사를 쓰고, 긍정이면 부정으로 쓰며 줄여서 쓴다.

03 There is/are 구문에서 부가의문문의 주어는 there로 쓴다.

04 긍정문인 일반동사 과거형의 부가의문문은 「didn't+주어?」로 쓴다.

05 (부정) 명령문의 부가의문문은 will you?로 쓴다.

06 일반동사가 있는 과거형의 긍정문은 부가의문문을 「didn't+주어?」로 만든다.

07 현재형의 일반동사이므로 don't, 주어가 Koreans이므로 they로 써야 한다.

08 긍정문에서 일반동사가 사용된 과거형으로, 부가의문문은 didn't로 쓰고 주어는 대명사로 쓴다.

09 일반동사가 있는 긍정의 현재형으로 부가의문문은 doesn't로 시작하며 B의 말에서 아이(kid)의 성별을 알 수 있다.

Level 3 Test
p. 90

01 ⑤
02 ②
03 ③
04 ① ⑤
05 ③
06 ④ ⑤
07 ②
08 ② ④
09 ③ ④
10 ②

11 do you → will you

12 ⓐ isn't this → isn't it ⓑ comes → come

13 will he

14 You didn't call me / did you

15 did you → didn't you / don't you → will you / shall we → will you

16 (A) is he (B) No, he isn't. 또는 No, he's not.

≫ 해설

01 ・일반동사이고 주어가 여성 3인칭 단수이므로 doesn't she
・won't가 부정의 조동사이므로 will they

02 B가 피자를 먹자고 하는 것으로 보아, B는 배가 고프므로 긍정의 대답을 해야 한다.

03 부가의문문에서는 주어를 대명사로 써야 하므로 can she로 써야 한다.

04 ① → aren't ⑤ → he

05 부가의문문을 만들 때 조동사는 그대로 쓰되 부정이면 줄여 쓰고 주어는 대명사로 쓴다. 그림에서 로봇은 바이올린을 연주하고 있으므로 긍정으로 대답해야 한다.

06 부가의문문이 shall we?이므로 Let's 또는 Let's not이 가능하다.

07 There is/are 구문의 부가의문문에서 주어는 there로 쓴다.

08 ② → doesn't he ④ → shall we

09 ③ 「Let+목적어 ∼」는 간접 명령문으로, 부가의문문은 will you?를 쓴다. ④ 일반동사의 과거형이므로 didn't she는 바르게 쓰였다.
① isn't he → is he ② don't they → won't they ⑤ do we → shall we

10 ⓔ hasn't she → doesn't she ⓕ do you → will you

11 부정 명령문의 부가의문문도 will you이다.

12 ⓐ this는 다시 쓸 때 it으로 쓴다. ⓑ will you를 보아 명령문인데 명령문은 동사원형으로 시작하므로 come으로 써야 한다.

13 조동사 won't는 부정이므로 긍정의 will로 쓰고, 주어가 남자 이름 단수이므로 대명사인 he로 써야 한다.

14 주어가 you이고 일반동사 과거형의 부정문으로 you didn't call me를 쓰고 부가의문문 didn't you?를 쓴다.

15 첫 번째 B의 말에서 일반동사가 있는 긍정의 과거형이므로 did you를 didn't you로 고쳐야 한다. 두 번째 A의 말은 명령문이므로 don't

you를 will you로 고쳐야 한다. 두 번째 B의 말에서 let me ∼도 간접 명령문이므로 shall we를 will you로 써야 한다.

16 (A) 부정의 be동사는 긍정의 be동사로 부가의문문을 만든다.
(B) 남자아이가 뱀을 무서워하지 않으므로 부정으로 답하면 된다.

UNIT 17 감탄문

1) What
2) 형용사
3) 형용사
4) 부사
5) How
6) 형용사/부사

Level 1 Test
p. 92

A 1 What
2 How
3 What
4 What
5 How

B 1 How
2 How
3 What
4 What
5 What beautiful eyes

C 1 a nice
2 you are
3 어색한 곳 없음
4 loudly the baby

D 1 What a big cat it is!
2 How slowly the snail moves!
3 How tall the tree is!
4 What an exciting game it is!

Level 2 Test
p. 93

01 ⑤
02 ④
03 ④
04 ②
05 ④
06 How cute

07 (1) 너의 발은 얼마나 크니?
(2) 너의 발은 참 크구나!

08 How white your teeth are!

09 a lucky person (you are)

≫ 해설

01 단수 명사(car)이면서 자음(nice)이므로 「What a+형용사+명사+주어+동사」로 써야 한다.

02 ④에서 How는 '어떻게'라는 의미의 의문사이고 나머지 문장에서는 감탄문의 How로 사용되었다.

03 What tall girls they are!이므로 두 번째 단어는 tall이다.

04 형용사(surprised)가 감탄의 대상이므로 「How+형용사/부사+주어+동사!」 순으로 쓰면 된다.

05 babies가 복수이므로 a를 빼야 한다.

06 형용사(cute)가 감탄의 대상이므로 How 감탄문을 쓰면 된다. 빈칸이 2개이므로 주어와 동사는 생략한다.

07 (1)은 의문문으로 How는 '어떻게'라는 의미의 의문사이다.
(2)는 감탄문으로 '참 ∼하구나'로 해석한다.

08 「How+형용사/부사+주어+동사」 순으로 쓰면 된다.

09 What으로 시작하므로 a lucky person을 쓰고 여기서 '주어＋동사'는 생략 가능하므로 괄호를 하면 된다.

Level 3 Test
p. 94

01 ②
02 ②
03 ① ②
04 ③ ⑤
05 ③
06 ③
07 ③
08 ③ ④
09 ① ②
10 ①
11 (1) How (2) What an
12 How short these shorts are!
13 (1) How expensive (2) an expensive watch
14 What pretty mugs you have!
15 What delicious pasta (it was)! 또는 How delicious (the pasta was)!

≫ 해설

01 ②는 What, 나머지는 How가 들어간다.

02 • 형용사(excellent)가 감탄의 대상이므로 How
• 복수 명사(chairs)가 감탄의 대상이므로 a를 빼고 What이 들어가야 한다.

03 「What (a/an)＋형용사＋명사(＋주어＋동사)」로 ①과 ②가 적절하다.

04 형용사(clever)가 있으므로 '주어＋동사' 어순에서 be동사가 온다.

05 형용사(dirty)가 감탄의 대상이므로 How dirty로 써야 한다.

06 What big eyes you have!에서 세 번째 오는 것은 eyes이다. eyes가 복수이므로 a나 an을 쓰지 않는다.

07 평서문에서 부사(slowly)를 감탄문으로 바꾼 것으로 ③이 적절하다.

08 「How＋형용사＋주어＋동사」 또는 「What＋a＋형용사＋명사＋주어＋동사」로 표현할 수 있다.

09 ③ How → What ④ pretty flower → a pretty flower ⑤ is your eraser → your eraser is

10 ⓐ~ⓔ 모두 틀린 부분이 없다.

11 (1)은 형용사(honest) 감탄문이고, (2)는 명사(boy) 감탄문으로 각각 How와 What을 쓰면 된다. honest가 모음으로 시작하므로 a 대신 an을 써야 한다.

12 형용사(short)가 감탄의 대상이므로 How 감탄문을 쓰면 된다. 주어(these shorts)를 바꾸지 말라고 했으므로 What 감탄문은 쓸 수 없다.

13 빈칸 수에 맞게 how 감탄문과 what 감탄문 두 가지로 표현하며 (2)는 expensive가 모음이라 an을 쓴다.

14 You have pretty mugs.의 감탄문으로 a와 how는 필요 없고 What pretty mugs you have!로 쓴다.

15 What 감탄문이면 「What (a/an)＋형용사＋명사(＋주어＋동사)!」로 쓰고, How 감탄문이면 「How＋형용사(＋주어＋동사)!」로 쓰면 된다. pasta는 셀 수 없는 명사이므로 What 감탄문에서 부정관사 a를 쓰지 않는다.

Review Test
p. 96

01 ③
02 ④
03 ④
04 ③
05 ③
06 ④
07 ⑤
08 ④
09 ②
10 ④

11 Which[What] sport
12 Whom do you live with?
13 What did you
14 Close your eyes and imagine your future.
15 Don't → Don't be
16 shall we
17 is she / No, she isn't. 또는 No, she's not.
18 ⓒ aren't they → don't they
19 How smart dolphins are!
20 What amazing students you teach! 또는 (What an amazing student you teach!)
21 What great music they play!
22 ⑤
23 Let's go back home, shall we?

≫ 해설

01 첫 번째는 '무엇'에 관해 묻고 있으므로 What을 쓴다. 두 번째는 나이에 대해 묻고 있으므로 How old를 쓴다. 세 번째는 '선택'에 관해 묻고 있으므로 Which가 적절하다.

02 Let's not 다음에는 동사원형을 쓴다. (eats → eat)

03 You are kind to others.의 명령문으로 Be가 들어가야 한다.

04 • 명령문이므로 부가의문문으로 will you?가 와야 한다.
• 조동사 won't가 쓰였으므로 부가의문문으로 will you?가 와야 한다.

05 대답이 직업을 말하고 있으므로 질문으로 ③이 적절하다.

06 대답이 '무엇'에 대한 답을 하고 있으므로 ④가 적절하다.

07 명령문은 동사원형으로 시작하고 일반동사가 있는 경우 be동사를 쓰지 않는다.

08 과거형 일반동사(came)가 있는 긍정문에 대한 부가의문문으로 ④가 옳다.

09 ②는 What, 나머지는 How가 들어간다.

10 (D) ⓐ There is의 부가 의문문은 isn't there?이고 부정 명령문의 부가의문문은 will you?이다. (A) ⓑ don't you → do you (B) ⓑ don't you → will you (C) ⓐ wasn't it → didn't it (E) ⓑ will I → will you

11 '무엇이 네가 제일 좋아하는 스포츠니?'는 '어떤 스포츠를 가장 좋아하니?'로 바꿔 쓸 수 있다.

12 who가 목적격일 때는 whom을 쓰고 '~와'는 with를 사용하여 표현하면 된다.

13 B가 '무엇'을 먹었는지 답하고 있으므로 What으로 물어봐야 한다.

14 명령문은 동사원형으로 시작한다.

15 부정 명령문은 don't 다음에 동사원형을 써야 하므로 are의 원형인 be를 써야 한다.

16 Let's (not) ~의 부가의문문은 shall we?이다.

17 be동사의 현재형이 있는 부정문은 「be동사＋주어(대명사)?」로 부가의문문을 만들며, 여자가 노래를 못하는 것으로 보아 부정의 답변을 하면 된다.

18 ⓒ 일반동사(grow)가 쓰였으므로 don't로 써야 한다.

19 형용사(smart)가 감탄의 대상이므로 How 감탄문을 쓴다. What smart dolphins they are!도 가능하지만 의미가 달라진다.

20 students가 복수이므로 a를 빼거나 a를 그대로 두고 student를 단수로 써야 한다.

21 what을 포함하라고 했으므로 what 감탄문을 쓰되, music은 셀 수 없는 명사이므로 부정관사 a/an을 쓰지 않는다.

22 ⓑ be going to의 의문문이므로 are ⓒ 명령문이므로 Believe
　 ⓔ 긍정문이면서 과거형 일반동사(caught)가 있는 문장의 부가의문
　 문으로 didn't로 고쳐야 한다.
23 제안할 때 사용하는 표현은 Let's이고 go back home을 쓴 후, 이의
　 부가의문문 shall we를 쓰면 된다.

[22~23]

> 한 아빠가 자신의 아이를 낚시 여행에 데리고 갔다. 그들은 한 시간 동안 낚시를 했다. 하지만 그들은 어떤 것도 잡지 못했다. 아들이 아빠에게 물었다. "아빠, 우리가 여기서 뭐 좀 잡을까요?" 아빠가 대답했다. "물론이지. 우리는 잡을 거야. 아빠를 믿어." 두 시간 후, 그들은 여전히 아무것도 잡지 못했다. 아빠가 말했다. "오늘 춥구나. 집으로 돌아가자. 그럴까?" 집에서 엄마가 물었다. "아들. 오늘 큰 거 잡았지, 그렇지?" "네. 물론이죠, 엄마. 큰 감기요 (감기에 걸렸어요), 아빠 덕분에요." 아들이 대답했다.

• 어휘 • fishing trip 낚시 여행 | fish 낚시하다 | catch 잡다, (감기에) 걸리다 |
thanks to ~ 덕분에

CHAPTER 06
형용사와 부사

UNIT 18 형용사

1) 한정적　　　2) 서술적　　　3) many
4) much　　　5) some　　　6) any
7) a few　　　8) a little　　　9) few
10) little　　　11) first　　　12) second
13) third　　　14) fourth　　　15) fifth
16) sixth　　　17) seventh　　　18) eighth
19) ninth　　　20) tenth　　　21) eleventh
22) twelfth　　23) thirteenth　24) fourteenth
25) twentieth　26) hundredth　27) thousandth
28) millionth

Level 1 Test
p. 100

A　1　≠　　　　　　2　≠
　　3　=　　　　　　4　≠
　　5　=　　　　　　6　≠

B　1　much　　　　2　many
　　3　lots of　　　4　A few
　　5　little　　　　6　some
　　7　any　　　　8　some
　　9　few

Level 2 Test
p. 101

01 ②　　　　　　　　02 ③
03 ②　　　　　　　　04 ④
05 ⓐ some → any
06 Do you spend a lot of time with your family?
07 one hundredth day
08 Few

》》 해설

01 much가 있으므로 셀 수 있는 명사는 쓸 수 없다.
02 • 부정문에는 any가 사용된다.
　 • 의문문에서의 some은 권유를 나타낸다.
03 year는 셀 수 있는 명사이므로 a few로 써야 한다.
04 19번째는 nineteenth, 5월 5일은 May fifth, 2029년은 two
　 thousand twenty-nine으로 읽는다.
05 부정문에서는 some 대신 any를 쓴다.
06 일반동사(spend)가 있는 의문문이므로 Do you spend 〜로 시작하
　 며, a lot of는 명사 앞에 위치하게 재배열하면 된다.
07 '100번째 날'은 순서를 가리키므로 서수로 써야 한다.
08 'Allison은 방문객이 거의 없었다.'이므로 부정을 나타내는 few가 적
　 절하다.

Level 3 Test
p. 102

01 ④ ⑤　　　　　　02 ① ② ③ ④
03 ④ ⑤　　　　　　04 ③
05 ③　　　　　　　06 ④
07 ②　　　　　　　08 ④
09 ②　　　　　　　10 ③
11 ① ④
12 lots of
13 A few students passed the hard test.
14 Ami has little time but lots of work.
15 The movie was nothing special.
16 ⓑ some → any
17 first grade

》》 해설

01 명사(guy)를 꾸미는 것은 형용사이므로 부사인 kindly(친절하게)는
　 적절하지 않고, honest는 모음으로 시작하므로 an을 써야 한다.
02 money는 셀 수 없는 명사라 ⑤는 답이 될 수 없다.
03 ④ Lot of → A lot of 또는 Lots of ⑤ sheeps → sheep (sheep
　 은 단복수의 형태가 동일하다.)
04 something은 형용사가 뒤에서 꾸며준다.
05 뒤의 문장에서 외롭다는 것으로 보아 부정의 의미가 있는 ③이 적절
　 하다.
06 셀 수 있는 명사를 꾸며 줄 때 a lot of는 many로 바꿔 쓸 수 있다.
07 소년은 사탕을 한 개 쥐고 있으므로 ②가 그림과 일치하지 않는다.
08 a lot of 또는 lots of로 써야 한다. plenty of도 가능하다.
09 He proposed to her many[a lot of, lots of, plenty of] times,
　 but her answer was always no.라고 영작할 수 있다. 필요 없는
　 단어는 much이다.
10 ⓐ some → any ⓒ some → any ⓓ something → anything

11 ① new something → something new ④ a little → a few

12 plenty of와 바꿔 쓸 수 있는 '많은'이라는 의미의 2단어는 lots of이다.

13 동사는 passed이고 주어가 students이며 이를 꾸며주는 a few를 앞에 쓰고 문장을 완성하면 된다.

14 time은 셀 수 없는 명사로 little로 수식하고, work는 lots of로 수식한다.

15 nothing은 형용사가 뒤에서 꾸며준다.

16 부정문에서는 any를 주로 쓴다.

17 grade는 '학년'을 나타내고 그림으로 보아 1학년이므로, 서수 first로 써야 한다.

UNIT 19 부사

1) 동사		2) 형용사		3) 부사	
4) 문장		5) +-ly		6) kindly	
7) slowly		8) y → i + -ly		9) easily	
10) happily		11) fast		12) early	
13) hard		14) late		15) pretty	
16) late		17) lately		18) hard	
19) hardly		20) near		21) nearly	
22) high		23) highly		24) too	
25) either		26) 잘		27) 건강한	
28) always		29) usually		30) often	
31) sometimes		32) seldom		33) never	

Level 1 Test

p. 104

A 1 quietly 2 great
3 easy 4 late
5 hard 6 fast
7 either 8 finally

B 1 어색한 곳 없음 2 hard
3 neither 4 highly
5 sometimes snows

Level 2 Test

p. 105

01 ⑤ 02 ②
03 ③ 04 ④
05 ③
06 too
07 ⓑ hard → hardly
08 (1) good (2) well
09 (1) The boss seldom praises his employees.
(2) 그 사장은 좀처럼 직원들을 칭찬하지 않는다.
10 (1) 그는 매우 늦었다.
(2) 나는 오늘 아침 늦게 일어났다.

>> 해설

01 lovely는 형용사로 동사(pushed)를 꾸밀 수 없다.

02 부정문에는 either, 긍정문에는 too를 쓴다. neither는 문장에 not이 있으므로 부적절하다.

03 near는 '가까운, 가까이'이고 nearly는 '거의'라는 뜻이다.

04 빈도부사의 위치는 일반적으로 조동사나 be동사 뒤, 일반동사 앞이다. sometimes는 문장의 처음에도 쓸 수 있다.

05 ⓑ 동사(cook)를 꾸며야 하므로 부사(well)가 필요하다. (good → well) ⓒ often is → is often ⓓ usefully → useful

06 • too는 형용사 앞에서 '너무'라는 의미의 부사로 쓰인다.
• too가 문장 뒤에 쓰이면 '역시, 또한'이라는 의미이다.

07 '그녀는 친구들을 거의 방문하지 않는다.'는 의미로 hard가 아닌 hardly로 써야 한다.

08 be good at은 '~을 잘하다'라는 의미이고 부사로는 well(잘)로 표현한다.

09 빈도부사는 일반동사 앞에 위치한다.

10 late가 형용사이면 '늦은'으로, 부사이면 '늦게'로 해석한다.

Level 3 Test

p. 106

01 ① 02 ④
03 ① 04 ④
05 ③ 06 ⑤
07 ② 08 ① ②
09 ③ 10 ④

11 The thirsty man drank the water quickly. 또는 The thirsty man quickly drank the water.

12 When do you usually put up Halloween decorations?

13 ⓒ He doesn't usually drive to work.

14 Lately, my daughter gets home late.

15 (A) She always takes a shower.
(B) She usually has breakfast.
(C) She seldom watches TV.

>> 해설

01 How often은 빈도를 묻는 것으로 빈칸에는 빈도부사가 와야 한다.

02 '버스가 보통은 늦지 않는다.'가 되어야 한다. never와 seldom은 부정문이라 들어갈 수 없다.

03 빈도부사는 일반동사 앞에 온다.

04 긍정문에 too, 부정문에는 either를 쓰거나 Me neither.와 같은 식으로 쓴다.

05 friendly는 형용사이고, [보기]와 나머지는 모두 부사이다.

06 always – usually – often – sometimes – seldom – never에서 선택지에 usually가 없으므로 두 번째로 자주 케이팝을 듣는 사람은 Nattapong이다.

07 hardly는 '거의 ~않는', hard는 '열심히'란 뜻으로 사용된 것을 찾으면 된다.

08 빈도부사는 일반동사 앞에 오고, 의문문인 경우는 주어 뒤에 온다.
① → I seldom see my cousins. ② → Is she often like this?

09 ⓐ quick → quickly ⓔ Lucky → Luckily ⓕ high → highly

10 Why is the store always crowded?로 영작 가능하며 의문문에서 빈도부사는 주어 뒤에 온다.

11 quick을 부사로 써야 하므로 quickly가 되어야 한다.

12 내용상 '할로윈 장식은 주로 언제 하나요?'이고 빈도부사 usually는 의문문인 경우 주어 뒤에 위치한다.

13 빈도부사는 조동사 뒤에 쓴다.

14 '최근에'라는 의미의 부사는 lately이고, '늦게'라는 의미의 부사는 late이다.

15 샤워는 매일 하므로 always, 아침은 5일 먹으므로 usually, TV는 하루만 보므로 seldom을 넣어 답변하면 된다.

Review Test

p. 108

01 ③	02 ②
03 ⑤	04 ③
05 ①	06 ④
07 ⑤	08 ②
09 ④	10 ⑤

11 plenty of
12 This is an interesting movie.
13 little / a lot of
14 four → fourth
15 somebody 또는 someone
16 Fortunate → Fortunately / suddenly → sudden
17 never
18 (1) passed　(2) passed / too　(3) failed　(4) pass
   (5) pass / either
19 Fast runners usually have pretty long legs.
20 ⓒ However, we got back home too late.
21 ③
22 They learned everything fast[quickly].

≫ 해설

01 forth → fourth / nineth → ninth / thirty-threeth → thirty-third

02 [보기]와 ⓐ, ⓒ는 명사를 직접 꾸며주는 한정적 용법으로 사용되었다. 나머지는 서술적 용법이다.

03 주어를 꾸며주는 형용사가 와야 한다. cloud는 명사이다.

04 money는 양을, dolls는 수를 나타내는 말과 함께 쓴다.

05 good은 형용사로만 사용된다.

06 hardly는 일반동사 앞에 위치한다. hardly 대신 hard(열심히)를 쓰면 빈칸 자리에 가능하다.

07 형용사가 명사를 직접 꾸밀 때는 명사 앞에 온다.

08 • 명사(shell)를 꾸미는 형용사가 필요하다.
   • 동사(listen)를 꾸미는 부사가 와야 한다.

09 lately는 '최근에'이므로 late(늦게)로 바꿔야 한다.

10 의문문일 경우 빈도부사는 주어 뒤에 온다. 여기서 주어는 Who이다.

11 plenty of는 수나 양에 모두 쓰인다.

12 interesting은 모음으로 시작하므로 한정적 용법으로 쓸 때 관사로 an을 써야 한다.

13 셀 수 없는 명사에서 '거의 없는'은 little, '많은'은 much[a lot of, lots of, plenty of]로 표현할 수 있다. 뒤의 빈칸이 3개이므로 a lot of를 써야 한다.

14 순서를 나타내는 말로 서수로 써야 한다. (11월의 네 번째 목요일)

15 somebody[someone]는 형용사가 뒤에서 꾸며주므로 The basketball team needs somebody[someone] tall and quick.로 영작한다.

16 Fortunate는 문장을 수식하는 부사 Fortunately로, suddenly는 명사 (attack)를 수식하는 형용사 sudden으로 써야 한다.

17 on time은 '제시간에'라는 뜻으로 늘 제시간에 온다는 내용은 절대 늦지 않는다는 것과 같으므로 never를 쓰면 된다.

18 긍정문에는 too, 부정문에는 either를 쓴다.

19 빠른(fast), 대개(usually), 꽤(pretty), 긴(long) 등을 찾아 쓰되, 빈도부사는 일반동사 앞에 쓰도록 한다.

20 lately는 '최근에'이므로 내용상 late(늦게)로 써야 한다.

21 ⓐ 2st → 2nd ⓑ did always → always did ⓓ too → either

22 learn의 과거형은 learned / fast는 형용사와 부사가 같은 형태로 fast가 적절하다.

[21~22]

> Ellie와 Janice는 2학년이었다. 그들은 가장 친한 친구였다. 그들은 항상 모든 것을 함께 했다. 그들은 매일 아침 학교에 같이 걸어갔다. 그들은 점심을 함께 먹었다. 그들은 같은 수업을 들었다. <u>그들은 모든 것을 빨리 배웠다.</u> 하지만 Ellie는 수학을 잘하지 못했다. Janice도 그것을 잘하지 못했다. 그들은 서로 많이 도왔다. 그들은 같은 고등학교에 가기를 원했다. 하지만 Ellie는 최근에 다른 도시로 이사했다.

＊어휘｜ grade 학년 | be good at ~을 잘하다 | each other 서로 | move 이사하다

CHAPTER 07
형용사와 부사

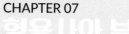

UNIT 20 비교 변화, 동등 비교

1) taller	2) tallest	3) larger
4) largest	5) busier	6) busiest
7) hotter	8) hottest	9) more famous
10) most famous	11) better	12) best
13) worse	14) worst	15) more
16) most	17) less	18) least
19) later	20) latest	21) latter
22) last	23) as	24) as
25) as[so]	26) as	

Level 1 Test

p. 112

A 1 as		2 much	
3 not as		4 yours	
B 1 어색한 곳 없음		2 heavy	

        3 not as[so]
C 1 as / as hers
  2 not as hard[difficult] as
  3 as easily as

Level 2 Test
p. 113

01 ②   02 ①
03 ⑤   04 ③
05 ③
06 I am not as hungry as you.
07 as not → not as
08 Your eyes are as big as his.
09 as heavy as

》》 해설
01 동등 비교에서 not의 위치는 평서문과 동일하다.
02 as ~ as 사이에는 원급이 온다.
03 ① so → as ② my → mine 또는 my puppy ③ clean → as clean ④ careless → carelessly
04 '너의 고양이만큼 많은 우유를 마신다'고 했으므로 동등비교 as ~ as를 사용한다. His cat drinks as much milk as yours[your cat]. 로 영작할 수 있다.
05 ③ ⓐ isn't → doesn't, much → many, so → as ⓑ many → much, wants → want로 고쳐야 한다.
06 동사가 am이라 주어는 I이고 「not ~ as ~ as...」 형식으로 쓰면 된다.
07 「as ~ as...」 구문을 뺀 후 not을 넣으면 된다. 여기서는 be동사(is)가 있으므로 is not으로 쓰면 된다.
08 as big as his eyes면 8단어가 되므로 소유대명사인 his로 써야 한다.
09 돈과 치킨의 무게가 같으므로 동등 비교를 사용하여 나타낸다.

Level 3 Test
p. 114

01 ⑤   02 ②
03 ②   04 ⑤
05 ⑤   06 ④
07 ④   08 ②
09 ③   10 ④
11 ④
12 ⓑ graceful → gracefully
13 bravely → brave
14 I need as much time as he does.
15 The balloon flew as high as the kite.
16 as much / as
17 was as clear as crystal

》》 해설
01 ⑤ 동사 flew를 수식해야 하므로 highly(매우)가 아니라 high(높이, 높은)이 필요하다. (→ Gomez flew as high as Superman.) ① My sister is not as old as me. ② Math is as boring as English. ③ Comics are not as funny as magazines.
02 「as ~ as...」 사이에는 원급이 온다. as ~ as...를 지우고 보면 부사 well이 필요하다.

03 '검정색 셔츠가 흰색 셔츠만큼 비싸지 않다'를 「not as ~ as...」를 이용하여 영작한 것을 찾으면 된다.
04 비교 대상이 같아야 하므로 your score 또는 yours로 해야 한다.
05 두 사람의 키가 같으므로 긍정의 동등 비교를 쓰면 된다.
06 「as ~ as ...」를 빼고 보면 동사(barks)를 수식하는 부사가 필요하다.
07 Marie는 Emma만큼 크지 않으므로 Marie가 작고, Lisa는 Emma만큼 크므로 둘의 키는 같다.
08 「as ~ as ...」를 빼고 보면 He has ~이므로 일반동사의 부정을 하면 된다.
09 ① me → mine 또는 my car ② beautiful → as beautiful ④ as not → not as ⑤ has not → doesn't have
10 expensive → as expensive
11 (A) ⓑ Jimmy → Jimmy's (B) ⓑ beautiful → beautifully (C) ⓑ heavily → heavy (E) ⓑ dangerously → dangerous
12 「as ~ as...」를 빼고 보면 동사(turned)를 수식할 부사가 필요하다.
13 「as ~ as...」를 빼고 보면 be동사가 보이므로 형용사로 써야 한다.
14 need가 동사이므로 I가 주어이고, 「as + 형용사 + 명사 + as」로 쓰면 된다.
15 원급을 사용하며 high는 형용사와 부사의 형태가 같음에 유의한다.
16 같은 액수의 돈을 갖고 있으므로 동등 비교를 사용하여 나타내면 된다.
17 호수가 수정처럼 맑은 그림으로 as clear as crystal로 쓰고, 과거이므로 was를 쓰면 된다.

UNIT 21 비교급

1) …보다 더 ~한[-히, -게]   2) 비교급
3) less   4) …보다 덜 ~한[-히, -게]
5) much   6) still
7) even   8) far

Level 1 Test
p. 116

A 1 quieter   2 older
  3 more careful   4 hard
  5 much

B 1 younger than you   2 much wiser than me
  3 less interesting than tennis
  4 less easy than that one

C 1 lazier   2 prettier
  3 large   4 어색한 곳 없음

D 1 younger than I[me]   2 isn't hotter than
  3 more than

Level 2 Test
p. 117

01 ⑤   02 ②
03 ③   04 ② ⑤
05 Is this ring smaller than that one?

06 (1) smaller than
   (2) bigger than
   (3) less big than
07 higher → high (또는 less 삭제)
08 more / than

>>> 해설

01 than이 왔으므로 비교급을 쓰며, dangerous의 비교급은 more dangerous이다.
02 모자가 작다고 했으므로 '더 큰(larger)' 사이즈를 원한다고 해야 한다.
03 '끔찍한(terrible)'이라고 했으므로 부정의 어구가 와야 한다. '음식은 나빴고, 서비스는 훨씬 더 나빴다'가 되어야 자연스럽다.
04 Ian이 Willy보다 키가 작고 뚱뚱하므로 ②와 ⑤가 답이다.
05 '~보다 더 …한'으로 비교급을 사용해 의문문을 만들면 된다.
06 (1) 체리가 사과보다 더 작다.
   (2) 사과는 체리보다 더 크다.
   (3) not을 사용하지 말라고 했으므로 열등 비교를 이용하면 된다.
07 less ~ than에서는 원급을 쓴다.
08 many를 활용해야 하므로 more ~ than으로 쓴다. (Vince는 A보다 F를 더 많이 받았다.)

Level 3 Test
p. 118

01	⑤	02	③ ④
03	④	04	③
05	⑤	06	⑤
07	③	08	② ④ ⑤
09	③		

10 less
11 nineteen (years old)
12 ⓑ heavy → heavily
13 This restaurant is a lot worse than that restaurant.
14 much stronger than
15 (1) lighter than the black suitcase[one]
   (2) heavier than the white suitcase[one]
   (3) as big as the black suitcase[one]

>>> 해설

01 '토론토가 부산보다 훨씬 덜 크다'는 '부산이 토론토보다 훨씬 크다'는 의미이다. a lot과 much는 비교급 강조 부사로 사용되었다.
02 than이 있으므로 비교급을 찾으면 된다.
03 Omar는 6시간 30분, Mark는 7시간 30분을 잔다.
04 ⓐ busyier → busier ⓔ you → yours 또는 your phone
05 '이 배가 더 싸다'고 했으므로 두 번째 문장은 ~ less cheap으로 써야 한다.
06 hardly는 '거의 ~ 않다'는 의미로 hard(열심히)로 바꾸어야 하는데 hard는 비교급에 more를 붙이지 않고 harder로 쓴다.
07 'Artie의 턱수염이 Hunter의 턱수염보다 더 길다'는 'Hunter의 턱수염이 Artie의 턱수염보다 덜 길다'와 같은 뜻으로 ③이 적절하다.
08 ② my grandpa's → my grandpa ④ more happy → happier ⑤ so → much[still, even, far, a lot]
09 Claire watches much[still, even, far, a lot] more films[movies] than Judy.으로 영작할 수 있으므로 ⓐ와 ⓓ는 필요 없다.

10 열등 비교는 less ~ than으로 표현한다.
11 Juan은 David보다 4살 많고, David는 Sarah는 보다 한 살 많은데 Sarah가 14살이므로, David는 15살이고 Juan은 19살이다.
12 more ~ than을 빼고 보면 rains heavy가 아닌 rains heavily가 되어야 한다.
13 비교 구문을 사용하고 강조 부사는 단어 수에 맞게 a lot을 쓰면 된다.
14 작은 차가 파손이 덜 되었으므로 큰 차보다 더 튼튼하다. 강조 부사는 m으로 시작하므로 much를 쓰면 된다.
15 (1)과 (2)는 단어 수에 맞게 비교급을 이용하면 되며, (3)은 동등 비교를 해야 단어 수가 맞다.

UNIT 22 최상급

1) …가장 ~한[-히, -게]   2) of
3) in   4) 복수
5) 가장 ~한 … 중 하나

Level 1 Test
p. 120

A 1 coldest   2 the biggest
    3 restaurants   4 of

B 1 longest   2 tougher
    3 most powerful   4 last

C 1 coldest   2 higher

D 1 worst day   2 the best
    3 respect the most

Level 2 Test
p. 121

01	③	02	②
03	⑤	04	④

05 the fastest of
06 (1) highest (2) biggest (3) smallest
07 one of the shortest shortstops
08 most cowardly

>>> 해설

01 「the+최상급+in+장소」의 형태로 ③이 옳다.
02 • 비교급 강조 부사가 필요하다.
   • 「the+최상급+in+장소」의 형태로 최상급이 들어간다.
03 첫 번째 마녀가 101살이므로 두 번째 마녀보다 훨씬 더 어리다.
04 「one of the+최상급+복수 명사」이므로 ④가 정답이다.
05 모든 다른 여자애들이 하니보다 더 느렸으므로 하니가 제일 빨랐다는 의미이다.
06 검정 블록은 가장 높이(highest) 있고, 회색 블록은 가장 크며(biggest), 하얀 블록은 가장 작다(smallest).
07 「one of the+최상급+복수 명사」 구조로 배열하면 된다.
08 Eric > Louis > Ethan 순으로 용감하다. 주어진 단어가 cowardly(겁 많은)이므로 'Ethan이 가장 겁이 많다'로 쓰면 된다.

01 ④   02 ④
03 ① ③   04 ④
05 ② ④   06 ③ ④
07 ③ ④   08 ④
09 ③ ⑤

10 ⓑ best → most

11 is one of the most important things of all (또는 is one of the most important of all things)

12 cuter / cute / Ki / cutest

13 The thinnest singer sang (the) most loudly.

14 (A) hardest   (B) harder   (C) harder

15 (1) as big as   (2) biggest   (3) bigger

16 Indifference is the scariest thing in the world.

≫ 해설

01 • late가 시간을 나타낼 때 late – later – latest(최신의)
    • bad – worse – worst

02 「one of the + 최상급」 다음에는 복수 명사를 써야 한다.

03 Geungnakjeon is the oldest building in Korean history.로 영작할 수 있으므로, most는 필요 없고 building은 단수가 필요하므로 ③도 필요 없다.

04 '소라가 반에서 가장 예의바르다'와 '반의 모든 소녀가 소라보다 더 예의바르다'는 같은 뜻이 아니다.

05 ② 'Lucy는 Daniel만큼 작지 않다'는 'Lucy가 더 크다'는 말이다.
    ④ 표에서 보면 Eric이 가장 키가 크다.

06 주어가 it이므로 보어로는 단수가 와야 하며, 「one of the + 최상급」 다음에는 복수 명사가 온다.

07 ① worse → worst ② most quiet → quietest ⑤ most longest → longest

08 ⓓ most biggest → biggest ⓕ of the library → in the library

09 ③ January is the coldest month of the year. ⑤ Jupiter is the biggest planet in our solar system. ① Dave can swim the most fastest. (→ most 삭제) ② Ryu is the most pitcher of all. (most → best) ④ Beavers are one of the most diligent animal. (animal → animals)

10 difficult의 최상급은 most difficult이다.

11 「one of the + 최상급 + (복수 명사) + of + 복수 명사」 순으로 쓰면 된다.

12 첫 번째는 than이 있으므로 비교급 cuter가 알맞다. 두 번째는 as ~ as가 있으므로 원급 cute가 알맞다. 마지막 두 빈칸은 내용상 Ki가 가장 귀엽고, 최상급이므로 cutest를 쓰면 된다.

13 thin의 최상급과 loudly의 최상급을 쓰고 부사의 최상급에는 the를 생략할 수도 있다.

14 (A) the 다음에는 최상급이 온다. (B) (C) than이 있으면 비교급을 쓴다. (A)와 (B)에서 hard는 '어려운'이라는 뜻의 형용사이고 (C)에서는 '열심히'라는 의미의 부사이다.

15 (2)는 the가 있으므로 최상급이 들어가고 (1)과 (3) 중에서 big이 들어가면서 원급이 가능한 것은 (1)이다. 나머지 (3)에 비교급을 쓰면 된다.

16 scary의 최상급은 scariest이다.

01 ③   02 ④
03 ⑤   04 ③
05 ③   06 ③
07 ② ⑤   08 ⑤
09 ②   10 ④

11 as much as

12 flew faster than

13 latest → last / more funnier → funnier

14 pays less / than

15 She plays the guitar much better than I.

16 Juri is the youngest (one) of my cousins.

17 best → most / things → thing

18 He is slimmer than Dave. → He is fatter than Dave.

19 ⓐ flowers → flower

20 worse / worst

21 ① ④

22 G27 understands me better than anyone

≫ 해설

01 ③은 규칙 변화이고 나머지는 불규칙 변화이다.

02 원급의 부정은 「not ~ as + 원급 + as …」이다.

03 「as + 원급 + as」를 쓰므로 ⑤에는 as가 들어가고 나머지는 비교급이므로 than이 들어간다.

04 Amy가 몸무게가 적게 나가므로 more than이 아니라 less than으로 해야 한다.

05 첫 번째 문장에 than이 있으므로 비교급을 찾는다.

06 than이 있으므로 bad 대신 비교급 worse로 써야 한다.

07 very는 원급을 수식하고 more는 faster가 비교급이라 불필요하다.

08 ⑤ The rock flew more highly than the roof. (more highly → higher) highly는 '매우'란 뜻이다. ① It was the happiest day of my life. ② New York is much bigger than Boston. ③ They walked as slowly as snails. ④ Kevin ran even farther than yesterday.

09 ⓑ Kyle이 Nicky보다 크다. ⓒ 제일 가벼운 사람은 Gong이다.

10 most가 있으므로, hard는 부적절하다.

11 '~만큼 …한[히]'는 「as + 원급 + as」로 쓰며 '많이'는 much로 표현하면 된다.

12 용이 공주보다 빨리 날지 못했으므로 공주가 더 빨리 날았다는 의미로 비교급을 써야 하며, fly의 과거형은 flew이다.

13 latest는 '최근의', last는 '지난'이란 뜻이고, funnier가 이미 비교급이므로 more를 빼야 한다.

14 네 번째 문장에서 '내가 항상 더 많은 돈을 낸다'고 했으므로 오타가 있는 두 번째 문장은 '그는 항상 나보다 더 적은 돈을 낸다'로 유추할 수 있다. 따라서 pays less ~ than을 넣으면 된다.

15 동사가 plays라 주어는 She이고, than이 있는 것으로 보아 비교급(better)이며, very는 비교급을 수식하지 못하고, the는 악기 앞에 쓰면 된다.

16 young의 최상급은 youngest이며, of 다음에는 복수 명사가 온다.

17 necessary의 최상급은 most necessary이고, 주어가 최상급 단수이므로 things를 thing으로 고쳐야 한다.

18 Ken은 Dave보다 뚱뚱하다.

19 The rose is a beautiful flower.를 최상급으로 만든 것으로 flower

는 단수가 되어야 한다.

20 ill/bad – worse – worst이다. 두 번째 문장은 (어제보다) 더 아파졌다는 말로 비교급을 써야 한다. 마지막 문장은 '최악의 하루였다'라고 마무리하는 것이 적절하다.

21 ⓑ 일반동사 do가 있는 의문문으로 do ⓒ 뒤에 than이 있으므로 비교급인 better ⓔ caring의 최상급은 most caring이다.

22 주어는 G27이고 동사와 목적어는 understands me이다. 내용상 '누구보다 잘'이란 말이 와야 하므로 well의 비교급을 써서 better than anyone으로 쓰면 된다.

[21~22]

나는 로봇 개발자이다. 나는 두 대의 로봇이 있다. 그들은 Yummy-O와 G27이다. 음, 그들이 무엇을 하냐고? Yummy-O는 나를 위해 식사를 요리하고, G27은 나를 위해 음악을 틀어준다. 그들은 정말 대단하다. Yummy-O는 나의 엄마보다 요리를 더 잘한다. 그녀는 세계에서 최고의 요리사이다. G27은 누구보다 나를 더 잘 이해해준다. 그는 세상에서 가장 사려 깊은 로봇이다. 그런 로봇 하나 갖고 싶니?

＊어휘 • developer 개발자 | meal 식사 | cook 요리사 | caring 사려 깊은

CHAPTER 08
to부정사

UNIT 23 명사적 용법

1) 동사원형
2) 명사/동명사
3) 주어
4) It
5) to learn
6) 보어
7) to be
8) 목적어
9) to be
10) should
11) 무엇을 ~할지
12) 어떻게 ~할지, ~하는 방법
13) 언제 ~할지
14) 어디에서 ~할지

Level 1 Test
p. 128

A 1 전치사　　　2 부정사
　 3 부정사

B 1 To bully　　2 live
　 3 catch　　　4 to be
　 5 To read

C 1 목적어　　　2 보어
　 3 목적어　　　4 주어

D 1 의사가 되는 것은　　2 친절하게 하는 것은
　 3 이야기하는 것을

Level 2 Test
p. 129

01 ④　　　　　　　02 ②
03 ②　　　　　　　04 ③
05 ②
06 (1) It / to use
　 (2) what I should say
07 trusting → trust
08 She likes to watch the stars at night.
09 It is dangerous to swim in the sea

≫≫ 해설

01 동사 plan의 목적어 역할을 하는 to부정사가 필요하다.

02 첫 번째는 보어로 쓰인 to부정사, 두 번째는 가주어 It, 세 번째는 목적어로 쓰인 to부정사이다.

03 [보기]와 ②는 명사적 용법 중 목적어 역할을 한다. ①, ④ 진주어 역할 ③ 보어 역할 ⑤ 주어 역할

04 ① → To remember ② → to the river ④ → To me ⑤ → to meet

05 when+to부정사: 언제 ~해야 할지

06 (1) 진주어인 to부정사를 뒤로 보내고 그 자리에 가주어 It을 쓴다.
　 (2) '의문사+to부정사' = 「의문사+주어+should+동사원형」으로 바꿔 쓸 수 있으며, '무엇을 말해야 할지'의 뜻이다.

07 '의문사+to부정사'로 쓰이므로 동사원형으로 고쳐야 한다.

08 like는 3인칭 단수 주어에 맞게 likes가 되어야 하고, 목적어로 to watch를 취해야 8단어가 된다.

09 「It ~ to...」 진주어-가주어 용법으로 「It is+형용사+to+동사원형 ~」으로 표현한다.

Level 3 Test
p. 130

01 ②　　　　　　　02 ②
03 ②　　　　　　　04 ②
05 ①　　　　　　　06 ①
07 ②　　　　　　　08 ①
09 ③　　　　　　　10 ②
11 It is dangerous to touch the jellyfish.
12 when I should call
13 wants to listen to *trot* songs
14 (A) ⓒ　(B) ⓐ　(C) ⓑ
15 I don't know how I should explain my feelings.

≫≫ 해설

01 「의문사+조동사(do)+주어+동사+to부정사?」의 어순으로 쓴다.

02 주어진 문장과 ②는 명사적 용법 중 목적어 역할을 한다. ① 주어 역할 ③ 보어 역할 ④ 진주어 역할 ⑤ 전치사+목적어 (나에게)

03 • 진주어가 to부정사이다.
　 • 「seem to+동사원형」(~처럼 보이다)에서 to부정사는 보어 역할을 한다.

04 ②는 전치사 to이고 나머지는 모두 to부정사로 사용되었다.

05 첫 번째는 want 다음에 to부정사가 온 것이다. 두 번째는 「be동사+-ing」의 진행형이다.

06 빈칸에는 '스키 타는 방법'이라는 말이 적절하므로 「how+to부정사」 형태의 how to ski가 알맞다.

07 주어 역할을 하는 명사적 용법으로 「to부정사+명사」의 형태로 '(명사)를 ~하는 것'이라고 해석된다.

08 to make cupcakes가 진주어이다. 가주어 It이 필요하다.

09 조건에 맞게 하려면 가주어-진주어 구문을 이용해야 한다. (→ It is impossible to live without water.)

10 ⓐ go → to go ⓑ be → to be

11 「It ~ to...」 진주어-가주어 용법으로 「It is+형용사+to+동사원형 ~」으로 표현한다.

12 「의문사+주어+should+동사원형」 순서로 '언제 내가 다시 전화해야 하는지'의 뜻이다.

13 주어 He가 3인칭 단수이므로 동사는 wants이고 want는 목적어로 to부정사를 취한다.

14 ⓐ-(B) to부정사의 명사적 용법 중 주어 역할. ⓑ-(C) to부정사의 명사적 용법 중 보어 역할. ⓒ-(A) to부정사의 명사적 용법 중 목적어 역할

15 '의문사+to부정사' = 의문사+주어+should+동사원형

UNIT 24 형용사적 용법, 부사적 용법

1) 나는 할 숙제가 많다.
2) 나는 마실 뭔가를 원한다.
3) 그는 앉을 의자가 없다.
4) 떠날 시간이다
5) ~하기 위해
6) 나는 공부하기 위해 도서관으로 갔다.
7) ~해서
8) 그녀는 그를 만나서 행복했다.
9) ~하기에
10) 그 질문은 답하기에 어렵다.
11) ~해서 …하다
12) 그는 살아서 100살이 되었다.
13) so
14) that
15) can't
16) 너무 ~해서 …할 수 없다
17) so
18) that
19) can
20) …할 만큼 충분히 ~하다

Level 1 Test

A 1 빌려줄 돈
2 끝낼[끝마칠]
3 도와줄
4 같이[함께] 살
5 할 심부름

B 1 원인
2 목적
3 결과

C 1 too nervous to talk
2 tired enough to sleep

Level 2 Test

01 ①
02 ④
03 ③
04 ①
05 Give me something warm to drink.
06 He was too tired to cook.
07 He woke up to hear the rain outside.
08 (1) small enough to
(2) so small that it can

≫ 해설

01 세 번째 문장에는 a chance to meet가 알맞다.

02 ④에서는 '~하기 위해'이고, 나머지는 감정 형용사 다음에 쓰인 '~해서'로 해석되는 원인의 의미이다.

03 [보기]와 ③은 형용사적 용법으로 ' ~할'로 해석되고, 나머지는 부사적 용법으로 '~하기에'로 해석된다.

04 어법상 어색한 문장이 없다.

05 형용사와 to부정사가 동시에 something을 수식할 때는 「something+형용사+to부정사」의 순서이다.

06 「too+형용사/부사+to부정사」 = 「so+형용사/부사+that+주어+can't ~」

07 to부정사의 부사적 용법의 '결과'이다. (그는 잠에서 깨어나 밖에서 나는 빗소리를 들었다.)

08 「형용사+enough+to부정사」 = 「so+형용사+that+주어+can+동사원형」 (내 스마트폰은 주머니에 들어갈 만큼 충분히 작다. / 내 스마트폰은 아주 작아서 주머니에 들어갈 수 있다.)

Level 3 Test

01 ②
02 ②
03 ②
04 ④
05 ③ ④
06 ②
07 ④
08 ⑤
09 to sit → to sit on[in]
10 I'm sorry to hear that
11 too late to get on the bus
12 Be careful not to use bad language with people.
13 (1) was too nervous to sleep
(2) kind enough to help
14 ②
15 The cow was so weak that it couldn't work.

≫ 해설

01 「anything+형용사+to부정사」의 순서이다.

02 ⓐ to not go → not to go

03 write on the paper는 '종이 위에 쓰는 것'이므로 전치사 on이 to부정사 뒤에 와야 한다.

04 ④는 명사적 용법이고 나머지는 형용사적 용법이다.

05 주어진 문장과 ③, ④는 부사적 용법(목적)이고 나머지는 형용사적 용법이다.

06 to live가 뒤에서 앞에 있는 a reason을 꾸며주는 형용사적 용법이다.

07 ④는 형용사적 용법이고 나머지는 부사적 용법이다.

08 ⓐ ~하기 위해(목적) ⓑ ⓔ ~하기에(형용사 수식) ⓒ ⓕ ~ 해서 …하다(결과) ⓓ ~할(명사 수식)

09 '위에 앉을 의자'이므로 전치사 on이 필요하다. 또는 '안에 앉을 의자'라는 의미로 전치사 in을 쓴다.

10 엄마가 아파서 집에 빨리 가야 한다는 안 좋은 소식을 듣고 '그런 이야기를 들어 마음 아프다'는 말이 자연스럽다.

11 「too+형용사/부사+to+동사원형」: 너무 ~해서 …할 수 없다

12 to부정사의 부정은 「not+to부정사」의 순서로 한다.

13 (1) 「too+형용사/부사+to부정사」 = 「so+형용사/부사+that+주어+can't」 (~너무 ~해서 …할 수 없다.)
(2) 「형용사/부사+enough+to부정사」 = 「so+형용사/부사+that+주어+can ~」 (…할 만큼 충분히 ~하다)

14 ⓐ to부정사의 형용사적 용법(먹을) ⓑ ⓓ to부정사의 부사적 용법 중 목적(~하기 위해) ⓒ to부정사의 명사적 용법(~하는 것) ⓔ to부정사의 부사적 용법 중 감정의 원인

15 「too+형용사/부사+to부정사」= 「so+형용사/부사+that+주어+can't/couldn't」(너무 ~해서 …할 수 없다) 시제는 과거이므로 과거시제에 일치시켜야 한다.

Review Test

01	③	02	⑤
03	②	04	②
05	④	06	④
07	②	08	②
09	①	10	①

11 (1) It / to cross (2) what they should choose
12 The kid doesn't have any friends to play with.
13 too shy / talk to him
14 Her dream is to become a vet.
15 It is hard to fix the car.
16 Is there anything funny to ask a student-teacher?
17 We don't have a baseball bat to play with.
18 not to play the game again
19 He grew up to become a boxing champion.
20 (1) too young to wear
   (2) so young that you can't
21 ① ⑤
22 They used soap to clean their bodies

》》 해설

01 ① Get up → To get up 또는 Getting up ② talk → to talk 또는 talking ④ be → to be ⑤ play → playing 또는 to play

02 [보기]는 '할아버지는 장기 두는 것을 좋아하신다'의 의미로 명사적 용법의 목적어 역할이고, ⑤는 가주어-진주어의 명사적 용법이다. ① 형용사적 용법 ② ③ ④ 부사적 용법

03 ②는 '그것'이라고 해석되는 인칭대명사이고, 나머지는 가주어이다.

04 ⓐ when leave → when to leave ⓑ where going → where to go ⓓ to write → to write with

05 ④는 목적어로 쓰인 명사적 용법이고, 나머지는 부사적 용법 중 '~하기 위해'의 목적의 의미이다.

06 It is time+to부정사 = It is time for+명사 (~할 시간이다)

07 ⓐ, ⓑ, ⓒ는 형용사적 용법이고 ⓓ, ⓔ는 부사적 용법이다.

08 • 「too ~ to...」 용법으로 to open이 알맞다.
   • want 다음에 목적어 역할을 하는 to open이 알맞다.

09 decide의 목적어로 명사적 용법의 to부정사가 먼저 오고, 뒤에는 '~하기 위해'의 의미로 쓰인 부사적 용법의 to부정사가 와야 한다.

10 [보기]와 ①은 형용사 수식을 하며 '~하기에'로 해석된다. ② 명사적 용법 ③ 부사적 용법(목적) ④ 부사적 용법(원인) ⑤ 부사적 용법(결과)

11 (1) 진주어인 to부정사를 뒤로 보내고 그 자리에 가주어 It을 쓴다.
   (2) '의문사+to부정사' = 「의문사+주어+should+동사원형」으로 바꿔 쓸 수 있으며 '무엇을 골라야 할지'의 뜻이다.

12 to play with(함께 놀 친구)는 to부정사가 앞에 있는 명사를 수식하는 형용사적 용법으로 any friends 다음에 와야 한다.

13 내용상 너무 수줍어서 그에게 말을 걸을 수 없었다는 의미이므로 too ~ too... 구문을 이용한다.

14 보어로 to부정사의 명사적 용법이 온다.

15 「It ~ to...」 진주어-가주어 용법으로 「It is+형용사+to+동사원형 ~」으로 표현한다.

16 「anything+형용사+to부정사」의 순서이다.

17 '가지고 놀 야구 방망이'이므로 to play 다음에 전치사 with를 추가한다.

18 to부정사의 부정은 「not+to부정사」의 순서로 한다.

19 to부정사의 부사적 용법의 '결과'이다.

20 too+형용사+to부정사 = so+형용사+that+주어+can't+동사원형

21 ① 가주어가 아니라 진주어로 쓰인 명사적 용법이다. ⑤ 주어가 복수(Most people)이므로 were not able to로 바꿔 쓸 수 있다.

22 주어(They)와 동사(used) 그리고 내용상 목적어인 soap를 쓰고 '~하기 위해'의 to부정사를 이용한다.

[21~22]

비누 없이 사는 것은 상상할 수 없다. 우리 모두는 깨끗해지기를 원한다. 오늘날 여러분은 어디에서나 비누를 얻을 수 있다. 하지만, 오래 전에 사람들은 비누가 없었다. 그들은 물로 그냥 씻었다. 물은 먼지만 씻어냈다. 누가 비누를 발명했는가? 이집트인들이 알칼리성 소금이 있는 동물과 채소 기름으로 비누를 만들었다. 그들은 신체를 깨끗이 하기 위해 비누를 사용했다. 하지만 그 당시에 비누는 비싼 품목이었다. 대부분의 사람들은 그것을 살 수가 없었다.

• 어휘 | unimaginable 상상할 수 없는 | soap 비누 | dirt 먼지 | then 그러면 | invent 발명하다 | expensive 비싼 | item 품목

CHAPTER 09
동명사

UNIT 25 동명사

1) ~하기, ~하는 것
2) 주어
3) 문장
4) 보어
5) be동사
6) 목적어
7) 동사
8) 전치사
9) 동명사
10) 내 취미는 돌을 모으는 것이다.
11) 현재분사
12) 나는 지금 돌을 모으고 있다.
13) ~하러 가다
14) ~하는 게 어때?
15) ~하느라 바쁘다
16) ~하느라 시간/돈을 쓰다
17) ~하고 싶다
18) ~하기를 고대하다

A 1 현재분사
2 동명사
3 현재분사
4 동명사

B 1 is busy watching
2 looking forward to meeting[seeing]
3 going camping

Level 2 Test

01 ④
02 ④
03 ③
04 ⑤
05 ③
06 lose → losing
07 Meeting new people is always exciting.
08 He is[He's] always busy doing his homework.
09 fishing
10 helping

≫ 해설

01 keep은 동명사를 목적어로 취한다.
02 ① to fish → fishing ② see → seeing ③ to write → writing
⑤ buy → buying
03 ③은 진행형으로 쓰인 현재분사이고 나머지는 동명사이다.
04 동명사 주어는 단수 취급한다.
05 ⓒ to smoke → smoking ⓓ were → was ⓕ Wait → Waiting
또는 To wait
06 give up (on)은 '~을 포기하다'라는 의미로 동명사를 목적어로 취한
다.
07 동사는 is이고 '~하는 것'이 주어이므로 Meeting으로 시작해서 배
열한다.
08 be busy+-ing에서 빈도부사(always)는 be동사 뒤에 쓰면 된다. 전
치사를 쓰지 말라고 했으므로 「be busy with+명사」는 쓸 수 없다.
09 그림에서 낚시하는 것을 유추할 수 있으며, 첫 번째 빈칸은 fishing이
be동사의 보어로, 두 번째 빈칸은 go+-ing(~하러 가다)의 의미로 쓰
였다.
10 전치사의 목적어로 동명사를 사용할 수 있다.

Level 3 Test

01 ③
02 ⑤
03 ③ ⑤
04 ⑤
05 ①
06 ③ ④
07 ⑤
08 ②
09 ②
10 ④
11 ⓑ ask → asking
12 usually enjoys skating
13 She went to bed without brushing her teeth.
14 was busy sweeping
15 Washing your hands before eating is a good habit.
16 Do you feel like ordering in?

≫ 해설

01 보어 역할을 할 수 있는 동명사가 알맞다.

02 「one of the+최상급+복수 명사」를 쓰고, 주어는 one이므로 단수
취급하며, 보어는 동명사로 쓰면 된다.
03 enjoy는 명사 또는 동명사를 목적어로 취한다.
04 목적어로 쓰인 동명사(watching)가 있는 문장으로 어색한 부분은 없다.
05 Sending an email to him will be a better choice than calling
him.으로 써야 한다.
06 ① to invite → inviting ② sold → selling ⑤ take → takes
07 ⑤는 현재분사이고 나머지는 동명사이다.
08 look forward to+-ing 구문이다. (visit → visiting)
09 ⓑ paint → painting ⓓ shoot → shooting
10 She usually spends ₩8,000 buying lunch.로 영작할 수 있으므
로 to는 필요하지 않다.
11 of가 전치사이므로 동명사를 써야 한다.
12 가능한 동사는 skates나 enjoys가 있는데 skates를 사용하면 세 단
어가 안 되므로 빈도부사, 일반동사(enjoys) 그리고 동명사를 쓰면 된
다.
13 without+-ing는 '~을 하지 않고'의 뜻이다.
14 be busy+-ing 형태로 쓴다.
15 손을 씻을 때 손이 두 개이므로 복수로 써야 하고, 동명사 주어는 단수
취급한다.
16 '~하고 싶다'는 「feel like+-ing」로 표현한다.

UNIT 26 동명사와 to부정사

1) enjoy
2) mind
3) give up
4) finish
5) practice
6) stop
7) keep
8) quit
9) dislike
10) want
11) wish
12) hope
13) expect
14) plan
15) promise
16) decide
17) would like
18) learn
19) begin
20) like
21) love
22) continue
23) hate
24) ~했던 것을 기억하다
25) ~할 것을 기억하다
26) ~했던 것을 잊다
27) ~할 것을 잊다
28) 한번 ~해보다
29) ~하기 위해 애쓰다
30) ~하는 것을 멈추다
31) ~하기 위해 (하던 일을) 멈추다

Level 1 Test

A 1 playing
2 to be
3 to win
4 to support 또는 supporting
5 to sell

B 1 to text
2 to look
3 waiting

Level 2 Test
p. 145

01 ⑤   02 ④
03 ①   04 ②
05 ⑤
06 to study → studying
07 quit stealing
08 (A) forget to bring   (B) did you

≫ 해설

01 hope는 목적어로 to부정사를 취한다.
02 내용상 전화하려고 노력한 것이므로 try to를 써야 한다. the line is busy는 통화 중이라는 뜻이다.
03 decide는 to부정사를, give up (on)은 동명사를 목적어로 취한다.
04 plan은 to부정사를 목적어로 취한다.
05 ⓐ to close → closing ⓓ to read → reading
06 like는 동명사와 to부정사를 모두 목적어로 취하지만 dislike는 동명사만 목적어로 취한다.
07 quit의 과거형은 quit이며 동명사를 목적어로 취한다. 경찰의 대사에서 stole을 활용하면 된다.
08 (A) forget+to ~: ~할 것을 잊다
(B) 과거 일반동사 부정의 부가의문문은 「did+주어(대명사)」이다.

Level 3 Test
p. 146

01 ① ② ④ ⑤   02 ④
03 ③   04 ②
05 ③   06 ②
07 ④   08 ③
09 ④   10 ① ②
11 to sneeze → sneezing
12 Why did you give up dancing?
13 forgot to bring
14 ⓒ → sharing ⓓ → to be
15 Would you like to donate a dollar?

≫ 해설

01 begin은 to부정사나 동명사 또는 명사를 목적어로 취한다.
02 • mind는 동명사를 목적어로 취한다.
  • feel like+-ing: ~하고 싶다
  • hope는 to부정사를 목적어로 취한다.
03 remember+-ing가 '~했던 것을 기억하다'이므로 folding으로 써야 한다.
04 forget+-ing는 '~했던 것을 잊다'이다.
05 stop+-ing로 해야 '~하는 것을 멈추다'가 된다. (to make → making)
06 like는 동명사와 to부정사를 둘 다 목적어로 취하지만 would like는 to부정사만 목적어로 취한다.
07 ⓑ getting → to get
08 keep과 practice 모두 동명사를 목적어로 취한다.
09 promise는 to부정사를 목적어로 취한다.
10 ① She disliked to be alone. (to be → being) ② They kept to talk about me. (to talk → talking) ③ Does he hate waking up early? ④ The writer loves writing with a pencil. ⑤ Don't

you remember meeting him there?
11 stop의 과거형은 stopped이고 stop+-ing가 '~하는 것을 멈추다'이다.
12 Why가 있으므로 의문문이며, give up+-ing로 사용된다.
13 우산을 가져올 것을 잊었으므로 과거형으로 쓴다. forget+to부정사: ~할 것을 잊다
14 mind는 동명사를, hope는 to부정사를 목적어로 취한다.
15 would like은 to부정사를 목적어로 취하고, 영영풀이는 '돈이나 물품을 사람이나 조직을 돕기 위해 주는 것'으로 donate이다.

Review Test
p. 148

01 ④   02 ③
03 ⑤   04 ① ⑤
05 ③   06 ③
07 ③ ⑤   08 ②
09 ①   10 ③
11 taking   12 ⓑ be → being
13 Getting up at 6 in the morning is not easy.
14 forgot to invite
15 runing → running / sking → skiing / swim → swimming
16 Collecting / is
17 tried to keep / started laughing[to laugh]
18 ⓐ to knit → knitting ⓔ Knit → Knitting 또는 To knit
19 Riding a roller coaster is fun.
20 ②

≫ 해설

01 be동사의 보어로 쓰일 수 있는 동명사가 적절하다.
02 decide는 to부정사를 목적어로 취한다.
03 ⑤는 문장의 주어이고 나머지는 동사의 목적어이다.
04 ① We went camp at the lake. (camp → camping) ⑤ Brushing your teeth are important. (are → is) ② Running is good for your health. ③ I'm looking forward to your visit. ④ After driving all night, we arrived.
05 remember to ~는 '~할 것을 기억하다'이므로 to meet을 meeting으로 바꾸어야 한다.
06 expect는 to부정사를, give up은 동명사를 목적어로 취한다.
07 주어 자리이므로 동명사나 to부정사를 쓴다. ④ money는 셀 수 없는 명사라 many로 수식할 수 없다.
08 Let's의 부정은 Let's not이며, go+-ing는 '~하러 가다'이다.
09 want는 to부정사를 목적어로 취한다.
10 ⓑ to take → taking ⓓ in → on (spend+목적어+on+명사) ⓕ to do → doing
11 전치사 뒤에는 동명사를 쓴다.
12 look forward to+-ing 형태로 쓴다.
13 주어가 '아침 6시에 일어나는 것은'이므로 동명사구 Getting up ~이 주어이고 동사는 isn't, 보어로 easy를 쓰면 된다.
14 Carrie를 초대할 것을 잊은 것이므로 「forget+to부정사」를 쓴다.
15 run의 -ing형은 running, ski의 -ing형은 skiing이고, swim은 enjoy A and B의 병렬 구조로 동명사 형태로 써야 한다.
16 동명사가 주어일 때 단수 취급한다.
17 침착하려고 노력하다가(tried to keep calm), 웃음이 터지기 시작하

는(started laughing[to laugh]) 모습이다.

18 ⓐ enjoy는 동명사를 목적어로 취한다. ⓔ 주어 자리이므로 동명사 또는 to부정사로 쓴다.

19 단어 수에 맞게 Ride를 명사로 써서 Riding a roller coaster로 쓰고 동명사는 단수 취급하므로 is를 쓴 후 보어 fun을 쓰면 된다.

20 ⓑ keep은 동명사를 목적어로 취하므로 waiting으로, ⓔ want는 to 부정사를 목적어로 취하므로 to go로 고쳐야 한다.

[19~20]

> 롤러 코스터를 타는 것은 재미있다. Christina와 친구들은 놀이공원에 갔다. 줄을 서는 것은 지루했다. 하지만 Christina와 친구들은 계속 기다리기로 결심했다. Christina는 시간을 보낼 방법을 찾으려 애썼다. 그녀는 사진을 찍었고, 발을 두드렸고, 친구들과 이야기를 했다. 그리고 나서 그녀의 스마트폰으로 게임을 했다. 나중에 그녀는 화장실에 갔다. 두 시간이 지났다. 그들은 여전히 줄을 서 있었다. 이제 그들은 집에 가고 싶어 했다.

• 어휘 • amusement park 놀이공원 | decide 결심하다 | pass time 시간을 보내다 | tap (톡톡) 두드리다

CHAPTER 10
문장의 형식

UNIT 27 There is 구문, 2형식(감각동사)

1) 단수　　2) 복수　　3) not
4) not　　5) is　　6) isn't
7) are　　8) aren't　　9) was
10) were　　11) ~하게 느끼다　　12) ~하게 들리다
13) ~한 냄새가 나다　　14) ~한 맛이 나다

Level 1 Test
p. 152

A 1 is　　2 Is
3 isn't　　4 were
5 weren't

B 1 Are there / there aren't　　2 Were there / there were

C 1 looks like　　2 sour
3 feels soft

D 1 tastes great　　2 smells like a pie
3 sounds amazing

---

01 ②　　02 ④
03 ①　　04 ⑤
05 ④

06 The perfume smells like sweet cotton candy.
07 terribly → terrible
08 There are two boys
09 There aren't any snow last night. → There wasn't any snow last night.

≫ 해설

01 • few(거의 없는) 다음에 복수 명사가 오므로 동사는 are가 알맞다.
   • some food는 단수 취급하므로 is가 알맞다.

02 대답에서 '그러나 개구리는 많이 있다'로 보아 앞에는 부정적인 답이 나와야 한다. Are there ~?로 질문하면 No, there aren't.로 답한다.

03 friend는 명사이고 형용사형은 friendly(상냥한)이다. 명사는 감각동사(look)의 보어가 될 수 없다.

04 빈칸 다음의 wonderful로 보아 형용사를 보어로 취하는 동사가 와야 함을 알 수 있다. 감각동사 look, smell, taste, sound, feel은 형용사를 보어로 취한다.

05 ⓒ looks → looks like ⓓ softly → soft

06 '달콤한 솜사탕(sweet cotton candy)'이 명사이므로 smells like로 써야 알맞다.

07 감각동사 smell 다음에 형용사형 terrible이 알맞다.

08 boy의 복수형은 boys이므로 two boys가 알맞고 동사는 are이다.

09 과거(어젯밤)이고 any snow는 단수 취급하므로 There wasn't가 알맞다.

Level 3 Test
p. 154

01 ②　　02 ①
03 ①　　04 ④
05 ③　　06 ⑤
07 ①　　08 ⑤
09 ⑤　　10 ③
11 ④　　12 ①
13 ① ② ③
14 There are two goldfish
15 No, there weren't
16 Your dog looks scare. → Your dog looks scary.

≫ 해설

01 • trash는 셀 수 없으므로 단수 취급한다.
   • any는 부정문에 쓰이고 셀 수 있는 명사일 경우 복수형과 함께 쓰이므로 여기서는 sheep(양들)이라는 뜻이다.

02 There is/are 복수 구문에 쓰인 there는 아무 뜻이 없지만, 부사로 쓰인 there는 '거기에'라는 의미가 있다. ①은 '우리는 거기에 갔다'라는 의미로 there는 부사로 쓰였다.

03 복수(several)이므로 there are로 쓰는 것이 맞다.

04 은행은 서점 옆에 있으므로 flower shop을 bookstore로 바꾸는 것이 알맞다.

05 ③ 'look like + 명사'로 쓰이므로 like가 필요하다. (→ The baby looks like an angel.) ① It tastes like chicken. ② What does

---

it smell like? ④ How often do you feel sad? ⑤ That does not sound very nice.

06 ⓔ rain은 셀 수 없으므로 Are를 Is로 고쳐야 한다.

07 lovely는 형용사형으로 '사랑스러운'이라는 뜻이다.

08 hear는 목적어로 명사가 필요하고, 비슷한 뜻이면서 형용사를 보어로 취하는 감각동사에는 sound가 있다.

09 감각동사 taste의 보어로 형용사가 와야 하므로 명사 spice를 형용사 spicy로 고쳐야 한다.

10 there로 물으면 there로 답한다.

11 ④ 명사 a good idea가 있으므로 like가 필요하다. (→ That sounds like a good idea.) ① Your scarf feels soft. ② The soup tasted great. ③ Do my shoes smell bad? ⑤ The moon looks like a cookie.

12 'taste+형용사' 또는 'taste like+명사'로 쓰인다. ① well이 형용사 이면 '건강한'이고 ③ less는 열등 비교로 적절하다.

13 ① worse는 bad의 비교급이므로 형용사형이 맞다. ② lonely는 형용사(외로운)이다. ③ 'taste+형용사'이므로 적절하다. ④ flower는 명사이므로 smells → smells like로 고쳐야 한다. ⑤ funnily → funny

14 fish의 복수형은 fish이므로 two goldfish가 알맞고 동사는 are이다.

15 뒤에 Nobody called you.를 보면 부정의 대답이 와야 함을 알 수 있다. Were there ~?에 대한 부정의 대답은 No, there weren't.이다.

16 감각동사 look의 보어로 형용사가 알맞으므로 scare(명사, 동사)는 scary(형용사)가 되어야 한다.

UNIT 28 4형식(수여동사), 5형식

1) 주어
2) (수여)동사
3) 간접 목적어
4) 직접 목적어
5) 직접 목적어(…을)
6) 전치사(to, for, of)
7) 간접 목적어(~에게)
8) give
9) bring
10) lend
11) send
12) sell
13) show
14) teach
15) write
16) hand
17) make
18) buy
19) cook
20) get
21) find
22) ask
23) 명사
24) 형용사
25) to부정사

Level 1 Test
p. 156

A 1 5형식 2 4형식
3 4형식 4 5형식

B 1 for 2 to
3 of 4 warm
3 special

C 1 Mr. King made a tree house for his daughter.
2 Did he find her a nice hotel?

D 1 The news made us angry.
2 Dad doesn't allow me to use his phone.

Level 2 Test
p. 157

01 ④ 02 ④
03 ① 04 ④
05 ③ ⑤
06 a violin for
07 (1) I will write Harley an email.
(2) I will write an email to Harley.
08 Mr. Gong advised me to continue with my studies.
09 Could you find a job for me?
10 My brother made cookies for his friends.

》》해설

01 find는 목적격 보어로 to부정사를 사용하지 않는다.

02 ④의 빈칸에는 for, ①, ②, ③, ⑤의 빈칸에는 to가 알맞다.

03 4형식을 3형식으로 바꿀 때는 간접 목적어와 직접 목적어의 자리를 바꾸고, 간접 목적어 앞에 전치사를 붙인다. ask는 전치사 of를 쓴다.

04 간접 목적어 앞에 for나 of가 있으므로 to를 취하는 gave는 올 수 없다.

05 ③ me → to me ⑤ to us → for us

06 4형식 문장을 3형식으로 바꿀 때는 간접 목적어와 직접 목적어 의 순서를 바꾸고, 간접 목적어 앞에 전치사를 넣는다. get은 전치사 for를 쓴다.

07 「주어+동사+간접 목적어+직접 목적어」의 4형식 문장이나 「주어+동사+직접 목적어+전치사+간접 목적어」의 3형식 문장으로 표현한다. write는 전치사 to를 쓴다.

08 advise는 목적격 보어로 to부정사를 취한다.

09 3형식 문장이므로 간접 목적어를 문장 뒤로 보내고, find동사는 전치사 for를 쓴다.

10 「수여동사(made)+직접 목적어+전치사(for)+간접 목적어」의 순서가 알맞다. (나의 오빠[형, 남동생]가 그의 친구들을 위해 쿠키를 만들었다.)

Level 3 Test
p. 158

01 ⑤ 02 ①
03 ① ② 04 ④
05 ① 06 ④
07 ② 08 ③
09 ③ 10 ① ⑤
11 to
12 a backpack for
13 He cooked an amazing meal for me.
14 ⓐ being → to be
15 It will make your soup tastier
16 We found him a little strange.

》》해설

01 cook동사는 전치사 for를, lend동사는 to를 쓴다.

02 「주어+동사+간접 목적어+직접 목적어」의 4형식 문장이나 「주어+

동사＋직접 목적어＋전치사＋간접 목적어」의 3형식 문장으로 표현한다. bring은 전치사 to를 쓴다.

03 send, show는 간접 목적어 앞에 to가 오고 ask는 of, find와 get은 for가 온다.

04 get동사는 간접 목적어 앞에 전치사 for를 쓴다.

05 3형식으로 전환할 때 give는 전치사 to를, ask는 전치사 of를 취한다.

06 gave동사 다음에 전치사 없이 간접 목적어 me를 그대로 쓰는 것이 맞다.

07 ⓒ to me → for me ⓔ comfortably → comfortable

08 send는 전치사 to를 간접 목적어 앞에 쓴다. (for him → to him)

09 3형식과 4형식에서 '만들다'의 의미로 쓰이고 '직접 목적어＋for＋간접 목적어'를 쓰는 동사는 make이다.

10 ① 대명사는 수여동사의 직접 목적어가 될 수 없으므로 to를 넣어 3형식으로 써야 한다. (→ Mr. Ahn didn't lend it to me.) ⑤ 목적격 보어는 형용사이므로 freshly가 아니라 fresh가 필요하다. (→ How can I keep vegetables fresh?) ② Please hand me two eggs. ③ They found the door open. ④ She will make coffee for us.

11 give동사는 전치사 to를 쓴다. (민주는 과학 경시대회에서 1등을 했다. 우리는 민주에게 큰 박수를 쳐 주었다.)

12 「수여동사(bought)＋직접 목적어＋전치사(for)＋간접 목적어」의 순서가 알맞다. (엄마가 나에게 배낭을 사주셨다.)

13 「수여동사(cooked)＋직접 목적어＋전치사(for)＋간접 목적어」의 순서가 알맞다.

14 tell은 목적격 보어로 to부정사를 취하므로 to be로 써야 한다.

15 「make＋목적어＋목적격 보어(형용사)」는 '～을 … 하게 만들다'라는 의미이다.

16 '～을 알게 되다; 그런 경우라고 발견하다'라는 의미의 영영풀이는 find를 의미하고, 과거형과 목적격 보어에 형용사(strange)넣어 영작한다.

Review Test

p. 160

01 ②   02 ④
03 ①   04 ②
05 ③   06 ③
07 ①   08 ①
09 ②   10 ②
11 There were seven children in the village.
12 looks like   13 He looks well.
14 allow   15 It may sound foolish.
16 May I ask a favor of you?
17 (1) to (2) for   18 softly → soft
19 Is there any interesting news in the newspaper?
20 Mom made me a funny boxed lunch.
21 ②   22 give a nice meal to them

≫ 해설

01 wine은 셀 수 없지만 셀 수 있는 유리잔이 두 잔이므로 복수 동사 are/were가 알맞고, Koreans는 복수형이므로 are/were가 알맞다.

02 give a call: 전화하다 / give a ride: 태워주다

03 B의 마지막 말에서 Joy가 피곤하다는 것을 알 수 있다. look 다음에 보어로 부사가 올 수 없으므로 ②와 ⑤는 내용에 관계 없이 틀리다.

04 are there ～?로 물어봤지만 one child가 단수이므로 there is ～로

답한다.

05 「look＋형용사」는 '～하게 보이다'라는 뜻이다. 내용상 세상이 아름다워 보이므로 bad는 올 수 없고, beautiful이 와야 한다.

06 look like 다음에 명사형이 와야 알맞다.

07 would like는 목적격 보어로 to부정사를 취한다.

08 「make＋목적어＋목적격 보어(형용사)」로, 목적격 보어로 부사는 올 수 없다.

09 ask동사는 간접 목적어 앞에 of가 오고 to를 쓰지 않는다.

10 ⓒ for Brad → to Brad

11 '일곱 명'은 복수이고 과거이므로 There were ～로 쓴다.

12 a tomato는 명사이므로 like가 와야 하고, 주어는 3인칭 단수이므로 looks로 써야 한다.

13 look well은 '좋아 보이다, 건강해 보이다'라는 뜻이다.

14 목적격 보어에 to부정사가 왔으므로 allow가 적절하다.

15 감각동사 sound는 보어로 형용사형을 취하므로 fool(명사: 바보) → foolish(형용사: 바보 같은)로 써야 알맞다.

16 ask동사는 간접목적어 앞에 of를 쓴다. 의문문이므로 조동사 (may)가 주어 앞에 나간다

17 4형식 문장을 3형식 문장으로 바꿀 때 teach는 전치사로 to를, buy는 for를 쓴다.

18 'sound＋형용사'로 쓰이므로 softly를 soft로 고쳐야 한다.

19 뉴스(news)는 셀 수 없는 명사이므로 단수 취급한다.

20 전치사를 쓰지 말라고 했으므로 「주어＋동사＋간접 목적어＋직접 목적어」의 4형식 문장으로 쓴다.

21 어법상 어색한 것은 ⓓ와 ⓔ이다. ⓓ 형용사 important를 수식하는 extreme을 부사인 extremely로 고쳐야 한다. ⓔ 'taste＋형용사'로 쓰이므로 like가 불필요하다. ⓐ like의 목적어로 쓰인 명사적 용법의 to부정사이다. ⓑ show A B → show B to A로 적절하다. ⓒ a lot of＋복수 명사로 적절하다.

21 give A B(A에게 B를 주다)구문에서 한 단어를 반드시 추가해야 하므로 give B to A 구문으로 쓰면 된다.

[21~22]

레바논에서, 사람들은 집에 손님을 맞이하는 것을 좋아한다. 그들은 음식과 함께 자신들의 친절함을 손님들에게 보여준다. 그들은 사람들은 자신의 집에 초대하고, 그들에게 맛있는 식사를 제공한다. 그들의 식사에 그들은 오이, 가지 그리고 토마토와 같은 많은 채소를 사용한다. 또한 그들의 문화에서 빵은 매우 중요하다. 만약 빵이 안 좋은 맛이 나기 시작하면, 그들은 그 빵에 입맞춤을 하고 버린다.

• 어휘 • kindness 친절함 | meal 식사 | cucumber 오이 | eggplant 가지 | extremely 매우 | culture 문화 | throw away 버리다

CHAPTER 11

전치사와 접속사

UNIT 29 시간 전치사, 장소 전치사

1) at 2) on 3) in
4) until 5) by 6) for
7) during 8) at 9) in
10) on 11) by 12) over
13) under 14) behind 15) by
16) into 17) out of 18) along
19) across from 20) through

Level 1 Test p. 164

A 1 in 2 during
3 until 4 for
5 on

B 1 for 2 behind
3 along

Level 2 Test p. 165

01 ③ 02 ④
03 ③ ⑤ 04 ③
05 ⑤
06 in front of
07 along the road
08 (1) on (2) at
09 on this weekend → this weekend

≫ 해설
01 연도 앞에 in을 쓴다.
02 between은 '~ 사이에'라는 뜻으로 뒤에 'A and B' 또는 복수 명사가 온다.
03 계절, 년도, 달 앞에는 in을 쓰고, 특정한 날 앞에는 on을 쓴다.
04 숫자로 표현된 기간 앞에는 for를 사용하고, night 앞에는 at을 쓴다.
05 ⓐ 달이 있더라도 날짜와 함께 있으면 on을 쓴다. ⓔ 숫자를 동반한 기간이 이어지므로 for를 쓴다. during은 방학, 휴가 등 특정 기간 앞에 쓴다.
06 behind와 의미상 대조를 이루는 in front of가 적절하다.
07 '~을 따라서'라는 의미의 전치사 along을 명사 the road 앞에 쓴다.
08 (1) 교통수단 위에 올라 타는 것이므로 on을 쓴다.
   (2) 좁은 의미로 우체국은 at을 쓴다.
09 시간 표현에서 this 앞에는 전치사를 쓰지 않는다.

Level 3 Test p. 166

01 ③ 02 ②

03 ① 04 ②
05 ④ 06 ③
07 ③ 08 ①
09 by
10 through
11 ⓓ by → for
12 for
13 until, during, at
14 Can I sit next to you?

≫ 해설
01 연도, 계절 앞에 사용하는 전치사는 in이다.
02 머무르는 것은 '계속'의 의미로 until이고, '특정 기간 동안'은 during이다.
03 during+특정 기간 / in+도시 / for+숫자로 나타낸 기간
04 개가 침대 밑에 있으므로 under가 알맞다
05 • 좁은 의미의 전치사 at이 필요하다.
   • in the sky: 하늘에
   • 4시까지 글쓰기를 끝내는 것은 동작의 완료이므로 by를 쓴다.
06 ⓑ 산 위를 날아가는 것이므로 on → over ⓓ in → on ⓕ in → on
07 우체국은 도서관이 아니라 빵집 건너편에 있다.
08 on은 날짜, 요일, 오전·오후·저녁·밤, 특정일 앞에 쓴다. ①의 midnight 앞에는 at이 적당하며 '자정에'라는 뜻이다.
09 '~까지'(시간의 완료 시점), '~ 옆에'(위치)라는 뜻의 전치사 by가 알맞다
10 소들이 군중을 통과하여 달리고 있으므로 through가 알맞다.
11 '10분 동안'이라는 의미가 되어야 하므로 전치사 for가 알맞다.
12 6시부터 9시까지 세 시간 동안 공부한 것이다. 숫자와 함께 쓰는 전치사 for가 알맞다.
13 ⓐ 의자 위에(on) ⓑ 너와 나 사이에(between) ⓔ 나무 아래에(under)에 해당하는 전치사를 쓰면 된다.
14 '옆에'를 의미하는 두 단어는 next to이다.

UNIT 30 등위 접속사, 종속 접속사

1) ~와, 그리고 2) 단어
3) 구 4) 절
5) 그러나 6) 단어
7) 절 8) 또는, 혹은
9) 단어 10) 구
11) 절 12) 그래서
13) 절 14) ~라는 것, ~라고
15) 주어 16) 보어
17) 목적어 18) ~할 때
19) ~하기 때문에 20) ~한다면

Level 1 Test p. 168

A 1 or 2 but
3 and 4 so
5 because

B 1 When 　　　　　　　　2 that
　3 that

C 1 that 　　　　　　　　2 or

Level 2 Test
p. 169

01 ② 　　　　　　　　02 ①
03 ① ④ 　　　　　　　　04 ②
05 ①
06 We hope (that) we can have fun at Everland.
07 because
08 When she listens to classical music / she falls asleep
09 and
10 If it rains tomorrow, I will wear my new rubber boots.

》 해설

01 해석: 나는 과일을 좋아하지만 나의 남동생은 좋아하지 않는다. / 그녀와 나는 사촌이다.
02 ①의 When은 '언제'를 뜻하는 의문사이고, 나머지는 '~할 때, ~하면'을 뜻하는 접속사이다.
03 ① '배고프고 피곤한 것'이므로 but → and ④ 「명령문,+or …」은 '~해라, 그렇지 않으면 …할 것이다'라는 의미이다. 서두르지 않으면 늦을 것이므로 and → or
04 때를 나타내는 부사절(after ~)에서는 미래의 일을 나타낼 때 미래 시제를 쓰지 않고 현재 시제를 쓴다. (→ finish)
05 「명령문+or…」: ~해라, 그렇지 않으면 …할 것이다
06 목적절을 이끄는 접속사 that은 생략 가능하다. 주절 We hope를 적고 that 목적절을 이어 적는다.
07 이유를 나타내는 접속사는 because이다. (옳은 것을 해라. 왜냐하면 그것이 옳으니까.)
08 '~할 때, ~하면'이라는 뜻의 시간의 부사절을 이끄는 종속접속사 when으로 두 문장을 연결할 수 있다.
09 「명령문, and+주어+동사 ~」=「If+주어+명령문, 주어+동사 ~」(…해라. 그러면 ~할 것이다)
10 조건을 나타내는 if절에서는 현재형이 미래의 뜻을 나타내므로 it rains라고 쓰고, 주절에는 미래 조동사 will을 써서 표현한다.

Level 3 Test
p. 170

01 ⑤ 　　　　　　　　02 ④
03 ③ 　　　　　　　　04 ①
05 ③ 　　　　　　　　06 ⑤
07 ① 　　　　　　　　08 ④
09 ⑤
10 (1) so 　(2) because
11 or
12 When she comes to my house again, I will light the candles for her.
13 that
14 If it snows tomorrow, I will build a snowman.
15 Take this pill, and you will feel better.

》 해설

01 조건 부사절에서 현재형이 미래를 대신하므로 어색한 부분이 없다.

02 미래 시제 will과 함께 쓰일 수 있으며 내용상 '좋은 점수를 받으면 행복할 것이다'라는 조건의 if가 알맞다.
03 ・'그가 잘 들을 수 없어서 누군가 도와줘야 한다.'라는 의미가 자연스러우므로 so가 알맞다.
　・'그녀는 가난한 학생을 돕기를 원했고 학교도 동의했다.'라는 의미가 자연스러우므로 and가 알맞다.
04 because: ~하기 때문에 (궁금했기 때문에 나는 그 돌을 만졌다.)
05 목적절을 이끄는 접속사 that만 생략 가능하다. ① ② ④ 지시형용사 ⑤ 보어절을 이끄는 접속사
06 '해가 질 때 아이들이 집에 간다'는 뜻으로 때를 나타내는 when이 알맞다.
07 ・'철자는 기억하지 못하지만 뜻은 안다'의 의미로 반대되는 내용이므로 but이 알맞다.
　・'아파서 침대에 누워 있었다'는 원인과 결과이므로 so가 알맞다.
08 ④ 때를 나타내는 부사절(when ~)에서는 현재형이 미래의 뜻을 나타내므로 현재형으로 바꾸어야 한다.
09 ⑤는 내용상 '그렇지 않으면'이 들어가므로 or가 적절하고 나머지는 and이다.
10 「원인, so+결과」=「결과+because+원인」 (나는 바빠서 일을 끝마칠 수 없었다.)
11 「명령문, or+주어+동사 ~」: …해라. 그렇지 않으면 ~할 것이다
12 when이 이끄는 부사절에서 미래의 일을 표현할 때는 현재 시제로 쓴다.
13 ・보어절을 이끄는 that (사실은 그녀가 아주 매력적이라는 것이다.)
　・진주어절을 이끄는 that (네가 규칙적으로 운동하는 것이 필요하다.)
14 조건을 나타내는 접속사 if는 현재형이 미래의 뜻을 나타내므로 it snows라고 문장 앞에 쓰고, 주절에는 미래 조동사 will을 써서 표현한다.
15 '명령문, and …' 구문으로 or를 빼고 배열하면 된다.

Review Test
p. 172

01 ② 　　　　　　　　02 ②
03 ① 　　　　　　　　04 ①
05 ① 　　　　　　　　06 ③
07 ③ 　　　　　　　　08 ①
09 ① 　　　　　　　　10 ①
11 ⓐ during → for ⓒ on this weekend → this weekend
12 through
13 for
14 for the airplane → by airplane
15 behind
16 After
17 and
18 that
19 If you scratch my back, I'll scratch yours.
20 (1) She bought her ticket early, so she could get a good seat.
　(2) Because she bought her ticket early, she could get a good seat. (또는 She could get a good seat because she bought her ticket early.)
21 ④
22 when they read and write

01 구체적인 시각, noon, night 앞에 쓰는 전치사는 at이다.

02 매일 얼마나 오랫동안 연습하는지 기간을 물어보고 있으므로 전치사 for로 답하는 것이 알맞다.

03 · until은 '~까지'라는 뜻으로 특정 시점까지의 동작의 계속을 나타낸다.
   · by는 '~까지'라는 뜻으로 특정 시점의 동작의 완료를 나타낸다.

04 for+구체적인 시간을 나타내는 말 / during+기간을 나타내는 말

05 일하고 난 후에 교회에 가는 것이고, after나 before 다음에는 will을 쓰지 않고 현재형을 써서 미래의 뜻을 나타낸다.

06 목적절을 이끄는 접속사 that은 동사 다음에 위치한다.

07 I feel down과 you are down 두 개의 절을 연결하는 접속사가 필요하다. '네가 우울할 때[우울하면] 난 우울해.'가 적절하므로 when이 답이다.

08 ⓕ so → because (나는 피곤했기 때문에 일찍 잠자리에 들었다.)

09 여러 가지가 나열되는 문장에서는 마지막 항목 앞에 접속사 and를 쓴다.

10 · 10월 17일 즉 날짜이므로 on
   · hurry to: 급히 ~로 가다
   · on the field: 경기장에
   · thanks to: ~ 덕분에

11 ⓐ 숫자와 함께 쓰이는 기간에는 for를 사용한다. ⓒ this는 on과 함께 쓰이지 않는다.

12 '~을 통과하여'라는 의미의 전치사는 through이다.

13 · for+시간: ~ 동안
   · make ~ for...: ···을 위해 ~을 만들다

14 교통수단을 나타낼 때 by를 쓰며 관사는 쓰지 않는다.

15 그림에서 소년이 커튼 뒤에 숨어 있으므로 '~ 뒤에'의 뜻을 가진 전치사 behind가 알맞다.

16 after는 '~한 후에'라는 뜻으로 시간의 부사절을 이끄는 접속사이고, before는 '~하기 전에'라는 뜻으로 역시 시간의 부사절을 이끄는 접속사이다.

17 · 「명령문, and...」: ~해라. 그러면 ···할 것이다
   · 계속되는 나열에 쓰이는 and(~와, 그리고)

18 · 「so ~ that... couldn't」: 너무 ~해서 ···할 수 없었다 (나는 너무 무서워서 눈을 뜰 수 없었다.)
   · 목적절을 이끄는 접속사 that (나는 우리가 우리 자신과 다른 사람들의 안전에 대해 신경을 써야 한다고 생각한다.)

19 조건을 나타내는 If절에서는 현재형을 써서 미래의 뜻을 나타낸다. 주절에는 미래의 뜻이므로 will을 쓴다.

20 「결과+because+원인」 = 「원인, +so+결과」 (그녀는 일찍 표를 샀기 때문에 좋은 자리를 얻을 수 있었다.)

21 ⓐ 서술적 용법으로 쓰인 형용사로 적절하고 ⓒ 과거 시제이므로 과거 동사가 쓰였으며 ⓔ 넓은 장소의 전치사 in은 적절하다. ⓑ 명사(kid)를 수식하므로 형용사 great으로 고쳐야 하고, ⓓ finish는 동명사를 목적어로 취한다.

22 '~할 때'의 접속사 when과 '그리고'의 and를 이용한다.

[21~22]

Louis Braille는 세 살 때 눈이 멀었다. 하지만 그는 뛰어난 어린이 발명가였다. 그는 자신만의 표기 체계인 점자를 위해서 솟아오른 점들은 사용했다. 그는 15세 때 마침내 시각 장애인들 위한 시스템을 만드는 것을 끝냈다. 그는 파리에서 선생님이 되었고, 시각 장애인 아이들을 위해 점자를 가르쳤다. 오늘날 전 세계의 사람들은 그들이 읽고 쓸 때 그 체계를 이용한다.

• 어휘 • blind 눈이 먼 | inventor 발명가 | raised 솟아오른 | dot 점 | own 자신만의 | writing system 표기 체계

내신공략

중학영문법 1 문제풀이책